高职高专"十一五"规划教材
江苏省精品教材系列

生物化工与制药专业英语

吴 昊 乔德阳 主编

U03359711

化学工业出版社
·北京·

本书系江苏省精品教材系列，全书共分 6 单元 21 章，讲述了生物化工的相关知识，及信息检索等内容，每章后都附有单词、短语解释，以及疑难长句注释，课后有练习题和原文的翻译参考。全书内容涉及面广，具有较强的实用性、可读性和趣味性，可提高读者的学习兴趣，帮助读者尽快掌握专业英语书刊的阅读技巧，了解文献检索及写作知识。

　　本书可作为高职高专院校各相关专业的教学用书，也可供从事相关工作的人员学习、阅读。

图书在版编目 (CIP) 数据

生物化工与制药专业英语 / 吴昊，乔德阳主编.
—北京：化学工业出版社，2009.8　(2023.4重印)
高职高专"十一五"规划教材　江苏省精品教材系列
ISBN 978-7-122-06247-5

Ⅰ．生…　Ⅱ．①吴…②乔…　Ⅲ．①生物工程：
化学工程-英语-高等学校：技术学校-教材②制药
工业-英语-高等学校：技术学校-教材　Ⅳ．H31

中国版本图书馆 CIP 数据核字（2009）第 114841 号

责任编辑：张双进　　　　　　　　　文字编辑：李　瑾
责任校对：凌亚男　　　　　　　　　装帧设计：王晓宇

出版发行：化学工业出版社（北京市东城区青年湖南街 13 号　邮政编码 100011）
印　　装：三河市延风印装有限公司
787mm×1092mm　1/16　印张 12　字数　326　千字　2023 年 4 月北京第 1 版第 9 次印刷

购书咨询：010-64518888　　　　　　售后服务：010-64518899
网　　址：http://www.cip.com.cn
凡购买本书，如有缺损质量问题，本社销售中心负责调换。

定　　价：36.00 元

前　言

随着生物技术应用领域的深入、生化制药产业的发展以及国际交流的日益紧密，社会对生物工程及制药人才的素质要求越来越高，既掌握专业技能，又能熟练地掌握专业英语的人才受到众多企业尤其是中外合资企业的欢迎。为适应新时期高职高专生化与制药专业对学生的能力培养和综合素质的要求，全国高等职业教育化工专业教材编审委员会和化学工业出版社组织全国部分高等院校编写本书。本教材被江苏省教育厅立项为江苏省高等学校精品教材进行建设。

本教材特点如下：

1. 从内容上改变已往专业英语教材难度大，内容晦涩，课文背景解释少的缺点，对文章中较长英语句子结构做了剖析与翻译，并附加文章背景知识与阅读材料。

2. 从形式上改变已往专业英语教材单词的注释都在文章后的方式，避免大量的单词引起学生的畏惧。本教材把单词注释与文章展开同步，不仅可以避免这一缺点，而且可以更好地通过阅读记忆单词。

本教材由徐州工业职业技术学院吴昊和乔德阳主编。全书分为 5 个单元共 21 章，参加编写的有：徐州工程学院曹丹丹编写第一单元第 1、2 章，南京化工职业技术学院沈建华编写第二单元第 3、4、5 章，天津渤海职业技术学院孙皓编写第三单元第 6 章，徐州工业职业技术学院吴昊编写第三单元第 7、8、9、11 章，徐州工业职业技术学院甘聘编写第三单元第 10 章，山西生物应用职业技术学院党莉编写第三单元第 12 章，徐州工业职业技术学院乔德阳编写第四单元第 13、15 章，徐州工业职业技术学院张达志编写第四单元第 14 章，常州工程职业技术学院吴玲编写第四单元第 16 章，徐州工业职业技术学院阮浩编写第四单元第 17、19 章，江苏省徐州医药高等职业学校江君编写第四单元第 18 章，徐州工业职业技术学院李宗磊编写第五单元第 20、21 章。全书由吴昊统稿。

本书编写过程中，参考了大量的相关书籍和资料，在此谨向作者致以由衷的谢意。本书编写得到了编者所在单位的大力支持和同事们的热情帮助，从而保证了编写出版工作的顺利进行，在此表示衷心的感谢。

由于编写时间紧迫和编者水平有限，疏漏和不妥之处在所难免，恳请广大读者和同行提出宝贵意见，以便进一步修改和完善。联系 E-mail：wuhao315425@163.com。

编者
2009 年 6 月

目　　录

Unit **1** Preface

Chapter 1   Translation skills

Great achievement has been made in bio-chemistry, which has been developing incredibly in many fields ever since the 20th century. However, in languages used to record the **voluminous** scientific documents, English **accounts for** more than 85%. Therefore being able to comprehend and translate English-written scientific documents and write abstract in English is the **essential** quality for practitioners of bioengineering, and also the important condition for them to be informed of the developments of their own specialities and exchange their achievement in scientific research.

English and Chinese belong to two language groups, which differ greatly in vocabulary and grammatical structure, therefore, the two different languages have their own characteristics in **wording**, word-order and structure. For example, in English, there are more postmodifiers while in Chinese, more premodifiers. Long sentences are often used in English, with the center of the sentence at the head, but in Chinese, short sentences are preferred, with the center at the end. In English, advanced modifiers are put behind the verb, however, in Chinese, they are placed in front of it. Passive voice is more often used than that in Chinese. Therefore, translation of scientific documents is not simply literal change. The translator should make his version logical, his language standard, his expression apt and his wording well-knit. And also the translator should know as much professional knowledge as possible and use the technical terms properly. The followings are some of the main translation skills used in the field of bio-chemistry.

1 Subordination

"Subordination" (the method of **differentiating**, and handling, of the **principal** and **subordinate** parts of a complex

Remarks Column

voluminous[vəˈljuːmɪnəs, vəˈluː-] *adj.* 卷数多的，长篇的
account for 占据
essential [iˈsenʃəl] *adj.* 本质的，实质的，基本的，提炼的，精华的

wording [ˈwəːdiŋ] *n.* 措词

differentiate [ˌdifəˈrenʃieit] *v.* 区别，区分

sentence[1] in the process of translation) is essential to achieving adequacy in translation.

E.g. **Biopharmaceutical** based medicines are typically **proteins**, **peptides** or genomic materials which are produced from living organisms, usually in **fermenters** or **bioreactors**.

The principal part of the sentence is "biopharmaceutical based medicines are typically proteins, peptides or genomic materials" and "which are produced from living organisms, usually in fermenters or bioreactors" is "subordinate part". Then the sentence can be translated into: 生物制药学是基于典型蛋白质、多肽和基因材料的医学，这些物质通常是来自发酵罐或生物反应器中带活性的生物体。

2 Amplification

A translator is not supposed to add any meaning to or **subtract** any meaning from the original work. This is a principle not to be violated in translation. However, it does not follow that a translator should refrain from supplying the necessary word (s) to make his version both accurate and in keeping with the usage of the language translated into. Because Chinese and English are two entirely different languages, whose creators and native speakers, moreover, have such entirely different historical and cultural background that many ideas, idiomatic expressions and "short-hand words"[2], etc. So well understood in the country of their origin, can hardly make sense to the people abroad, if translated literally without the necessary "amplification"[3].

E.g. interruption 中断现象
neutralization 中和作用
transmission 传送方式
measurement 测量方法

3 Omission

True, a translator has no right to subtract any meaning from or add any meaning to the original work. But it does not follow that a translator should **refrain from** omitting any words at all in translation. In fact, one of the marker differences in syntax[4] between English and Chinese is the omission of words in sentence. What is regarded a natural or indispensable form of repetition in one language may be regarded as **superfluous** or even "a **stumbling** block" in the other.

E.g. A gas distributes *itself* uniformly throughout a container. 气体均匀地分布在整个容器中。

4 Conversion

The fact that Chinese and English differ greatly determines

principal ['prinsəp(ə)l, -sip-] *adj.* 主要的，首要的
subordinate [sə'bɔ:dinit]*adj.* 次要的，从属的，下级的
biopharmaceutical['baɪəu,fɑ:mə's ju:tɪkəl]*adj.*生物制药学
protein ['prəuti:n]*n.*[生化]蛋白质
peptide ['peptaɪd]*n.*肽
fermenter [fə'mentə]发酵罐，发酵槽
bioreactor [,baiəuri(:)'æktə]生物反应器
amplification[,æmplifi'keiʃ ən]*n.*增加
subtract [səb'trækt]*v.* (～ from)减去，减

refrain [ri'frein]*vi.* (～ from)节制，避免，制止
superfluous [,sju:'pə:fluəs]*adj.*多余的，过剩的，过量的
stumble ['stʌmbl]*v.*绊倒，使困惑，蹒跚，结结巴巴地说话，踌躇
mechanically [mi'kænikəli]*adv.*机械地

that in doing translation the translator should not follow the "parts of speech"[5] of the original **mechanically**. As a matter of fact, a word in one language belonging to a certain "part of speech" has often to be converted into a different "part of speech" to conform to the usage of the language to be translated into.

E.g. Each of the **dosage** units is designed to contain a specified quantity of medication for *ease and accuracy* of dosage administration.

每一种剂量单位都要设计成含有指定量的药物以简便而准确地给药。（English *n.*—Chinese *adv.*）

5 Inversion

"Inversion" means the necessary or even **inevitable** change of word-order in a sentence according to the usage of the language to be translated into. This "change of word-order" is necessary because, first of all, each language has its own "natural word-order" and its own **peculiarities** in word-order; secondly, "inversion", as a **stylistic** device[6], is often used for emphasis.

E.g. A patient should be warned of any expected minor side effects.

须警告病人可预期的所有微小的副作用。（from passive voice to active voice[7]）

6 Division

"Division" means the necessary splitting of a long sentence into short sentence. To split a sentence at will is definitely a mistake in translation. But that does not mean "splitting the sentence" is absolutely **impermissible**. Because in English, especially in ESP, long sentences are usually used while in Chinese short sentences are preferred. Therefore, "division" as a translation technique is often called for to change the original syntactic structure.

E.g. Another extraction system having potential in the downstream processing of proteins is *that* of reverse **micelles** which are **thermodynamically** stable aggregates of **surfactant molecules** and water in organic **solvents**.

可用于蛋白质下游工艺的另一种萃取系统为反胶束，该系统形成热力稳定的聚集体，而聚集体是由表面活性剂分子与有机溶剂中水相所组成的。

dosage ['dəusidʒ]*n.*剂量，配药，用量

inevitable [in'evitəbl]*adj.*不可避免的，必然的

peculiarity [pi,kju:li'æriti]*n.*特性，怪癖

stylistic [stai'listik]*adj.*格式上的，体裁上的

impermissible [,impə'misəbl]*adj.*不许可的，不允许的

micelle [mi'sel, mai-]*n.*[化][物][生]胶束，胶囊，微胞，微团，胶态离子

thermodynamics ['θə:məudai'næmiks]*n.* [物] 热力学

surfactant [sə'fæktənt]*n. & adj.* [化]表面活性剂(的)

molecule ['mɔlikju:l]*n.* [化]分子，些微

solvent ['sɔlvənt]*adj.*溶解的，有偿付能力的，有溶解力的 *n.*溶媒，溶剂，解决方法

Notes

[1] **complex sentence** 复合句

复合句（complex sentence）由一个主句（principal clause）和一个或一个以上的从句（subordinate clause）构成。主句是全句的主体，通常可以独立存在；从句则是一个句子成分，不能独立存在。从句不能单独成句，但它也有主语部分和谓语部分，就像一个句子一样。所不同在于，从句须由一个关联词（connective）引导。

复合句可分为：

（1）定语从句（the attributive clause）；

（2）状语从句（the adverbial clause）；

（3）名词性从句（the noun clause）

[2] **short-hand words** 速记词汇

[3] **if translated literally without the necessary "amplification"** 如果没有增译只按照字面翻译。

[4] **syntax:** 句法

In linguistics, **syntax** is the study of the principles and rules for constructing sentences in natural languages. In addition to referring to the discipline, the term *syntax* is also used to refer directly to the rules and principles that govern the sentence structure of any individual language. 句子的结构方式，表示其在句子中相互关系的词形式的排列。

[5] **part of speech** *n.*（名词）【复数】 parts of speech

One of a group of traditional classifications of words according to their functions in context, including the noun, pronoun, verb, adjective, adverb, preposition, conjunction, and interjection, and sometimes the article. 词类，词性：一组传统的词语类别之一，根据它们在上下文中的功能划分，包括名词、代词、动词、形容词、副词、介词、连词和感叹词，有时还包括冠词。

[6] **stylistic device**: In literature and writing, a **stylistic device** is the use of any of a variety of techniques to give an auxiliary meaning, idea, or feeling to the literal or written. 修辞格是人们在组织、调整、修饰语言，以提高语言表达效果的过程中长期形成的具有特定结构、特定方法、特定功能、为社会所公认、符合一定类聚系统要求的言语模式，也称语格、辞格、辞式等。

[7] **from passive voice to active voice** 从被动语态到主动语态

汉语科技说明文中被动语态较少，但英语中，为了比较客观地进行描述和讨论，避免主观武断，被动语态应用得较广。如：All biotechnological processes are carried out within a containment system or bioreactor. Recently, however, many novel forms have been designed and they may play an increasingly active part in biotechnology.

Exercises

1. Put the following into Chinese

Proteins are the most abundant biological macromolecules，occurring in all cells and all parts of cells. Proteins also occur in great variety；thousands of different kinds，ranging in size from relatively small peptides to huge polymers with molecular weights in the millions，may be found in a single cell. Moreover，proteins exhibit enormous diversity of biological function and are the most important final products of the information pathways discussed in Part Ⅲ of this book. Proteins are the molecular instruments through which genetic information is expressed.

2. Put the following English sentences into Chinese and pay attention to the italicized words.

（1）*Traveling* very fast, light from the sun takes a little more than eight minutes to reach the earth.

（2）As most metals are malleable and ductile, *they* can be beaten into plates and drawn into wires.

（3）Only small amount of enzymes *are required* to carry out chemical reactions even on an industrial scale.

（4）Since the 1940s much other fermentation has been *commercialized*.

（5）Chlorine is very active *chemically*.

（6）Salt and sugar are both *soluble* in water.

3. Put the following words into English

生物制药学　　蛋白质　　肽　　发酵罐　　减去　　抑制
剂量　　　　　必然的　　热力学　　表面活性剂　分子　　溶剂

4. Cloze

Animal and plant cells contain approximately 10000 kinds of molecules (referred to ＿（1）＿ biomolecules). One of these, water, may constitute 50%~95% of a cell's content ＿（2）＿ weight, while ions ＿（3）＿ sodium (Na^+), potassium (K^+), magnesium (Mg^{2+}), and calcium (Ca^{2+}) may account ＿（4）＿ another 1%. Almost all ＿（5）＿ kinds of molecules in ＿（6）＿ organisms are organic. Organic molecules are principally ＿（7）＿ six elements: carbon, hydrogen, oxygen, nitrogen, phosphorus, and sulfur. However, the properties of one element, carbon, are responsible ＿（8）＿ the ＿（9）＿ infinite variety ogorganic molecules. Carbon atoms can form four strong covalent bonds, either to other carbon atoms ＿（10）＿ to atoms of other elements.

（1）A. as　　　　　B. with　　　　C. for　　　　　D. in　　　　　（　　　）
（2）A. in　　　　　B. with　　　　C. by　　　　　D. on　　　　　（　　　）
（3）A. except　　　B. besides　　　C. in spite of　　D. such as　　　（　　　）
（4）A. to　　　　　B. in　　　　　C. for　　　　　D. with　　　　（　　　）
（5）A. other　　　　B. the other　　C. another　　　D. the　　　　　（　　　）
（6）A. alive　　　　B. living　　　C. live　　　　　D. lively　　　（　　　）
（7）A. consisted of　B. made with　C. composed of　D. formed in　　（　　　）
（8）A. to　　　　　B. for　　　　　C. in　　　　　D. with　　　　（　　　）
（9）A. mostly　　　B. most　　　　C. almost　　　D. all most　　（　　　）
（10）A. nor　　　　B. with　　　　C. for　　　　　D. or　　　　　（　　　）

参考译文

20世纪以来，生物化学科学以惊人的发展速度，在众多领域中取得了巨大的发展，获得了很多突破性成就。然而，在记载这些浩如烟海的科技文献所使用的语言中，英语占到85%以上。因此，能够理解和翻译这些科技文献并能为撰写的论文写出英文摘要，成为一个生化工作者所应具备的基本素质。同时也是他们了解本专业的发展动向和交流学术成果的重要条件。

英汉两种语言属于两种不同的语系，无论在词汇还是在语法结构上都有巨大的差异，因此英汉两种语言的句子在措词、语序、结构等方面都各有特点。比如：英语多后置定语，而汉语前置定语较多。英语多长句（句子中心在句首），汉语多短句（句子中心在句尾）。英语中状语多放于谓语之后，而汉语则习惯放在动词之前。英语多被动语态，汉语多主动语态。因此对英文文献的翻译并非是简单对应的词汇罗列，译者更应注意逻辑思维严密，语言准确，表达清晰，措词严谨。同时译者也应掌握相当的专业知识，恰当地运用专业词汇及专业术语。以下是一些翻译的基本技巧。

1. 分清主从

分清主从是指在翻译过程中对复合句的主句和从句进行区分和处理，这种方法对准确翻译非常重要。

2. 增译

翻译人员对原文不应该在意义上进行任何程度的增删，这点是在翻译中不能违反的原则。然而，这并不是说翻译人员不能使用必要的词汇使译文既准确又符合译文语言的习惯。因为英语和汉语是两种完全不同的语言。此外，创造并使用这两种语言的人具有不同的历史和文化背景，以至于很多概念、习语和"速记语"等在本国很容易理解而对其他国家的人来说如果没有进行必要的增译而只是根据字面意思来翻译的话，就几乎没什么意义。

3. 省译法

确实，翻译人员没有权力增删原文的任何含义，但并不是说译者就不应该在翻译过程中省略任何词汇。事实上，在句法上，英汉两种语言的显著区别之一就是在句中对词语的省略。一种语言中被认为是很自然或绝对必要的重复形式在另一种语言中则被认为是多余甚至是难以理解的。

4. 转换

英汉两种语言有很大的区别，这一事实就决定了在翻译过程中译者不应该机械地按"词性"翻译。事实上，一种语言中属于某种"词性"的一个词汇在翻译成另一种语言时常被转换成不同的词性以符合该语言的习惯。

5. 语序调整

语序调整是指在翻译中根据被译成的语言的习惯进行的必要甚至是不可避免的语序改变。这种语序改变之所以必要是因为：首先，每种语言都有自己的自然语序以及自己的语言特点；其次，语序调整作为一种修辞格经常用于表示强调。

6. 长句拆译

长句拆译指的是在翻译中必要的时候把长句分译成短句。在翻译中任意拆分一个长句是不可取的，但并不是说"拆句"都是不合理的。因为在英语尤其是专业英语中，长句非常常见，而汉语更倾向于用短句表达。因此，翻译中经常要用到"长句拆译"这一技巧以改变原来的句子结构。

Chapter 2　Special English word-formation

With the fast development of science and technology, many new words are created in order to describe the new phenomenon, inventions, discoveries and so on. Generally speaking, the word-formation methods of **ESP (English for Specific Purposes**[1]**)** fall under the following categories:

1　Conversion

Conversion means using a form that represents one part of speech as another part of speech without changing the form of the word. In effect, zero affix is added. Therefore, it is also called **zero derivation**[2]. For example: island *n.*（小岛）—*v.*（隔离）, coordinate *v.*（协调）—*n.*（坐标）. One distinct form of conversion in ESP is to use noun as **attribute**[3].

E.g. growth factor 生长因子　ketone bodies 酮体

point mutation 点突变　signal transduction 信号转导

2　Composition(Compounding)

Compounding is a process of word-formation by which two independent words are put together to make one word. Words formed by compounding are called compounds.

E.g.　brain + power—brainpower

power +plant—powerplant

green + house—greenhouse

Sometimes, a hyphen is used to combine the two words:

E.g.Calcium-binding 钙结合　**alanine-glucose** 丙氨酸-葡萄糖

conveyer-belt 传送带　machine-made 机制的

In English, many technical terms are composed of two or more words, which are called compound technical terms. Each of the component part seems to be independent, but in fact, the composition has a total different concept.

E.g. salvage pathway 补救合成途径　Okazaki fragment 冈崎片段

feedback inhibition 反馈抑制　housekeeping gene 管家基因

3　Affixation

The process by which words are formed by adding affixes to a root is called affixation. English affixes can be divided into **prefixes** and **suffixes**. Affixes that come before the root[4] are called prefixes. Most prefixes, when added to words, effect a change in meaning,

Remarks Column

conversion [kən'və:ʃən]*n.*转类法

attribute[ə'tribju(:)t] *n.*定语

compounding ['kɔmpaundiŋ]*n.*合词法

alanine ['ælə,ni:n]*n.* [化]丙氨酸

glucose ['glu:kəus]*n.*葡萄糖

feedback ['fi:dbæk]*n.* 反馈, 反应

affixation [,æfik'seiʃən]*n.*词缀法

prefix['pri:fiks]*n.* [语]前缀

suffix ['sʌfiks]*n.* [语]后缀

but without converting one word-class to another.

E.g. degenerate（简并）*v.*—de + generate (generate *v.*)

anticodon（反密码子）*n.*—anti + codon (codon *n.*)

ultrasonic（超声的）*a.*—ultra+ sonic (sonic *a.*)

Affixes that come after the root are called suffixes. Some suffixes, when added to words, can transform one word-class into another.

E.g. liquidize（液化）*v.*—liquid + ize (liquid *n.*)

induction（诱导）*n.*—induce + tion (induce *v.*)

nicotinic（烟碱的）*a.*—nicotin+ ic (nicotin *n.*)

4　Abbreviation (Shortening)

Shortening is frequently used in word-formation especially in English for science and technology. There are two kinds of shortening, clipped words and **initialisms**.

Clipped words are those created by clipping part of a word, leaving only a piece of the old word. The shortening may occur at the beginning of a word (telephone—phone, helicopter—copter); at the end of the word (professional—pro, laboratory—lab); at both ends of the word (detective—tec, influenza—flu)

Initialisms are words formed from the initial letters of words and pronounced as letters. For example: mitogen-activated-protein kinase—MAPK（有丝分裂原激活蛋白激酶），epidermal growth factor—EGF（表皮生长因子）. Apart from clipped words and initialisms, there is another kind of abbreviation — half-abbreviation. It only shortens the first component of a word which is made up of two components or the first two components of a word made up of three, leaving the last word unchanged.

E.g. **complementary** DNA—cDNA（互补 DNA）

heterogeneous nuclear RNA—hnRNA（不均一核内 RNA）

5　Blending

Another source of word formation which creates a word by combining parts of other words is called blending: smog, brunch, helicox. Each of these is made up of the first part of one word and the second part of another: smoke + fog = smog（烟雾）；breakfast+ lunch= brunch（早午餐）；helium + oxygen= helicox.（供深水呼吸用的氢氧混合剂）

Blending has been used to create a lot of new words in order to meet the development of modern science and technology.

E.g.　biorhythm = biological + rhythm（生理节奏）

lidar = light + radar（激光雷达）

mascon = mass +concentration（质量密集）

abbreviation[əˌbriːviˈeiʃən]*n.*缩略法

initialism [iˈniʃəliz

(ə)m]*n.* [语]词首字母缩略词

complementary [kɔmpləˈmentəri] *adj.*补充的，补足的

heterogeneous [ˌhetərəuˈdʒiːniəs] *adj.*异类的

blending [ˈblendiŋ]*n.* 拼缀法

concentration[ˌkɔnsenˈtreiʃən] *n.*集中，集合，专心，浓缩，浓度

Notes

[1] ESP (English for Specific Purposes)：专门用途英语

专门用途英语是把基本英语知识和某个特殊用途（比如化学、物理、生物、商务、电子等）连接起来，不断吸收时代的新信息，能够满足学生对其他专业知识的要求。

[2] zero derivation 零位派生

不改变词的形态，只是使词从一种词类转化为另一种词类，从而使该词具有新的意义和作用，成为一个新词，这种构词的方法叫做词类转化法(conversion)。也有人把这种构词方法叫做"零位后缀派生法"（derivation by zero suffix），又简称"零位派生法"(zero-derivation)。零位派生法这个名称在一定程度上说明转化法只是派生法的一种特殊形式。

[3] Noun as attribute：名词作定语

作定语的名词往往是说明其中名词的材料、用途、时间、地点、内容、类别等。作定语用的名词一般没有与之相应的同根形容词。它既可以是有生命的，也可以是无生命的；既可以是可数的，也可以是不可数的。例如：a city streets 城市街道，plant fat 植物脂肪，a love story 爱情故事等。注意：被修饰的名词变复数时，一般情况下，作定语用的名词不需要变为复数形式，但由 man 或 woman 作定语修饰的名词变成复数时，两部分皆要变为复数形式。例如：

man doctor—men doctors 男医生

woman singer—women singers 女歌手

[4] root: 词根

词根是一个词的根本部分。它和前缀、后缀共同组成英语构词的三个要素。它表示一个单词的基本意义，是同词根共有的可以辨认出来的部分。例如：在 eulogize（称赞），prologue（序言），monologue（独白），dialogue（对话），apologize（道歉），logogram（标语）等词中，我们可以认出一个共同部分就是"log"，它表示一个共同的基本意义"言"。这个共同的部分"log"就是这些单词的词根。一个词根可以派生出许多新词。

Exercises

1.Make a semantic analysis of the relationship between noun attributes and the words they qualify.

Example: anxiety neurosis = neurosis caused by anxiety

soap suds, mosquito net, fire squad, fertility site, influenza virus, battle fatigue, brisk mason, voter enthusiasm, surface vessel, investment money, donor blood, export reject.

2.Explain the term "conversion". Pick out examples of conversion I the sentences below to illustrate your explanation:

（1）So she believed me and doctored my battered face, pleased that she could be useful.

（2）The train was telescoped as a result of the collision.

（3）We cannot mandate a solution to inflation.

（4）He preferred moderns like Micro and Klee.

（5）The television drearies the ball game.

（6）Heart transplants began 10 years ago. Why have British doctors done only four since then?

3. Translate the following words into English

转类法　　缩略法　　葡萄糖　　前缀　　后缀　　定语

反馈　　　词缀法　　　补充的　　　异类的　　　集中　　　拼缀法

4. Cloze

All life processes consist of chemical reactions catalyzed ＿（1）＿ enzymes. The reactions in a living organism, which are known collectively ＿（2）＿ metabolism, result ＿（3）＿ highly coordinated and purposeful activity. The primary functions of metabolism are: ① acquisition and utilization of energy, ②synthesis of molecules ＿（4）＿ for cell structure and functioning (i.e., protein, nucleic acids, lipids, and carbohydrates), and ③ removal ＿（5）＿ waste products.

＿（6）＿ first glance the thousands of reactions the occur in cells appear overwhelmingly complex. However, several characteristics of metabolism allow us to vastly simplify this picture.

① While ＿（7）＿ number of reactions is very large, the number of reaction types is relatively small.

② The mechanisms ＿（8）＿ in biochemical reactions [i.e., the means ＿（9）＿ chemical changes occur] are relatively simple.

Reactions of central importance in biochemistry [i.e., ＿（10）＿ used in energy production and the synthesis and degradation of major cell components] are relatively few in number.

（1） A. in   B. by   C. to   D. with
（2） A. to   B. for   C. as   D. with
（3） A. with   B. for   C. in   D. to
（4） A. to need   B. needing   C. need   D. needed
（5） A. in   B. of   C. to   D. against
（6） A. With   B. To   C. At   D. In
（7） A. a   B. the   C. some   D. small
（8） A. to use   B. to be used   C. using   D. used
（9） A. in which   B. which   C. by which   D. with which
（10） A. they   B. the ones   C. these   D. those

参考译文

随着科技的快速发展，人们通过创造新的词汇来表示新的科学技术现象和发明。一般来讲，专业英语的构词方式主要包括以下几种。

1. 转类法

转类法指的是无需借助词缀就实现词性的转换，又被称为零位派生。例如：名词 island（小岛）转化成动词 island（隔离），动词 coordinate（协调）转化成名词 coordinate（坐标）。专业英语转类构词法中一个较突出的现象是名词作定语修饰另一个名词。如：growth factor 生长因子，ketone bodies 酮体，point mutation 点突变，signal transduction 信号转导。

2. 合词法

合词法是把两个独立的词合称为一个词。用这种方法构成的新词叫做复合词。例如：

brain + power—brainpower　脑力

power +plant—powerplant　发电站

green + house—greenhouse　温室

有的合成词的两个成分之间要有连字符。例如：

calcium-binding 钙结合　alanine-glucose 丙氨酸-葡萄糖

conveyer-belt 传送带　machine-made 机制的

英语中有很多术语属于由两个以上的词组成，叫复合术语。它们的构成部分虽看似独立，但实际上合起来构成一个完整的概念，因此应该把它们看成是一个术语。例如：

salvage pathway　补救合成途径　Okazaki fragment 冈崎片段

feedback inhibition 反馈抑制　housekeeping gene 管家基因

3. 词缀法

通过在词根上加词缀组成一个新词的构词方式叫词缀法。英语词缀分前缀和后缀两种。加于词根前的叫前缀。一般来说，前缀只改变词的意义，不改变其词类。例如：

degenerate（简并）*v.*—de + generate (generate 是动词)

anticodon（反密码子）*n.*—anti + codon (codon 是名词)

ultrasonic（超声的）*a.*—ultra+ sonic (sonic 是形容词)

加在词根后面的词缀叫后缀。加后缀构成的新词可能改变也可能不改变词意，但一般改变词性。例如：

liquidize（液化）*v.*—liquid + ize (liquid *n.*)

induction（诱导）*n.*—induce + tion (induce *v.*)

nicotinic（烟碱的）*a.*—nicotin+ ic (nicotin *n.*)

4. 缩略法

缩略法是科技英语中非常常见的一种构词法。主要分为缩短词和首字母缩略词两种。

缩短词是去掉一个单词的一部分而产生的词。有可能去除单词的头部，如 telephone—phone, helicopter—copter; 有可能去除单词的尾部，如 professional—pro, laboratory—lab; 有可能去除单词的两头，如 detective—tec, influenza—flu。

首字母缩略词是取每个单词的首字母，然后按字母读音发音。如 mitogen-activited-protein kinase—MAPK（有丝分裂原激活蛋白激酶），epidermal growth factor—EGF（表皮生长因子）。

除了缩短词和首字母缩略词以外，还有一种半缩略词。这类词只缩略两个成分组成的词的第一成分或三个成分组成的词的前两个部分，最后一个成分保持不变。

如：complementary DNA—cDNA（互补 DNA）

heterogeneous nuclear RNA—hnRNA（不均一核内 RNA）

5. 拼缀法

对原有的两个词进行剪裁，取舍其中的首部或尾部，然后连成一个新词，这种方法叫拼缀法，如 smog（烟雾）由 smoke 和 fog 拼缀而成，brunch（早午餐）由 breakfast 和 lunch 组成。

为了适应现代科学和技术的发展，利用拼缀法构成了不少新词。如：

biorhythm = biological + rhythm（生理节奏）

lidar = light + radar（激光雷达）

mascon = mass +concentration（质量密集）

Reading material

Glossary of Prefixes, Roots, Suffixes

a-/an-　无，非

ace-/acet/aceto　乙酸的

acid　酸

acryl　丙烯酰基

acyl　酰基

aer-　需氧的，好氧的

albi　白色

alcohol　醇

-aldehyde/-al　醛

alk　烃

alky-　烷基

allyl-　烯丙基

-amide 酰胺
-amine 胺
amino- 氨基的
-an 聚糖
-ane 烷
anhydrous 无水的
-ant 剂
anti- 抗，反对
apo- 离，脱，远
aqu- 水
aryl 芳（香）基
asco- 子囊
-ase 酶
aspergill 曲霉
-ate 正盐，酯
auto- 自动
bacilli- 杆菌
benzyl- 苯甲基，苄基
bi- 二，双
bi-/bis- 二元的，酸式的
bio- 生物
brady- 徐缓
bronch- 支气管
but(a)- 丁，丁基
by- 旁，副
carboxyl 羧基
card- 心脏
cary/caryo 核
cephal/cephalo 头
cetyl 十六（烷）基
chloro- 氯
chol- 胆，胆汁
chrom- 有色的
-cide 杀…剂
cis- 顺式
co-,com- 共同
coccus 球菌
contra- 反，逆
cry(o)- 冷，低温，冰冻
cyan 氰
cyan(o)- 青紫，绀，氰(基)
cycl-/cyclo 环，圆

cyst- 膀胱，囊
cyto-/cyt- 细胞的
de- 除去，分解，降低
deca- 十
dent- 牙
deoxy- 脱氧
derm- 皮，膜
dermato- 皮，膜
di- 二、双、联
dia- 离，通过
dis- 去，除去
dys- 有病的
-ectasis 扩张
ecto-/ex-/exo- 外的
en-/endo- 内的
-ene 烯
entero- 肠道的
epl- 在…上
erythro- 红
ester 酯
eth- 乙
ether 醚
ethinyl 乙炔基
eu- 优，真
ex- 出，外，离
extra- 外的
facultative 兼性的
febri- 烧，热
fibr- 纤维
flav 黄色的
gastr- 胃
-gen 原
gen- 基因的，遗传的
glyc- 糖，糖原，甘（油，
         氨酸）
glycer-/glycerol 甘油，丙
                  三醇
-gram 图
hem-/hemato- 血
hemi- 半，单侧
hepat-/hepato- 肝
hept-/hepta- 七，庚

hetero- 杂，异
hexa- 六，己
hexadeca- 十六
homo-/hom- 均匀，相同
-hydrate 水合物
hydro-/hydra- 氢，水
hydroxide 氢氧化物
hydroxyl 羟基，氢氧(基)
hyper- 高，超(出)
hypo- 次，亚，低
-ic acid 正酸
-ide 化物
immuno- 免疫性的
in- 内
-in 素
inter- 间
intra- 内的
ion- 离子
iso- 异构，相等
-ite 亚盐
-itis 炎
karyo-/caryo- 核
keto- 酮基
lact-/lacti-/lacto 乳，乳酸糖
lauryl 十二（烷）基
leuc- 白色，白细胞
lip-/lipo- 脂肪的，类脂
-lith 石
lymph- 淋巴
-lyte 产物
mal- 坏，错误
-megaly 巨大
meso- 内消旋
meta-/m- 间位的
-meter 仪，计
meth- 甲
-mia 血症
micro- 微
mono- 单一的
mort- 死
multi- 多
mycete- 霉菌

myco- 真菌

-necrosis 坏死

neo- 新

nephro- 肾

nerv-/nervi-/nervo- 神经的

nitr- 含氮的

nitril 腈

nitro- 硝基

nitroso- 亚硝基

nona- 九，壬

nucle- 核（的），核酸

oct(a)- 八，辛

-oid 类似物

-ol 醇

ole 油

oligo- 寡，少

-oma 肿瘤

-one 酮

orth(o)/o- 邻位的

-ose 糖

-osis 病态

-oste(o) 骨

-ous acid 亚酸

-oxide 氧化物

p-/para 对

path (o)- 病

-pathy 病

-penia 缺乏，不足

penicill 青霉

pent(a)-/amyl- 五，戊

penta 五

per- 高，过

peri- 周（围），近

phago-/-phage 噬

phenoxy 苯氧基

phenyl 苯基

-philic 亲，好，嗜

-phobic 厌，嫌，疏

photo- 光

plano- 浮动的，平面，水平

plasm 原生质

-plast 体，质

poly- 多，聚

pre- 先，前

pri- 伯，一级

pro- 原

prop- 丙

prote- 蛋白质的

pseudo- 单，假

psycho- 精神，心理

pyro- 焦，火热，焦性

radio- 放射

ribo- 核糖

saccharo- 糖

sapro- 腐败

-sclerosis 硬化

sec- 仲，二级

sept- 隔膜

-side 苷

-some 体

staphyl 葡萄球菌

-stat 抑制…剂

stereo- 立体的

strept- 链，链霉

sub- 亚，下，不足

terpin 萜

tert- 叔，三级

tetra- 四

therm-/thermo- 热

thi 硫

trans- 反，转

tri- 三

-type 型

-um/-ium …金属

uni 单

uro- 尿

vinyl 乙烯基

-yl 基

-yne 炔

Unit 2 Fundamental chemistry

Chapter 3 Elements and compounds

Elements are pure **substances** that can not be decomposed into simpler substances by ordinary chemical changes. At present there are 109 known elements. Some common elements that are familiar to you are **carbon**, **oxygen**, **aluminum**, **iron**, **copper**, **nitrogen**, and gold. The elements are the building blocks of matter just as the numerals 0 through 9 are the building blocks for numbers. To the best of our knowledge, the elements that have been found on the earth also comprise the entire universe.

Pure substances composed of two or more elements are called **compounds**. Because they contain two or more elements, compounds, unlike elements, are capable of being decomposed into simpler substances by chemical changes. The ultimate chemical decomposition of compounds produces the elements from which they are made.

The **atoms** of the elements in a compound are combined in whole number ratio, not in fractional parts of an atom. Atoms combined with one another to form compounds which exist as either **molecule** or **ions**. A molecule is a small, **uncharged** individual unit of a compound formed by the union of two or more atoms, if we subdivide a drop of water into smaller and smaller particles, we ultimately obtain a single unit of water known as a molecule of water. We cannot subdivide this unit further without destroying the molecule, breaking it up into its elements. Thus, a water molecule is the smallest unit of the compound water.

There are over three million known compounds, with no end in sight as to the number that can and will be prepared in the future. Each compound is unique and has characteristic physical and chemical properties. Let us consider in some detail the compound water. Water is a colorless, **odorless**, tasteless liquid that can be changed to a solid, ice at 0℃ and to a gas, steam at 100℃. It is composed of two atoms of **hydrogen** and one atom of oxygen per molecule, which represents 11.2 percent hydrogen and 88.8 percent oxygen by **mass**. Water reacts chemically with **sodium** to produce **hydrogen gas** and **sodium hydroxide**, with **lime** to produce **calcium hydroxide**, and with **sulfur trioxide** to produce **sulfuric acid**. No other compound has all these exact physical and chemical properties; they are characteristic of water alone.

Expressions and Technical Terms
hydrogen gas 氢气
sodium hydroxide 氢氧化钠
calcium hydroxide 氢氧化钙
sulfur trioxide 三氧化硫
sulfuric acid 硫酸

Notes

[1] special background　物质都是由被称为元素（element）的基本物质所组成。元素是同种原子（atom）的总称，同种原子具有相同的原子序数和核电荷数。化学反应中不能将原子分解成更小的单位。纯净物可以分为单质（elementary substance）和化合物（compound）。单质只含一种元素，而化合物含有两种或两种以上的元素。

[2] Elements are pure substances that can not be decomposed into simpler substances by ordinary chemical changes. 元素是纯的物质，不能通过一般的化学变化分解成为更简单的物质。that 从句为定语从句，翻译时将定语从句转换成谓语，也可译为元素是不能通过一般的化学变化分解成为更简单的物质的纯的物质，只是这样翻译显得句子结构不匀称。

[3] The elements are the building blocks of matter just as the numerals 0 through 9 are the building blocks for numbers. 元素是组成物质的基本单元，就像 0 到 9 的数字是组成数的基本单元一样。building block 原意为建筑物的砖块，比喻为基本单元。numeral 为数字之意，指 0～9 这 10 个阿拉伯数字，number 是一般意义上的数，如 123 由 1、2 和 3 三个阿拉伯数字组成。

[4] The ultimate chemical decomposition of compounds produces the elements from which they are made. 化合物化学分解的最终结果是生成组成该化合物的元素。from which they are made 为定语从句，修饰 the elements，词组 be made from 的介词 from 提到 which 之前，they 指代 compounds。

[5] A molecule is a small, uncharged individual unit of a compound formed by the union of two or more atoms, if we subdivide a drop of water into smaller and smaller particles, we ultimately obtain a single unit of water known as a molecule of water. 化合物中的一个分子是由两个或者更多的原子结合而成的很小且不带电荷的单元，当我们把一滴水分成越来越小的部分，我们最终得到一个称之为水分子的单元。formed by the union of two or more atoms 过去分词做后置定语，也可以用相应的定语从句来表示，即 which are formed by the union of two or more atoms。known as a molecule of water 的语法地位与之相同。

[6] No other compound has all these exact physical and chemical properties; they are characteristic of water alone. 没有其他的化合物具有所有这些确切的物理和化学性质，这些性质是水所特有的。be characteristic of 是词组，"属于…所特有的"，"…的特性是"。

Exercises

1. Put the following into Chinese

When carbon unites with oxygen, it forms a colorless, odorless, and tasteless gas called carbon dioxide, which is heavier than air and will extinguish flame. Carbon dioxide is like nitrogen in many ways, but if it is mixed with limewater, it causes the clear liquid to become milky, while nitrogen does not. This is the test for carbon dioxide. Carbon dioxide is a source of plant food. Plants have the power to take this gas from the air, combine it with water, and make it into their tissues; in fact it is from this source that all organic carbon comes.

2. Put the following into English

元素　分子式　二氧化碳　硝酸钠　氧气　硫酸　氯化银

氢离子　氨气　氢氧化钾　无机化合物　无色无味

3. Cloze

All matters is ___(1)___ of basic substances called elements. An element cannot be broken down into simpler units by ___(2)___ reactions; it contains only one kind of atom, which has a specific number of nuclear ___(3)___. An atom is the smallest characteristic unit of an element.

A compound is a substance that can be split into ___(4)___ of more elements. Water is a compound because it can be split into its ___(5)___, hydrogen and oxygen. The formula of a compound ___(6)___ information about the kinds and numbers of ___(7)___ that make up each molecule of that compound. A formula contains the ___(8)___ of the kinds of atoms in each molecule and ___(9)___ that indicate the number of each kind of atom in the molecule. For example, the formula of glucose, $C_6H_{12}O_6$, contains six carbon atoms, ___(10)___ hydrogen atoms, and six oxygen atoms.

（1）A.composed　　B. consisted　　C. consisting　　　D.composing　　　　　（　　）
（2）A.phisical　　B.chemical　　C.biological　　D. general　　　　（　　）
（3）A.size　　B. weight　　C. density　　D.charge　　　　（　　）
（4）A. one　　B.two　　C. three　　D. many　　　　（　　）
（5）A.atom　　B.particles　　C.components　　D. ions　　　　（　　）
（6）A. says　　B.calls　　C.gives　　D. writes　　　　（　　）
（7）A.atoms　　B.molecules　　C. ions　　D. groups　　　　（　　）
（8）A. signs　　B.shapes　　C. symbols　　D. figures　　　　（　　）
（9）A. scripts　　B.subscripts　　C.numbers　　D. characters　　　　（　　）
（10）A. six　　B. twelve　　C.ten　　D. eleven　　　　（　　）

参考译文

　　元素是单纯的物质，不能通过一般的化学变化分解成为更简单的物质。目前已知有109种元素。一些你熟悉的常见元素是碳、氧、铝、铁、氮和金。元素是组成物质的基本单元，就像0到9的数字是组成数的基本单元一样。就我们所知，已经在地球上发现的元素也是组成整个宇宙的元素。

　　两种或者更多种元素结合成的单纯物质称为化合物。化合物与元素不同，由于其中含有两种或者更多种的元素，所以能够由化学变化分解成为更简单的物质。化合物化学分解的最终结果是生成组成该化合物的元素。

　　化合物中各个元素的原子以整数比的形式组成，而不是以某个原子的小数形式。一些原子与另一些其他原子结合成的化合物或者以分子存在，或者以离子存在。化合物中的一个分子是由两个或者更多的原子结合而成的很小且不带电荷的单元，当我们把一滴水分成越来越小的部分，我们最终得到一个称之为水分子的单元。这个水分子由结合在一起的两个氢原子和一个氧原子组成。我们不能将水分子进一步再分，分裂成元素。因而水分子是水这种化合物的最小单元。

已知的化合物超过 3000000 种，在今后还会制备出新的化合物，其种类还要增加。每一种化合物是唯一的（与其他的化合物有区别的）并且有其独特的物理和化学性质。让我们从某些具体内容来考察两种化合物——水和氧化汞。水是无色、无臭、无味的液体，在 0℃下变成固体即冰，而在 100℃变为气体即蒸汽。水的每个分子由一个氧原子和两个氢原子结合而成，氢和氧的质量百分数分别为 11.2 和 88.8。水与钠反应生成氢气和氢氧化钠，与石灰反应生成氢氧化钙，与三氧化硫反应生成硫酸。其他的化合物不具有所有这些准确的理化性质，这些性质是水所特有的。

Chapter 4　Organic solvent

Organic solvents are a chemical class of compounds that are used routinely in industries. They share a common structure (at least 1 carbon atom and 1 hydrogen atom), low **molecular weight**, **lipophilicity**, and **volatility**, and they exist in liquid form at **room temperature**.

Table 4-1: Some operations and formulations with some associated solvents

paints and lacquers	toluene, xylene, methyl ethyl ketone
adhesives	cyclohexanes, acetones
antifreeze	ethylene glycol
degreasing	trichloroethylene, perchloroethylene
drycleaning	perchloroethylene
printing	turpentine, white spirits, xylene

The physical properties of an organic solvent have great bearing on the **safe handling procedures** for that chemical and play a large role in determining the degree of fire and explosion hazard associated with its use. Important properties are listed below.

Boiling point

This is an indicator of how readily the chemical becomes a gas (**vapourises**). The lower the boiling point, the more readily it vapourises.

Flash point

The lower the flash point, the greater the **flammability**. A solvent with a flash point of 23℃ or less is highly flammable; a flash point between 23℃ and 61℃ represents moderate flammability. A flash point of more than 61℃ is low flammability.

Table 4-2: Some highly flammable organic solvents (flashpoint of 23℃ or below)

acetaldehyde	diethyl ether	petroleum ether
acetone	ethanol	propanol
acetonitrile	ethyl acetate	pyridine
benzene	*n*-hexane	tetrahydrofuran
carbon disulphide	methanol	toluene
cyclohexane	methyl ethyl ketone	vinyl acetate
cyclohexene	pentane	

Explosive limits

Remarks Column

lipophilicity *n.*亲油性
volatility [ˌvɔləˈtiliti]*n.*挥发性
formulation[ˌfɔːmjuˈleiʃən]*n.*制剂
lacquer [ˈlækə]*n.*漆
toluene [ˈtɔljuiːn]*n.*甲苯
xylene [ˈzailiːn]*n.*二甲苯
adhesive[ədˈhiːsiv]*n.*黏合剂
cyclohexane [ˌsaikləuˈheksein]*n.* 环己烷
acetone [ˈæsitəun]*n.*丙酮
antifreeze[ˈæntiˈfriːz]*n.*抗冻剂
trichloroethylene [traiˌklɔːrəuˈeθˌliːn]*n.*三氯乙烯
perchloroethylene [pəˌklɔːrəuˈeθliːn] *n.*全（四）氯乙烯
turpentine [ˈtəːpəntain]*n.*松节油
vapourise *v.*蒸发
flammability[ˌflæməˈbilətI]*n.*可燃性
ignite [igˈnait]*v.*自燃
ether [ˈiːθə]*n.*醚；乙醚
trichloroethane [traiˌklɔːrəuˈeθein]*n.*三氯乙烷
acetaldehyde[ˌæsiˈtældəhaid] *n.*乙醛
ethanol [ˈeθənɔːl]*n.*乙醇
propanol *n.*丙醇
acetonitrile[ˌæsitəuˈnaitril] *n.*乙腈
pyridine [ˌpirəˈdainə] *n.*嘧啶
benzene [ˈbenziːn]*n.*苯
n-hexane *n.* 正己烷

tetrahydrofuran [ˌtetrəˌhaidrəˈfjuərən]*n.* 四氢呋喃
cyclohexene[ˌsaikləu ˈheksiːn] *n.* 环己烯
pentane [ˈpentein]*n.* 戊烷

The lower explosive limit (LEL) is the lowest concentration of solvent in air that will **ignite**. The upper explosive limit (UEL) is the highest concentration of solvent in air that will ignite. As a rule of thumb, the greater the range between the LEL and the UEL, the greater the fire hazard. For example:

ether   LEL = 1.9%   UEL = 36.0%

1,1,1-trichloroethane   LEL = 8.0%   UEL = 10.5%

Based on these values only, ether presents a greater fire hazard than the 1,1,1-trichloroethane formulation. However, to determine the fire hazard accurately, flash point and vapour pressure would also need to be considered.

Vapour density

A vapour which is heavier than air (vapour density greater than 1) will tend to collect in pools and spread near ground level and in confined spaces. A vapour which is lighter than air (vapour density less than 1) will tend to rise.

Expressions and Technical Terms

organic solvent 有机溶剂
molecular weight 分子量
room temperature 室温
methyl ethyl ketone 甲乙酮（丁酮）
ethylene glycol 乙二醇
white spirit 石油溶剂油
safe handling procedure 安全操作规程
boiling point 沸点
flash point 闪点
explosive limits 爆炸极限
vapour density 蒸气密度
diethyl ether 二乙醚
petroleum ether 石油醚
ethyl acetate 乙酸乙酯
carbon disulphide 二硫化碳
vinyl acetate 醋酸乙烯酯

Notes

[1] special background   有机溶剂（organic solvent）是一大类在生活和生产中广泛应用的有机化合物，分子量不大，能溶解一些不溶于水的物质（如油脂、蜡、树脂、橡胶、染料等），其特点是在常温常压下呈液态，具有较大的挥发性，在溶解过程中，溶质与溶剂的性质均无改变。它存在于涂料、黏合剂、漆和清洁剂中。有机溶剂包括多类物质，如链烷烃、烯烃、醇、醛、胺、酯、醚、酮、芳香烃、氢化烃、萜烯烃、卤代烃、杂环化物、含氮化合物及含硫化合物等，多数对人体有一定毒性。

[2] They share a common structure (at least 1 carbon atom and 1 hydrogen atom), low molecular weight, lipophilicity, and volatility, and they exist in liquid form at room temperature.它们具有共同的结构（至少含有 1 个碳原子和 1 个氢原子）、低的分子量、亲油性以及挥发性，且在室温下它们以液体形式存在。本句为并列复句，前一个分句介绍了有机溶剂的几个特点，后一个分句说明有机溶剂在常温下的物理状态。

[3] The physical properties of an organic solvent have great bearing on the safe handling procedures for that chemical and play a large role in determining the degree of fire and explosion hazard associated with its use. 有机溶剂的物理性质对于该化学物质的安全操作规程具有重要的意义且对确定与它的使用联系在一起的火灾和爆炸的程度具有很大的作用。have great bearing on 词组，"对于…具有重要的意义"，play a large role in 词组，"在…方面起很大作用"。

[4] As a rule of thumb, the greater the range between the LEL and the UEL, the greater the fire hazard.一般说来，爆炸极限下限和爆炸极限上限之间的范围越宽，引起火灾的可能性就越大。as a rule of thumb，词组，"一般说来"。整个句子是 the more…, the more…的结构，表示"越…就越…"。

[5] A vapour which is heavier than air (vapour density greater than 1) will tend to collect in pools and spread near ground level and in confined spaces. 如果蒸气比空气重（蒸气相对密度大于1），它将会不断沉积，然后在接近地面的水平上扩散且只在有限的空间内扩散。collect in pool 意为不断聚集，根据原文，密度比空气大的蒸气，将会（向下）沉积，然后再向四周扩散，且扩散的范围

不会太广。

Exercises

1. Put the following into Chinese

（1）Based on these values only, ether presents a greater fire hazard than the 1,1,1-trichloroethane formulation.

（2）The lower the boiling point, the more readily it vapourises.

（3）A solvent with a flash point of 23℃ or less is highly flammable; a flash point between 23℃ and 61℃ represents moderate flammability. A flash point of more than 61℃ is low flammability.

2. Put the following into English

黏合剂　　　三氯乙烯　　乙二醇　　　四氢呋喃　　　戊烷　　　　　环己烯
挥发性　　　亲油性　　　可燃性　　　爆炸极限上限　安全操作规程

3. Reading comprehension

After my last lecture, someone asked me to repeat the explanation of acids and bases. For those of you who didn't understand the first time, here it is again. The terms acid and base apply to two groups of compounds with opposing sets of characteristics. An acid is defined as a substance that releases protons, particles that have a positive electrical charge. A base is a substance that combines with these positively charged protons. Because of their electrical charges, a strong base or acid in solution can readily conduct electricity. Another important fact that you should know is that when equal amounts of an acid and a base of the same strength are mixed, they neutralize each other. In a moment, we will go to the lab and see for ourselves how neutralization works.

（1）Who is the speaker mostly to be? （　　）

（A）A neuclear physicist

（B）A chemical sales-person

（C）A chemistry professor

（D）An electrical engineer.

（2）What was the speaker asked to be? （　　）

（A）Provide a demonstration

（B）Explain a concept again

（C）Divide the group in two

（D）Concentrate on what was said

（3）What is one characteristic of acids and bases that can be inferred from the talk? （　　）

（A）Acids are more concentrated than bases

（B）Bases mixed with water make acids

（C）They are essentially of equal strength

（D）They both have electrical charge

（4）What is a proton? （　　）

（A）A strong acid in solution

（B）A neutralized solution

（C）Equal amounts of weak acids and bases

（D）Two groups of compounds with similar characteristics

（5）What happens when equal amounts of an acid and base of the same strength are mixed? （　　）

（A）The produce a neutral solution

（B）They separate into two layers

（C）They increase in strength

（D）They form two groups of compounds

参考译文

有机溶剂是一类工业上常用的化合物。它们具有共同的结构（至少含有 1 个碳原子和 1 个氢原子）、低的分子量、亲油性以及挥发性，且在室温下它们以液体形式存在。

表 4-1　一些具有某种功能的有溶剂

涂料和漆	甲苯　二甲苯　甲乙酮
黏合剂	环己烷　丙酮
抗冻剂	乙二醇
脱脂剂	三氯乙烯　全氯乙烯
干洗剂	全氯乙烯
打印（墨）剂	松节油　石油溶剂油　二甲苯

有机溶剂的物理性质对于该化学物质的安全操作规程具有重要的意义且对确定与它的使用联系在一起的火灾和爆炸的程度具有很大的作用。

沸点

沸点是化学品变成气体（挥发）难易程度的表征。沸点越低，它越容易挥发。

闪点

闪点越低，可燃性就越大。闪点小于或等于 23℃ 的溶剂高度可燃；闪点在 23℃ 和 61℃ 之间代表中等程度的可燃性。闪点高于 61℃ 则可燃性低。

表 4-2　一些高度可燃的有机溶剂（闪点小于或等于 23℃）

乙醛　二乙醚　石油醚	二硫化碳　甲醇　甲苯
丙酮　乙醇　丙醇	环己烷　甲乙酮　醋酸乙烯酯
乙腈　乙酸乙酯　嘧啶	环己烯　戊烷
苯　正己烷　四氢呋喃	

爆炸极限

爆炸极限下限（LEL）是空气中该溶剂自燃的最低浓度。爆炸极限上限（UEL）是空气中该溶剂自燃的最高浓度。一般说来，爆炸极限下限和爆炸极限上限之间的范围越宽，引起火灾的可能性就越大。例如：

乙醚　LEL = 1.9%　UEL = 36.0%

1,1,1-三氯乙烷　LEL = 8.0%　UEL = 10.5%

仅仅根据这些数值，可以得出这样的结论：乙醚比 1,1,1-三氯乙烷制剂具有更大的引起火灾的可能性。但是，为了精确地确定引起火灾的可能性，也要考虑闪点和蒸气压力。

蒸气密度

如果蒸气比空气重（蒸气相对密度大于 1），它将会不断沉积，然后在接近地面的水平上扩散且只在有限的空间内扩散。如果蒸气比空气轻（蒸气相对密度小于 1），它将会上升。

Chapter 5 Biochemical reaction

Consider the simple reaction of nitrogen to make **ammonia**:

$$N_2 + 3H_2 \rightleftarrows 2NH_3$$

About half of the world's production of ammonia is carried out industrially and half biologically. At first glance, the two processes look quite different. The industrial reaction takes place at 500°C and uses gaseous hydrogen and a metal **catalyst** under high pressure. The biochemical reaction takes place in the soil, uses **bacterial** or plant reactors, and occurs at moderate temperature and normal **atmospheric pressure** of nitrogen. These differences are so substantial that, historically, they were interpreted by supposing that biological systems are infused with a **vital spirit** that makes life possible. However, the biochemical reaction can be done with a purified **enzyme**. Like almost all biochemical reactions, the **biological synthesis** of ammonia requires a specific biochemical catalyst—an enzyme—to succeed. Enzymes are usually **proteins** and usually act as true catalysts; they carry out their reactions many times. The biological reduction of nitrogen is more similar to than different from its industrial counterpart: the energy change from synthesis of a mole of ammonia is identical in both cases, the **substrates** are the same, and the detailed chemical reaction is similar whether the catalyst is a metal or the **active site of an enzyme**.

Although there are many possible biochemical reactions, they fall into only a few types to consider: 1) **oxidation and reduction**, for example, the **interconversion** of an alcohol and an aldehyde; 2) movement of functional groups within or between molecules, for example, the transfer of **phosphate groups** from one oxygen to another; 3) addition and removal of water, for example, **hydrolysis** of an **amide linkage** to an **amine** and a **carboxyl group**; 4) **bond-breaking reaction**s, for example, **carbon-carbon bond breakage**.

The complexity of life results, not from many different types of reactions, but rather from these simple reactions occurring in many different situations. Thus, for example, water can be added to a **double bond** as a step in the breakdown of many different compounds, including **sugars**, **lipids**, and **peptides**.

Remarks Column

ammonia ['æməunjə]n.氨

catalyst ['kætəlist]n.催化剂
bacterial [bæk`tɪərɪəl]n.细菌
enzyme ['enzaɪm]n.酶
protein ['prəuti:n]n.蛋白质
substrate['sʌbstreit]n.底物
interconversion[,intə(:)kən'və:ʃən]n.相互转化
hydrolysis[hai'drɔlisis]n.水解
amine ['æmi:n] n. 胺
sugar ['ʃugə] n. 糖
lipid ['lipid]n. 脂
peptide ['peptaɪd] n. 多肽

Expressions and Technical Terms
atmospheric pressure 气压
vital spirit 生命的精气
biological synthesis 生物合成
active site of an enzyme 酶的活性部位
oxidation and reduction 氧化和还原
phosphate groups 磷酸基团
amide linkage 酰胺键
carboxyl group 羧基
bond-breaking reactions 键断裂反应
carbon-carbon bond breakage 碳-碳键断裂
double bond 双键

Notes

[1] special background　生物化学反应（biochemical reaction）也是一种化学反应。化学反应过程中两个或两个以上的物质相互作用，从而生成新物质。通常可以通过颜色变化、气味产生、气体释放、沉淀生成、能量变化来判断化学反应发生与否。而生物化学反应通常指发生在活的有机体内的化学反应。通常需要酶的参与。生物化学反应也可以在实验室中利用生化试剂进行，而该生化试剂可以来自活的有机体，也可以是实验室制备的。

[2] The biochemical reaction takes place in the soil, uses bacterial or plant reactors, and occurs at moderate temperature and normal atmospheric pressure of nitrogen.该生物化学反应发生在土壤中，使用细菌或植物作为反应器，且反应在常温和常压下进行。uses bacterial or plant reactors 指该生物化学反应发生的场所为细菌内或植物内，例如豆科植物的根瘤菌即具有生物固氮功能。normal atmospheric pressure of nitrogen 为介词 at 的宾语，意为通常气压的氮气，翻译时应注意句子的结构分析。

[3] These differences are so substantial that, historically, they were interpreted by supposing that biological systems are infused with a vital spirit that makes life possible.这些差异是如此巨大，因此历史上曾经有人认为生物系统是因为具有"生命的精气"才使得生命现象成为可能。vital spirit 意为"生命的精气"或"生命力"，是一种生物学史上的错误观点，即认为有机体含有特殊的生命力，是对有机体和无生命物体之间的差异的错误解释。

[4] The biological reduction of nitrogen is more similar to than different from its industrial counterpart: the energy change from synthesis of a mole of ammonia is identical in both cases, the substrates are the same, and the detailed chemical reaction is similar whether the catalyst is a metal or the active site of an enzyme.氮的生物还原类似于而非区别于工业上氮的还原：在两种情形下生成一摩尔氨的能量变化是相同的，反应物是相同的，而且不管催化剂是金属还是酶的活性部位，该具体的化学反应都是类似的。More A than B 词组，意为"与其说是 B，毋宁说是 A"，或"是 A 而非 B"。Substrate 本意指酶的底物，在句中也指化学反应中的反应物。whether the catalyst is a metal or the active site of an enzyme 意为不管起催化作用的是金属催化剂（化学反应）还是酶的活性部位（生物化学反应）。

[5] Movement of functional groups within or between molecules, for example, the transfer of phosphate groups from one oxygen to another，分子内或分子间官能团的转移，例如，磷酸基团从一个氧原子转移到另一个氧原子上。句中所举的例子，在生化反应中经常出现，磷酸化和脱磷酸化经常发生，其化学本质是磷酸酯键的断裂和形成。

[6] The complexity of life results, not from many different types of reactions, but rather from these simple reactions occurring in many different situations.生命的复杂性不是（有机体具有）很多不同类型的反应的结果，而是（有机体内）这些简单的反应在很多不同的情形下发生的结果。根据原文，要进行适当增译，才能把原文的意思表达清楚。

Exercises

1. Put the following into English

| 相互转化 | 磷酸基团 | 酰胺键 | 羧基 | 有机体 |
| 水解 | 氧化和还原 | 碳碳键断裂 | 生物合成 | 酶的活性部位 |

2. Put the following into Chinese

The ultimate basis for controlling biochemical reactions is the genetic information stored in the cell's DNA. This information is expressed in a regulated fashion, so that the enzymes responsible for carrying out the cell's chemical reactions are released in response to the needs of the cell for energy production, replication, and so forth. The information is composed of long sequences of subunits, where each subunit is one of the four nucleotides that make up the nucleic acid.

3. Cloze

Life on earth ultimately depends on nonliving energy ___（1）___. The most obvious of these is the sun, whose energy is ___（2）___ here on Earth by photosynthesis (the use of the light energy to carry out the synthesis of biochemicals especially sugars). Another source of energy is the ___（3）___ of the Earth itself. Microorganisms living in deep water, the soil, and other environments without sunlight can ___（4）___ their energy from chemosynthesis, the oxidation and reduction of inorganic molecules to yield biological energy.

The goal of these energy-storing processes is the production of carbon-containing ___（5）___ compounds, whose carbon is reduced (more electron-rich) than carbon in CO_2. Energy-yielding metabolic processes oxidize the reduced carbon, yielding energy in the process. The organic compounds from these processes are synthesized into ___（6）___ structures, again using energy. The sum total of these processes is the use of the original energy source, that is, light from the sun, for the maintenance and ___（7）___ of living organisms, for example, humans.

The energy available from these reactions is always ___（8）___ the amount of energy put into them. This is another way of saying that living systems ___（9）___ the Second Law of Thermodynamics, which states that spontaneous reactions run "downhill," with an increase in entropy, or ___（10）___, of the system. (For example, glucose, which contains six carbons joined together, is more ordered than are six molecules of CO_2, the product of its metabolic breakdown.)

（1）A.resouces   B.form   C. sources   D.synthesis   （   ）
（2）A.seize   B. captured   C.got   D.reached   （   ）
（3）A. makeup   B.make up   C.make from   D. matters   （   ）
（4）A.absorb   B.release   C.delete   D. derive   （   ）
（5）A.inorganic   B.mineral   C. organic   D.general   （   ）
（6）A. easy   B. complex   C.simple   D.couple   （   ）
（7）A.grow   B.addition   C.reply   D. replication   （   ）
（8）A. more than   B. less than   C.equals   D. relevant to   （   ）
（9）A. obey   B.counteract   C.belong to   D. break away from （   ）
（10）A.normal   B. order   C. disorder   D.beautiful   （   ）

参考译文

考虑一个简单的由氮制备氨气的反应：

$$N_2 + 3H_2 \rightleftharpoons 2NH_3$$

全球大约一半的氨气是通过工业生产的，而另一半是生物合成的。粗一看，这两个过程似乎大不相同。该工业反应在500℃下发生且在高压下使用气态氢和金属催化剂。而生物化学反应发生在土壤中，使用细菌或植物作为反应器，且反应在常温和常压下进行。这些差异是如此巨大，因此历史上曾经有人认为生物系统是因为具有"生命的精气"才使得生命现象成为可能。但是，该生物化学反应可通过使用纯化的酶来加以完成。与几乎所有的生物化学反应一样，氨的生物合成需要特定的生物化学催化剂——酶——才得以完成。酶通常为蛋白质且通常作为真正的催化剂而起作用；它们可以多次重复进行它们的催化反应。氮的生物还原类似于而非区别于工业上氮的还原：在两种情形下生成一摩尔氨的能量变化是相同的，反应物是相同的，而且不管催化剂是金属还是酶的活性部位，该具体的化学反应都是类似的。

尽管可能有许多生物化学反应，但可以将它们分成少数几类来加以考虑：① 氧化还原反应，例如，乙醇和乙醛的相互转化；② 分子内和分子间官能团的转移，例如磷酸基团从一个氧原子转移到另一个氧原子上；③ 水的加合或去除，例如酰胺键水解为胺和羧基；④ 键断裂反应，例如碳碳键断裂。

生命的复杂性不是（有机体具有）很多不同类型的反应的结果，而是（有机体内）这些简单的反应在很多不同的情形下发生的结果。因而，举例而言，作为很多不同的化合物包括糖、脂，以及多肽的分解过程中的一个反应步骤，水可以与这些化合物中的双键进行加成。

Reading material

Chemical Reaction

A chemical reaction is a process that always results in the **interconversion** of chemical substances. The substance or substances initially involved in a chemical reaction are called **reactants**. Chemical reactions are usually characterized by a chemical change, and they **yield** one or more **products**, which usually have properties different from the reactants. Classically, chemical reactions **encompass** changes that strictly involve the motion of electrons in the forming and breaking of **chemical bonds**, although the general concept of a chemical reaction, in particular the notion of a **chemical equation**, is applicable to **transformations** of **elementary particles**, as well as nuclear reactions.

1. Chemical **kinetics**

The rate of a chemical reaction is a measure of how the concentration or pressure of the involved substances changes with time. Analysis of reaction **rates** is important for several applications, such as in **chemical engineering** or in **chemical equilibrium** study. Rates of reaction depend basically on:

（1）Reactant concentrations, which usually make the reaction happen at a faster rate if raised through increased **collisions** per unit time.

（2）**Surface area** available for contact between the reactants, in particular solid ones in **heterogeneous systems**. Larger surface area leads to higher reaction rates.

（3）Pressure, by increasing the pressure, you decrease the **volume** between molecules. This will increase the **frequency** of collisions of molecules.

（4）**Activation energy**, which is defined as the amount of energy required to make the reaction start and carry on **spontaneously**. Higher activation energy implies that the reactants need more energy to start than a reaction with a lower activation energy.

（5）Temperature, which **hastens** reactions if raised, since higher temperature increases the energy of the molecules, creating more collisions per unit time.

（6）The presence or absence of a **catalyst**. Catalysts are substances which change the **pathway (mechanism)** of a reaction which in turn increases the speed of a reaction by lowering the activation energy needed for the reaction to take place. A catalyst is not destroyed or changed during a reaction, so it can be used again.

（7）For some reactions, the presence of **electromagnetic radiation**, most notably **ultraviolet,** is needed to **promote** the breaking of bonds to start the reaction. This is particularly true for reactions involving **radicals**.

Reaction rates are related to the concentrations of substances involved in reactions, as **quantified** by the rate law of each reaction. Note that some reactions have rates that are independent of reactant concentrations. These are called **zero order reactions**.

2. Reactions and energy

Chemical energy is part of all chemical reactions. Energy is needed to break chemical bonds in the starting substances. As new bonds form in the final substances, energy is released. By comparing the **chemical energy** of the original substances with the chemical energy of the final substances, you can decide if energy is **released** or **absorbed** in the overall reaction.

New Words

interconversion ［,intə(:)kən'və:ʃən]*n.* 相互转化

reactant [ri:'æktənt]*n.*反应物

yield [ji:ld]*v.*生成

product ['prɔdəkt]*n.*产物，生成物

encompass [in'kʌmpəs]*v.*包括，包含

transformation [,trænsfə'meiʃən]*n.*转变

kinetics [kai'netiks]*n.*动力学

rate [reit]*n.*速率

collision [kə'liʒən]*n.*碰撞

volume ['vɔlju:m]*n.*体积

frequency ['fri:kwənsɪ]*n.*频率

spontaneous [spɔn'teinjəs]*adj.*自发的

hasten ['heisn]*v.*加快

catalyst ['kætəlist]*n.*催化剂

pathway ['pɑ:θwei]*n.*途径

mechanism ['mekənizəm]*n.*机理

ultraviolet ['ʌltrə'vaiəlit]*n.*紫外线

promote [prə'məut]*v.*促进

radical ['rædikəl]*n.*自由基

quantify ['kwɔntifai]*v.*定量

release [ri'li:s]*v.*释放

absorb [əb'sɔ:b]*v.*吸收

Expressions and Technical Terms

chemical bond 化学键

chemical equation 化学方程式

elementary particle 原子

nuclear reaction 核反应

chemical engineering 化学工程

chemical equilibrium 化学平衡

surface area 表面积

heterogeneous system 非均相系统

activation energy 活化能

electromagnetic radiation 电磁辐射

zero order reaction 零级反应

chemical energy 化学能

Unit **3** Biochemical engineering

Chapter 6   Introduction

6.1   The nature of biotechnology

Biotechnology is an area of applied bioscience and technology which involves（涉及，包括）the practical application of biological organisms, or their subcellular components to manufacturing and service industries and to environmental management. Biotechnology utilizes **bacteria**, **yeasts**, **fungi, algae**, plant cells or cultured mammalian cells as constituents of industrial processes. Successful application of biotechnology will **result** only **from** the integration of a multiplicity of scientific disciplines and technologies, including microbiology, biochemistry, genetics, molecular biology chemistry and chemical and process engineering.

Biotechnological processes will normally involve the production of cells or biomass, and the achievement of desired chemical transformations. The latter may be further subdivided into:

(a) formation of a desired end product (e. g. enzymes, **antibiotics**, organic acids, **steroids**);

(b) decomposition of a given starting material (e. g. **sewage disposal**, destruction of industrial wastes or **oil spillages**).

The reactions of biotechnological processes can be **catabolic**, in which complex compounds are **broken down** to simpler ones (**glucose** to ethanol), or **anabolic** or biosynthetic, whereby simple **molecules** are **built up** into more complex ones (antibiotic synthesis). Catabolic reactions are usually exergonic（放能的）**whereas** anabolic reactions are normally endergonic（吸热的）.

Biotechnology includes **fermentation** processes (**ranging**

Remarks Column

bacteria [bæk'tiəriə]*n.*细菌
yeast [ji:st]*n.*酵母；发酵物 barm
fungi ['fʌndʒai, 'fʌŋgai]*n.*真菌类
(包括霉菌、食用伞菌、酵母菌等),
似真菌的，由真菌引起的
algae ['ældʒi:]*n.*藻类
genetics [dʒi'netiks]*n.*遗传学

antibiotics *n.*抗生素，抗生学
steroid ['stiərɔid]*n.*类固醇

catabolic [ˌkætə'bɔlik]*adj.*分解代
谢的，异化的
glucose ['glu:kəus] *n.* [化]葡萄糖
anabolic [əˈnæbəlik]*adj.*合成代谢
的 of or relating to anabolism
molecule ['mɔlikju:l] *n.* 分子

from beers and wines to bread, cheese, antibiotics and **vaccines**), water and waste treatment, parts of food technology, and an increasing range of novel applications ranging from biomedical to metal recovery from low grade ores. Because of its versatility（全面性）, biotechnology will exert a major impact in many industrial processes and **in theory** almost all organic materials could be produced by biotechnological methods. Predictions of future worldwide **market potential** for biotechnological products in the year 2000 have been **estimated at** nearly US $ 65bn (Table **6-1**). However, it must also be appreciated that many important new bio-products will still be synthesized chemically from models **derived from** existing biological molecules, e. g., new drugs based on the interferons（干扰素）. Thus the interface between bioscience and chemistry and its relationship to biotechnology must be broadly **interpreted**.

A high proportion of the techniques used in biotechnology **tend to** be more economic, less energy demanding and safer than current traditional industrial processes and for most processes the residues are **biodegradable** and **non-toxic**. **In the long term** biotechnology offers a means of solving some major world problems, **in particular** those related to medicine, food production, pollution control and the development of new energy sources.

Table 6-1　Growth potential for worldwide biotechnological markets by the year 2000

Market sector	$ (million)
Energy	16350
Foods	12655
Chemicals	10550
Health care (pharmaceuticals)	9080
Agriculture	8546
Metal recovery	4570
Pollution control	100
Other (i.e. unexpected developments)	3000
Total	**64851**

From T. A. Sheets Co. (1983). Biotechnology Bulletin November.

whereas [(h)wɛər'æz]*conj.*但是，然而

fermentation [ˌfəːmen'teiʃən]*n.* 发酵 zymosis

vaccine ['væksiːn]*n.*疫苗；痘苗

interpret [in'təːprit]*vt.*解释；说明 *vt. & vi.*口译；翻译 analyze

biodegradable [ˌbaiəudi'greidəbl] *adj.*生物所能分解的

non-toxic　*adj.* 无毒的

Expressions and Technical Terms
result from　产生于
sewage disposal　污水处理
oil spillage　石油泄漏
break down　分解
built up　组合
in theory　理论上
market potential　市场潜力
estimate at　估计，猜测…为
derived from　由…起源
tend to　趋向
In the long term 从长远观点来看
in particular　尤其，特别

Notes

[1] special background　生物技术（biotechnology）系以生命科学为基础，利用生物体系和工程原理进行生物制品的生产和新物种的研制的综合性科学技术，又称生物工程。主要包括基因工程、细胞工程、酶工程和发酵工程四个领域。传统的生物技术如微生物发酵技术，已在食品、制

药和轻工业等部门广泛应用，并形成了庞大的产业。生物技术的显著应用不仅在健康行业，在其他产业中的研发投入也十分突出。依靠生物技术，农业上用更少的土地生产更多的健康食品；制造业可以减少环境污染、节省能耗；工业可以利用再生资源生产原料，以保护环境。

[2] Successful application of biotechnology will result only from the integration of a multiplicity of scientific disciplines and technologies, including microbiology, biochemistry, genetics, molecular biology chemistry and chemical and process engineering. 生物技术的成功应用只有通过多种理论学科结合才能实现，这包括微生物学、生物化学、遗传学、分子生物化学、化学和过程工艺的知识。including 以动词的 ing 形式作后置定语修饰 disciplines and technologies。

[3] Biotechnological processes will normally involve the production of cells or biomass, and the achievement of desired chemical transformations. 生物工艺过程一般包括细胞或者生物物质的产生和所期望化学转变的成功实现。desired 是过去分词作定语修饰 chemical transformations。

[4] Biotechnology has been defined as a subject that uses biological organism, systems or processes to manufacture industrial products. 生物工程是应用生物有机体、生物系统或生物过程来制造工业产品的学科。这里 that 引导的是定语从句，修饰的是 subject。

[5] Biotechnology is in reality a subject of great antiquity, having its origin in ancient microbial processes such as brewing, wine making, and fermented milk products as cheese and yoghurts. 生物工程在应用微生物方面有很悠久的历史。例如酿酒，发酵乳制品奶酪、酸乳等。现在分词短语 having… 表示伴随状况，作状语。

[6] It cannot be ascertained whether these microbial processes arose by accidental observation or by intuitive experimentation but their further and continued development were early examples of man's abilities to use the vital activities of organisms for his own needs. 现在还不能确定这些微生物过程的发现是基于偶然的观察还是直接的实验，但是微生物过程的进一步和持续发展确是人类运用生物有机体的活动满足自己需求的早期例证。这里 whether 引导的是定语从句，修饰的是 it。

Exercises

1. Put the following into Chinese

Although not normally thought of as biotechnology, agriculture clearly fits the broad definition of *"using a biological system to make products"* such that the cultivation of plants may be viewed as the earliest biotechnological enterprise. Agriculture has been theorized to have become the dominant way of producing food since the Neolithic（新石器时代）Revolution. The processes and methods of agriculture have been refined by other mechanical and biological sciences since its inception. Through early biotechnology, farmers were able to select the best suited and highest-yield crops to produce enough food to support a growing population. Other uses of biotechnology were required as crops and fields became increasingly large and difficult to maintain. Specific organisms and organism by-products（副产品）were used to fertilize（施化肥），restore nitrogen（氮），and control pests. Throughout the use of agriculture, farmers have inadvertently altered the genetics of their crops through introducing them to new environments and breeding them with other plants——one of the first forms of biotechnology.

2. Put English sentences into Chinese

（1） Exploiting micro-organisms as sources of oils and fats; oil making with enzyme, interesterification（酯交换）with enzyme, hydrolysis（水解）with enzyme, hydrogenation（氢化）with enzyme, the use of microbial lipases（脂肪酶）to improve the flavour of butter fat; the techniques for genetic engineering both microorganisms of oils and fats and oil plants become evident.

（2） Composting is one of ways to handle the wastes, which is a fermentation process under the conditions with appropriate moisture, C/N ratio, and oxygen.

（3） Bioscience refers to acquisition of biological knowledge whereas biotechnology refers to application of biological knowledge.

3. Cloze

Brewing is the production of alcoholic beverages and alcohol fuel through fermentation. The term is used __(1)__ the production of beer, although the word "brewing" is also used to describe the fermentation process used to __(2)__ wine and mead. It can also refer to the process of producing sake（理由）and soy sauce（酱）. "Brewing" is also sometimes used to refer __(3)__ any chemical __(4)__ process.

Brewing specifically refers to the process of steeping, such as with tea and water, and extraction, usually through heat. Wine and cider（苹果汁）technically aren't brewed, rather vinted（用水果酿造酒）, as the __(5)__ fruit is pressed, and then the liquid extracted. Mead（蜂蜜酒）isn't technically brewed, as heating often isn't used in the mixing process, and the honey is __(6)__ entirely, as opposed __(7)__ being heated with water, and then discarded, as are hops and barley in beer, and or tea leaves for tea, and coffee beans for coffee. Spices __(8)__ technically be brewed into a mead though.

Brewing has a very long history, and archeological evidence suggests __(9)__ this technique was used in ancient Egypt. Descriptions of __(10)__ beer recipes can be found in Sumerian writings, some of the oldest known writing of any sort.

The brewing industry is part of most western economies.

（1）A. for   B. on   C. to   D. of   (   )
（2）A. form   B. make   C. create   D. produce   (   )
（3）A. with   B. as   C. to   D. to   (   )
（4）A. max   B. mixed   C. mix   D. mixing   (   )
（5）A. all   B. entire   C. total   D. full   (   )
（6）A. use   B. used   C. using   D. unused   (   )
（7）A. with   B. for   C. to   D. of   (   )
（8）A. could   B. can   C. will   D. would   (   )
（9）A. which   B. that   C. what   D. how   (   )
（10）A. several   B. various   C. different   D. many   (   )

4. Put the following into English

| 放热的 | 生物技术 | 石油泄漏 | 污水处理 | 发酵 | 合成代谢的 |
| 抗生素 | 遗传学 | 酵母 | 有机物 | 分解 | 干扰素 |

5. Writing

You should write a composition on the title "biotechnology in China" (no more than 200 words).

参考译文

生物技术的本质（特性）

生物技术是属于应用生物科学和技术的一个领域。它包含生物或其亚细胞组分在制造业、服务业和环境管理等方面的应用。生物技术运用细菌、酵母、真菌、藻类、植物细胞或者培养的哺乳动物细胞作为工业过程的组成部分。生物技术的成功应用只有通过多理论学科与技术的综合才得以实现，这包括微生物学、生物化学、遗传学、分子生物化学及化学过程工程。

生物工艺过程一般包括细胞或者生物物质的产生和所期望化学转变的成功实现。这些化学转变可进一步细分为以下几个方面。

（1）目标产物的生成（例如酶、抗生素、有机酸和类固醇类物质）；

（2）起始原料的分解（例如污水处理、工业用水或者溢出石油的处理）。

生物工艺过程中的反应可以是分解过程，在这一过程中复杂化合物被分解成简单的物质（例如葡萄糖降解成乙醇）；也可以是合成代谢或者生物合成，在这一过程中简单的分子组合成更加复杂的分子（例如抗生素的合成）。通常情况下，分解反应是放热的，而合成反应是吸热的。

生物技术包括发酵过程（范围涵盖从啤酒、白酒到面包、奶酪，还有抗生素和疫苗）、水和废物处理、部分食品工艺学，还包含了生物医学和低级矿中回收金属等不断增长的全新领域。由于其全面性，生物技术将在诸多工业过程产生重要影响；并且从理论上而言，几乎所有的有机物都可以通过生物技术的方法生产得到。预计到 2000 年，在全球市场生物技术产品的产值将达到近650 亿美元（表 6-1）。然而，必须意识到许多重要的新的生化产品仍旧根据已存在的生物分子结构通过化学方法合成得到（例如基于干扰素的新药开发），因此生物科学和化学的结合与生物技术的关系得到进一步的阐述。

表 6-1　到 2000 年全球生物技术市场的增长潜力

市场领域	美元（百万）
能源	16350
食品	12655
化学品	10550
健康保健（药品）	9080
农业	8546
金属回收	4750
污染控制	100
其他（未预期的发展）	3000
总计	64851

数据来源：11 月生物技术报告（1983）。

与目前传统的工业过程相比，在生物技术中用到的大部分技术是趋向于更经济、更低的能耗和更安全，并且大多数工艺生产过程中产生的废物是可以生物降解和无毒的。长期来看，生物技术为解决目前一些重要的世界难题，尤其是那些涉及药物、食品生产、污染控制和新能源发展的难题提供了一种途径。

6.2 Historical evolution of biotechnology

Contrary to popular belief biotechnology is not a new pursuit but in reality **dates far back** into history. In practice, four major developmental phases can be identified in arriving at modern biotechnological systems.

Biotechnological production of foods and beverages

Activities such as baking, **brewing** and wine making are known to date back several millennia. The recognition that these processes were being affected by living **organisms,** yeasts, was not formulated until the 17th century, by Anton van Leeuwenhoek. Definitive proof of the fermentative abilities of these **minute** organisms came from the seminal studies of Pasteur between 1857 and 1876. Pasteur can **justifiably** be considered as the father of biotechnology.

Biotechnological processes initially developed under non-sterile conditions

Many important industrial compounds such as ethanol, acetic acid（乙酸）, organic acids, butanol（丁醇） and **acetone** were being produced by the end of the 19th century by microbial fermentation procedures that **were open to** the environment.

Other outstanding examples of non-sterile biotechnology are waste **water treatment** and **municipal** composting of solid wastes. Biotechnological treatment of waste waters represents **by far** the largest (but least recognized) fermentation capacity practised throughout the world (Table **6-2**)

Table 6-2   Total UK fermentation capacity

Product	Total capacity (m^3)
Waste water	2800000
Beer	128000
Baker's yeast	19000
Antibiotics	10000
Cheese	3000
Bread	700

From Dunhill(1981).

The introduction of sterility to biotechnological processes

A new direction in biotechnology came in the 1940s with the introduction of complicated engineering techniques to the mass **cultivation** of micro-organisms to ensure that the particular biological process could **proceed with** the exclusion of **contaminating** micro-organisms. Thus by prior sterilization of the

Remarks Column

brewing ['bruːiŋ]*n.*酿造

organism ['ɔːgənizəm] *n.*有机物, 有机体；生物

minute [mai'njuːt] *adj.*极小的；极详细的 small

justifiable ['dʒʌstifaiəbl] *adj.*有理由的 capable of being justified; understandable

sterile ['sterail] *adj.*无菌的, 消过毒的

acetone ['æsitəun]*n.*丙酮

municipal [mju(ː)'nisipəl] *adj.*市的，市政的 of or relating to a town

cultivation [ˌkʌlti'veiʃən] *n.*培养, 教养，耕作，中耕 the planting, culture

contaminate [kən'tæmineit] *vt.*把…弄脏，污染 to make impure

medium and the bioreactor and **with engineering provision for** the exclusion of incoming contaminants only the chosen **biocatalyst** was present in the reactor.

New dimensions and possibilities for biotechnological industries

Within the last decade there have been outstanding developments in **molecular biology** and **process control** which have created new and exciting **opportunities** not only to create new dimensions but also to improve greatly the efficiency and economics of the established biotechnological industries.

What then are these new innovations? (Table **6-3**).

Table 6-3　Techniques stimulating the development of biotechnology

Recombinant DNA manipulation	Tissue culture
Protoplast fusion	**Monoclonal antibody** preparation
Protein structural modification ("**protein engineering**")	Immobilized enzyme and cell catalysis
Sensing **with the aid of** biological molecules	Computer linkage of reactors and processes
New biocatalytic reactor design	

(a) Genetic engineering. Manipulation of the **genome** of industrially important organisms by sexual recombination and by **mutation** has long been part of the innovative repertoire of the industrial geneticist. New **recombinant DNA** techniques involve breaking living cells gently, the extraction of DNA, its **purification** and subsequent selective **fragmentation** by highly specific enzymes; the sorting, analysis, selection and purification of a **fragment** containing a required gene; **chemical bonding** to the DNA of a carrier molecule and the introduction of the **hybrid** DNA into a **selected cell for** reproduction and cellular synthesis.

(b) Enzyme technology. Isolated enzymes have long been a part of many biotechnological processes and their catalytic properties are **being further-utilized with** the development of suitable immobilization techniques allowing reuse of the biocatalyst. Of particular, importance has been the development of high **fructose syrups** (annual production 3 million tonnes) using immobilized **bacterial** glucose isomerase（异构酶）.

(c) Biochemical engineering. Bioreactors play a central role in biotechnological processes by providing a link between the starting materials or **substrates** and final products (Fig. **6-1**). Major advances have been made in bioreactor designs, in process monitoring techniques and in computer control of fermentation processes. However, the application of process control in

medium ['miːdjəm] n.生活条件,环境

biocatalyst [ˌbaiəu'kætəlist]n.生物催化剂 a chemical initiates or increases the rate of a biochemical reaction

opportunity[ˌɔpə'tjuːniti]n.机会,时机　possibility

protein ['prəutiːn] n.蛋白质

modification [ˌmɔdifi'keiʃən]n.更改,改变,修改 the act of modifying or the condition of being modified

immobilize [I'məubIlaIz]vt.使不动,使固定 to make or become immobile

genome['dʒiːnəum] n.基因组，染色体组 the full complement of genetic material within an organism

mutation [mju(ː)'teiʃən]n.突变；变异，变种 the act or process of mutating; change; alteration

purification [ˌpjuərifi'keiʃən] n.净化

fragmentation[ˌfrægmen'teiʃən]n.分裂、破碎

fragment ['frægmənt]n.碎片；片段

hybrid ['haibrid]n.杂交生成的生物体、杂交植物（或动物）；crossbreed

fructose ['frʌktəus] n.果糖

syrup['sirəp]n.糖浆，糖汁；类药品

bacterial[bæk'tIərIəl] adj.细菌的

substrate ['sʌbstreit] n.酶作用物，培养基

Expressions and Technical Terms

contrary to　和…相反，违反

date back　回溯至

be open to　开放

non-sterile　非无菌的

water treatment　水处理

by far　更，尤其

· 33 ·

biotechnological industries is many years behind that in operation in the chemical process industry. New approaches to the processing of the products of biotechnology (downstream processing) will improve the economics of all processes.

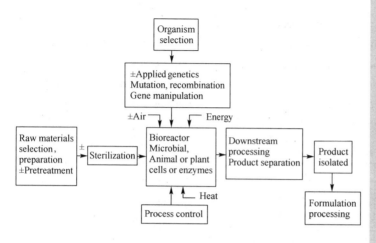

Fig. 6-1   Schematic overview of a biotechnological process

proceed with 继续做

with provision for 考虑到

process control 过程控制

molecular biology 分子生物学

What then 下步怎么办

Protoplast fusion 原生质体融合

Monoclonal antibody 单克隆抗体

Tissue culture 组织培养

protein engineering 蛋白质工程

with the aid of 借助于

Genetic engineering 遗传工程

recombinant DNA 重组 DNA

chemical bonding 化学键连接

select for 为…而选

be with 在…方面先进

Biochemical engineering 生化工程

In a word 总而言之

Notes

[1] special background 基因工程(genetic engineering) 所谓基因工程是在分子水平上对基因进行操作的复杂技术，是将外源基因通过体外重组后导入受体细胞内，使这个基因能在受体细胞内复制、转录、翻译表达的操作。它是用人为的方法将所需要的某一供体生物的遗传物质——DNA大分子提取出来，在离体条件下用适当的工具酶进行切割后，把它与作为载体的 DNA 分子连接起来，然后与载体一起导入某一更易生长、繁殖的受体细胞中，以让外源物质在其中"安家落户"，进行正常的复制和表达，从而获得新物种的一种崭新技术。

[2] An organism produced by genetic engineering, in which DNA from distinct parent species is combined to produce an individual with a double chromosome complement. 嵌合体在遗传工程中所产生的有机体，在此过程中将不同亲本种类的 DNA 结合起来产生具有双重染色体配对的个体。in which 引导的是非限制性定语从句，修饰 genetic engineering。

[3] Many important industrial compounds such as ethanol, acetic acid（乙酸）, organic acids, butanol（丁醇） and acetone were being produced by the end of the 19th century by microbial fermentation procedures **that** were open to the environment. 到 19 世纪末，许多重要的工业产品，例如乙醇、乙酸、有机酸、丁醇和丙酮是通过微生物发酵过程产生，这些发酵过程是在没有密闭的条件下进行的。这里 that 引导的是定语从句，修饰的是 fermentation procedures。

[4] A new direction in biotechnology came in the 1940s with the introduction of complicated engineering techniques to the mass cultivation of microorganisms to ensure that the particular biological process could proceed with the exclusion of contaminating microorganisms. 在 20 世纪 40 年代，随着

复杂工程技术引入到微生物的群体培养中，以保证生物反应过程在无杂菌的条件下进行，生物技术新的时代开始到来。"contaminating microorganisms"指的是"杂菌"的意思。

[5] Within the last decade there have been outstanding developments in molecular biology and process control which have created new and exciting opportunities **not only** to create new dimensions **but also** to improve greatly the efficiency and economics of the established biotechnological industries. 最近十年来，在分子生物学和过程控制方面取得了显著的进展。这些新进展不仅对生物技术产业的发展方向创造了激动人心的新机会，而且还极大地提高了它的效率和经济性。这里"not only…but also…"表示"不仅…而且…"。

[6] Manipulation of the genome of industrially important organisms by sexual recombination and by mutation has long been part of the innovative repertoire of the industrial geneticist.通过有性结合与基因突变来控制重要的工业用有机体一直被看做是遗传学者的创新性工作。在这里 has long been 用现在完成时表示从过去发生并一直延续到现在的状态。

[7] Isolated enzymes have long been a part of many biotechnological processes and their catalytic properties are being further-utilized with the development of suitable immobilization techniques allowing reuse of the biocatalyst.游离酶很长时期已成为生物技术过程的一部分，它们的特性随着合适固定化技术的发展得到进一步开发利用，使得其重复利用。"allowing reuse of the biocatalyst"现在分词表示伴随状况。

Exercises

1. Put the following into Chinese

Bioscientists and engineers' of various specializations will make their individual contributions to biotechnology. The term biotechnologist has crept into our vocabulary as an all-embracing description of scientists or engineers engaged in applying their skills and knowledge to the processing of biological materials. However, the use of this term should be discontinued as it can only lead to confusion. In contrast a biochemical engineer is a process engineer whose role is to transfer the knowledge of the biological scientist into a practical operation. A biochemical engineer will have been trained in the scientific and engineering principles underlying the design and operation of biological operations. A "complete biotechnologist" will never exist, since no one can be expert in the skills of microbiology, biochemistry, molecular biology, chemical and process engineering, etc. However, for those who practise in this subject every effort must be made to understand the language of the other component subjects. The lack of a common language between specialists in different disciplines is undoubtedly the major obstacle in realizing the full potential of biotechnology.

2. Put English sentences into Chinese

(1) The major problems encountered in the application of biotechnology are: sterilization of feed to bioreactors; recovery of products from bioreactor downstream; computerized monitoring of bioreactors and the development of highly efficient bioreactors.

(2) Organic solvents denatured or deactivated the biocatalyst, however when it was suspended in an aqueous solution containing 6% (V/V) methanol, the residual activity was(98.8%) after 20 h.

(3) One of the most advanced applications of membrane（薄膜）processes in biotechnology is their use in the immobilization of biocatalysts (enzymes and whole cells).

3. Cloze test

Biotechnology is being (1) to engineer and adapt organisms especially microorganisms in an effort to find sustainable ways (2) clean up contaminated environments. The elimination of a (3) range of pollutants and wastes from the environment is an (4) requirement to promote a sustainable development of our society with low environmental impact. Biological processes play a major role in the removal of contaminants and biotechnology is (5) advantage of the astonishing catabolic versatility of microorganisms to degrade/convert such compounds. New methodological breakthroughs in sequencing, genomics, proteomics, bioinformatics and imaging are producing (6) amounts of information. In the field of Environmental Microbiology, genome-based global studies open a new era providing unprecedented *in silico* views of metabolic and regulatory networks, (7) well as clues to the evolution of degradation pathways and (8) the molecular adaptation strategies to (9) environmental conditions. Functional genomic approaches are increasing our understanding of the relative importance of different pathways and regulatory networks to carbon flux in particular environments and for particular compounds and they will certainly accelerate the development (10) bioremediation technologies and biotransformation processes.

（1）A. using   B. used   C. uses   D. use   （   ）
（2）A. in   B. from   C. to   D. down   （   ）
（3）A. ample   B. wide   C. broad   D. roomy   （   ）
（4）A. entire   B. total   C. absolute   D. complete   （   ）
（5）A. taking   B. take   C. taken   D. taked   （   ）
（6）A. large   B. vast   C. big   D. great   （   ）
（7）A. so   B. as   C. with   D. in   （   ）
（8）A. to   B. from   C. in   D. by   （   ）
（9）A. changed   B. chenge   C. change   D. changing   （   ）
（10）A. to   B. of   C. in   D. by   （   ）

4. Put the following into English

无菌的   培养   生物催化剂   蛋白质   基因组
突变   过程控制   分子生物学   水处理   组织培养
生化工程   酶固定   排除   葡萄糖   微生物

5. Writing

You should write a composition on the title "Applications of biotechnology". (no more than 200 words).

参考译文

生物技术的发展历史

与公众的普遍认识相反，生物技术不是一个新兴的学科，而是有着比较长的发展历史。在形成现代的生物技术系统之前，其发展历史可划分为四个阶段。

食品和饮品的生物技术产品

烘培、酿造和酿酒活动已有近千年的历史。这些过程是受到鲜活的有机体和酵母的影响而产生的，但是对这些过程直到 17 世纪才被安东·范·列文虎克明确阐述出来。关于这些微生物体的发酵能力是巴斯德在 1857 到 1876 年间对种子的研究中证实的。所以，巴斯德被认为是生物技术之父。

生物技术在非无菌条件下的发展

到 19 世纪末，许多重要的工业产品，例如乙醇、乙酸、有机酸、丁醇和丙酮是通过微生物发酵过程产生，这些发酵过程是在没有密闭的条件下进行的。

另外一个非无菌的生物工艺过程的典型例子是污水处理和城市固体废物处理。到目前为止，污水的生物技术处理是全球最大的（但很少被认识到）发酵应用方面（表 6-2）。

表 6-2 英国总发酵能力

产　品	总发酵能力（m³）	产　品	总发酵能力（m³）
污水	2800000	抗生素	10000
啤酒	128000	奶酪	3000
烘焙酵母	19000	面包	700

数据来源：Dunhill（1981）。

无菌生物技术的出现

在 20 世纪 40 年代，随着复杂工程技术引入到微生物的群体培养中，以保证生物反应过程在无杂菌的条件下进行，生物技术新的时代开始到来。所以，应先对培养基和生物反应器进行杀菌，并且保证反应设备能够隔绝外来污染，只允许所需的生物催化剂存在于体系中。

生物技术的新发展方向

最近十年来，在分子生物学和过程控制方面取得了显著的进展。这些新进展不仅对生物技术产业的发展方向创造了激动人心的新机会，而且还极大地提高了它的效率和经济性。

这些新的技术有哪些呢（表 6-3）？

表 6-3 推动生物行业发展的技术

DNA 重组操作	组织培养
原生质体融合	单克隆抗体制备
蛋白质结构修饰（蛋白质工程）	固定化酶和细胞的催化
生物分子传导技术	反应器和反应过程的计算机控制技术
新型生物催化反应器设计	

（a）基因工程。通过有性结合与基因突变来控制重要的工业用有机体长期被看做是遗传学者的创新性工作。新的重组 DNA 技术包括：活体细胞的轻微破碎、DNA 的提取和纯化，随后是用高效专一的酶进行选择性分裂；排序、分析、选择和纯化含有目的基因的片段；与载体细胞进行 DNA 的化学键连接、引入杂交基因到一个选择的细胞实现复制和细胞合成。

（b）酶技术。游离酶很长时期已成为生物技术过程的一部分，它们的特性随着合适固定化技术的发展得到进一步开发利用，使得其重复利用。例如，使用固定化细菌葡萄糖异构酶开发利用高果糖浆（年产 300 万吨）。

（c）生化工程。生化反应器通过提供起始原料物质和最终产物，或底物与产物之间的链接在生物工艺过程中扮演了中间角色（图 6-1）。主要的进步取决于生物反应器的设计，例如过程中的检测技术和发酵过程的计算机控制。然而，多年来生物工艺工业生产的控制技术还是落后于化学工业。生物工艺产物处理（下游处理）的新方法将提高整个过程的经济性。

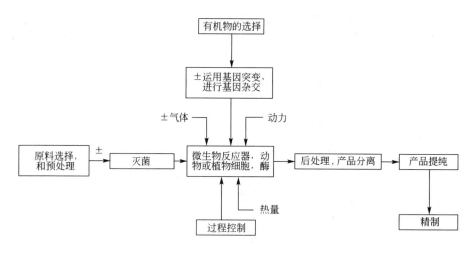

图 6-1　生物工艺过程简图

Biotechnology

Biotechnology is technology based on biology, especially when used in agriculture, food science, and medicine. United Nations Convention on Biological Diversity defines biotechnology as: Any technological application that uses biological systems, living organisms, or **derivatives** thereof, to make or **modify** products or processes for specific use.

Biotechnology is often used to refer to genetic engineering technology of the 21st century, however the term encompasses a wider range and history of procedures for modifying biological organisms **according to** the needs of humanity, going back to the initial modifications of native plants into improved food crops through artificial selection and **hybridization**. Bioengineering is the science upon which all biotechnological applications are based. With the development of new approaches and modern techniques, traditional biotechnology industries are also acquiring new horizons enabling them to improve the quality of their products and increase the productivity of their systems.

Before 1971, the term, *biotechnology*, was primarily used in the **food processing** and agriculture industries. Since the 1970s, it began to be used by the Western scientific establishment to refer to laboratory-based techniques being developed in biological research, such as recombinant DNA or **tissue** culture-based processes, or **horizontal gene transfer** in living plants, using **vectors** such as the *Agrobacterium* bacteria to transfer DNA into a host organism. In fact, the term should be used in a much broader sense to describe the whole range of methods, both ancient and modern, used to manipulate organic materials to reach the **demands of** food production. So the term could be defined as, "The application of **indigenous** and/or scientific knowledge to the management of (parts of) microorganisms, or of cells and tissues of higher organisms, so that these supply goods and services of use to the food industry and its consumers".

Biotechnology combines disciplines like genetics, molecular biology, biochemistry, **embryology** and cell biology, which are **in turn** linked to practical disciplines like **chemical engineering**,

information technology, and **biorobotics**. Patho-biotechnology describes the exploitation of **pathogens** or pathogen derived compounds for beneficial effect.

Biotechnology has applications in four major industrial areas, including health care (medical), crop production and agriculture, non food (industrial) uses of crops and other products (e.g. biodegradable plastics, **vegetable oil**, biofuels), and environmental uses.

For example, one application of biotechnology is the directed use of organisms for the manufacture of organic products (examples include beer and milk products). Another example is using naturally present bacteria by the mining industry in **bioleaching**. Biotechnology is also used to recycle, treat waste, clean up sites contaminated by industrial activities (**bioremediation**), and also to produce biological weapons.

A series of derived terms have been coined to identify several branches of biotechnology, for example:

- **Bioinformatics** is an interdisciplinary field which addresses biological problems using computational techniques, and makes the rapid organization and analysis of biological data possible. The field may also be referred to as *computational biology*, and can be defined as, "conceptualizing biology in terms of molecules and then applying informatics techniques to understand and organize the information associated with these molecules, on a large scale." Bioinformatics plays a key role in various areas, such as functional **genomics**, structural genomics, and **proteomics**, and forms a key component in the biotechnology and **pharmaceutical** sector.

- **Blue biotechnology** is a term that has been used to describe the **marine** and **aquatic** applications of biotechnology, but its use is relatively rare.

- **Green biotechnology** is biotechnology applied to agricultural processes. An example would be the selection and **domestication** of plants via **micropropagation**. Another example is the designing of **transgenic** plants to grow under specific environmental conditions or in the presence (or absence) of certain agricultural chemicals. One hope is that green biotechnology might produce more environmentally friendly solutions than traditional industrial agriculture. An example of this is the engineering of a plant to express a **pesticide**, thereby eliminating the need for external application of pesticides. An example of this would be **Bt corn**. Whether or not green biotechnology products such as this are ultimately more environmentally friendly is a topic of considerable debate.

- **Red biotechnology** is applied to medical processes. Some examples are the designing of organisms to produce antibiotics, and the engineering of genetic cures through genomic manipulation.

- **White biotechnology**, also known as industrial biotechnology, is biotechnology applied to industrial processes. An example is the designing of an organism to produce a useful chemical. Another example is the using of enzymes as industrial catalysts to either produce valuable chemicals or destroy hazardous/polluting chemicals. White biotechnology tends to consume less in resources than traditional processes used to produce industrial goods.

- The investments and economic output of all of these types of applied biotechnologies form what has been described as the **bioeconomy**.

New Words

derivative [di'rivətiv]*n.*派生物，引出物 *adj.*模仿他人的，衍生的，派生的

modify['mɔdifai]vt. & vi.修改，更改　vt.修饰

hybridization[,haibridai'zeiʃ ən]n.杂交，杂种培植，配种

tissue ['tisju:]n.组织；薄纸,棉纸；一套，一系列

vectors　　n.向量，带菌者

agrobacterium　　n.农杆菌

indigenous[in'didʒinəs]adj.土生土长的；生来的，固有的

embryology[,embri'ɔlədʒi]n.胚胎学

biorobotics　　n.生物机器人技术

pathogens ['pæθədʒəns]n.病原体(物)

bioleaching　　n.生物过滤

bioremediation[,ri,midi'eiʃ ən]n.(利用微生物净化有毒废物场或受污染水域等的)生物治理

bioinformatics n.分析复杂生物资料的学科

proteomics　　n.蛋白质组学

genomics　　n.基因组学

pharmaceutical[,fɑ:mə'sju:tikəl]adj.制药的；配药的

marine[mə'ri:n]adj.海的，海产的，海生的；海军的；海事的，海运的 n.水兵；海军陆战队士兵

aquatic [ə'kwætik]adj.水生的，水产的，水栖的，水中的

domestication [dəu,mesti'keiʃ ən]n.驯养，驯服，教化

micropropagation [,maikrəu'prɔpə'geiʃ ən]n.微繁殖，组织栽培法：栽培植物组织的栽培方法，其产物会由单一植物组织中以无性生殖培养繁殖出来

transgenic　　基因改造的，基因被改变的(gene-altered)

pesticide['pestisaid]n.杀虫剂

investment[in'vestmənt]n.投资

bioeconomy　　n.生物经济

Expressions and Technical Terms

according to　根据、按照

food processing　食品加工；食品热杀菌

horizontal transfer　横向转移

demands of　要求…需求…

in turn　依次，轮流的

chemical engineering　化学工程

information technology　信息技术

vegetable oil　植物油

milk product　奶制品、乳制品

Bt corn　Bt 玉米（转 Bt 基因抗虫玉米）

Chapter 7 Amino acids, peptides, and proteins[1]

Proteins are the most **abundant** biological macromolecules, occurring in all cells and all parts of cells. Proteins also occur in great variety; thousands of different kinds, **ranging** in size **from** relatively small peptides **to** huge polymers with molecular weights in the millions, may be found in a single cell[2]. Moreover, proteins **exhibit** enormous diversity of biological function and are the most important final products of the information pathways discussed in Part III of this book. Proteins are the molecular **instrument**s through which genetic information is expressed.

Relatively simple **monomeric** subunits provide the key to the structure of the thousands of different proteins. All proteins, **whether** from the most ancient lines of bacteria **or** from the most complex forms of life, are constructed from the same **ubiquitous** set of 20 amino acids, covalently linked in characteristic linear sequences. Because each of these amino acids has a side chain with **distinctive** chemical properties, this group of 20 precursor molecules may be regarded as the alphabet in which the language of protein structure is written.

What is most **remarkable** is that cells can produce proteins with **strikingly** different properties and activities by joining the same 20 amino acids in many different combinations and sequences. From these **building block**s different organisms can make such widely diverse products as enzymes, hormones, antibodies, transporters, muscle fibers, the lens protein of the eye, feathers, spider webs, rhinoceros horn, milk proteins, antibiotics, mushroom poisons, and **myriad** other substances having distinct biological activities (Fig. 7-1). Among these protein products, the enzymes are the most varied and specialized. **Virtually** all cellular reactions are catalyzed by enzymes.

Protein structure and function are the topics of this and the next three chapters. We begin with a description of the fundamental chemical properties of amino acids, peptides, and proteins.

Remarks Column

abundant[ə'bʌndənt]*adj.*丰富的，充裕的，丰富，盛产，富于

monomeric[ˌmɔnə'merik]*adj.* 单体的

instrument['instrumənt]*n.*工具，手段，器械，器具，手段

ubiquitous *adj.*到处存在的，(同时)普遍存在的

distinctive [dis'tiŋktiv]*adj.*与众不同的，有特色的

remarkable[ri'mɑːkəbl]*adj.*不平常的，非凡的，值得注意的，显著的

striking['straikiŋ]*adj.*（1）显著的，惊人的；（2）打击的；（3）罢工的

building block *n.*（儿童游戏用的）积木

lens protein   透镜蛋白

rhinoceros *n.* 犀牛

distinct[dis'tiŋkt] *adj.*清楚的，明显的，截然不同的，独特的

myriad ['miriəd]*adj.*无数的，种种的 *n.*无数，无数的人或物

virtually ['vɜːtjuəli]*adv.*事实上，实质上

erythrocyte [i'riθrəusait]*n.*红细胞，红血球

hemoglobin[ˌhiːməu'gləubin]*n.* 血红素

keratin ['kerətin]*n.*角蛋白

vertebrate ['vɜːtibrit]*n.*脊椎动物

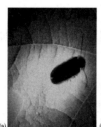

Fig. 7-1   Some functions of proteins.

(a) The light produced by fireflies is the result of a reaction involving the protein **luciferin** and ATP, catalyzed by the enzyme **luciferase**. (b) **Erythrocytes** contain large amounts of the oxygen-transporting protein **hemoglobin**. (c) The protein **keratin**, formed by all **vertebrates**, is the chief structural component of hair, scales, horn, wool, nails, and feathers. The black rhinoceros is nearing extinction in the wild because of the belief **prevalent** in some parts of the world that a powder derived from its horn has **aphrodisiac** properties. In reality, the chemical properties of powdered rhinoceros horn are no different from those of powdered **bovine hoove**s or human fingernails.

*adj.*有椎骨的，有脊椎的，
prevalent ['prevələnt] *adj.*普遍的，
流行的
aphrodisiac [,æfrəu'diziæk] *adj.* 引
起性欲的
Expressions and Technical Terms
product yield 产品收率
dispose of   处理
originate from   来源于，起源于
contribute to 对⋯贡献，有助于
take⋯into consideration 对⋯考虑
globular protein   球蛋白
as such 同样地
peptide bond   肽键
glucosidic bond 糖苷键
ester bond   酯键
covalent bond 共价键
bovine hoof 牛蹄

Notes

[1] special background   蛋白质是生命的物质基础，是肌体细胞的重要组成部分，是人体组织更新和修补的主要原料，没有蛋白质就没有生命。蛋白质是由 20 多种氨基酸组成，以氨基酸组成的数量和排列顺序不同，人体中蛋白质多达 10 万种以上。它们的结构、功能千差万别，形成了生命的多样性和复杂性。

与其他生物大分子（如核酸和多糖）一样，蛋白质是生物体中的必要组成成分，参与了细胞生命活动的每一个进程。

蛋白质能够在细胞中发挥多种多样的功能，涵盖了细胞生命活动的各个方面：发挥催化作用的酶；参与生物体内的新陈代谢的调剂作用，如胰岛素；一些蛋白质具有运输代谢物质的作用，如离子泵和血红蛋白；发挥储存作用，如植物种子中的大量蛋白质，就是用来萌发时的储备；许多结构蛋白被用于细胞骨架等的形成，如肌球蛋白；还有免疫、细胞分化、细胞凋亡等过程中都有大量蛋白质参与。

[2] Proteins are the most abundant biological macromolecules, occurring in all cells and all parts of cells. Proteins also occur in great variety; thousands of different kinds, ranging in size from relatively small peptides to huge polymers with molecular weights in the millions, may be found in a single cell. 蛋白质是所有细胞及细胞组分中最丰富的生物大分子。蛋白质以不同种类形式（成千上万种）存在，从小分子肽到成百万分子量的聚合体，也存在于单细胞体中。occurring 和 ranging 是现在分词，作伴随状语，主语都是 Proteins。range from⋯to⋯是一固定短语，表示从某到某的一系列范围。

[3] All proteins, whether from the most ancient lines of bacteria or from the most complex forms of life, are constructed from the same ubiquitous set of 20 amino acids, covalently linked in characteristic linear sequences. 所有的蛋白质，无论是最古老的细菌株还是最复杂的生命形式，其结构都由（自然界）普遍存在的 20 种氨基酸通过共价连接的线性序列组成。这里 whether from the most ancient

lines of bacteria or from the most complex forms of life 是插入语，该句的主语是 All proteins，linked 是过去分词，表示方式状语。

[4] What is most remarkable is that cells can produce proteins with strikingly different properties and activities by joining the same 20 amino acids in many different combinations and sequences. 最令人注意的是细胞通过连接这 20 种氨基酸组成不同的序列能产生显著不同活性的蛋白质。这里 What is most remarkable 是主语，表示令人注意的是。That 引导的是表语从句。

Exercises

1. Put the following into Chinese

The words protein, polypeptide, and peptide are a little ambiguous and can overlap in meaning. Protein is generally used to refer to the complete biological molecule in a stable conformation, whereas peptide is generally reserved for a short amino acid oligomers often lacking a stable three-dimensional structure. However, the boundary between the two is not well defined and usually lies near 20–30 residues. Polypeptide can refer to any single linear chain of amino acids, usually regardless of length, but often implies an absence of a defined conformation.

2. Cloze

Proteins are the most abundant biological （1）, （2）in all cells and all parts of cells. Proteins also occur in great variety; thousands of different kinds, ranging in size （3）relatively small peptides to huge polymers with molecular weights in the millions, may be found in a single cell. （4）, proteins exhibit enormous diversity of biological function and are the most important final products of the information pathways discussed in Part Ⅲ of this book. Proteins are the molecular instruments （5）which genetic information is expressed.

Relatively simple （6） subunits provide the key to the structure of the thousands of different proteins. All proteins, whether from the most ancient （7） of bacteria （8） from the most complex forms of life, are constructed from the same ubiquitous set of 20 amino acids, covalently （9） in characteristic linear sequences. Because each of these amino acids has a side chain with（10）chemical properties, this group of 20 precursor molecules may be regarded as the alphabet in which the language of protein structure is written.

（1）A. micromolecules　　B. macromolecules　　C. small molecules　　D. middle molecules（　　）

（2）A. occurring　　　　　B. occurs　　　　　　C. occurred　　　　　D. occur　　　　　　（　　）

（3）A. in　　　　　　　　B. of　　　　　　　　C. from　　　　　　　D. with　　　　　　（　　）

（4）A. However　　　　　B. Wherever　　　　　C. Whereas　　　　　D. Moreover　　　　（　　）

（5）A. of　　　　　　　　B. for　　　　　　　　C. through　　　　　D. in　　　　　　　（　　）

（6）A. nomenclative　　　B. monomerous　　　　C. monomer　　　　　D. monomeric　　　（　　）

（7）A. lines　　　　　　　B. lots　　　　　　　　C. mass　　　　　　　D. structure　　　　（　　）

（8）A. to　　　　　　　　B. or　　　　　　　　C. in　　　　　　　　D. by　　　　　　　（　　）

（9）A. links　　　　　　　B. link　　　　　　　　C. linked　　　　　　D. linking　　　　（　　）

（10）A. distinguishing　　B. distinguished　　　　C. distinct　　　　　D. distinctive　　　（　　）

3. Put the following into English

蛋白质　遗传信息　亚基单体　共价连接　酶　激素　抗体　运输体　肌肉纤维　羽毛

蜘蛛网　犀牛角　牛乳蛋白　抗生素　蘑菇毒　荧光素　脊椎动物

4. Writing

Write summary of this text (no more than 200 words).

参考译文

蛋白质是所有细胞及细胞组分中最丰富的生物大分子。蛋白质以不同种类形式（成千上万种）存在，从小分子肽到成百万分子量的聚合体，也存在于单细胞体中。而且蛋白质具有不同的生物功能，是信息传递最重要的终端产品（见本书第三部分）。蛋白质是遗传信息表达的分子工具。

相对小的亚基单体是成千上万种不同蛋白质结构的关键，所有的蛋白质，无论是最古老的细菌株还是最复杂的生命形式，其结构都由（自然界）普遍存在的20种氨基酸通过共价连接的线性序列组成。由于每个氨基酸都具有一个（表示）化学特性的侧链，因此这20种前体分子可以看做是蛋白质结构这个语言的字母（可以用蛋白质英文字母表示）。

最令人注意的是细胞通过连接这20种氨基酸组成不同的序列能产生显著不同活性的蛋白质。通过这些单体有机体组成如此多的不同产品，例如酶、激素、抗体、运输体、肌肉纤维、眼晶状体蛋白、羽毛、蜘蛛网、犀牛角、牛乳蛋白、抗生素、蘑菇毒以及无数具有显著生物活性的其他物质（见图7-1），在这些蛋白质产品中，酶最具易变性和选择性，事实上所有细胞反应都是由酶催化的。

图 7-1　蛋白质的功能

（a）萤火虫发光是荧光素这个蛋白质与 ATP 结合，由荧光素酶催化的结果。（b）红细胞含有大量的传氧血红素蛋白。

（c）脊椎动物角蛋白是毛发、鳞片、角、羊毛、指甲和羽毛的主要组成部分。黑犀牛正面临灭绝，因为世界上某些地区盛行相信犀牛角具有引起性欲的特性。实际上，犀牛角粉末与牛蹄或人指甲粉末的化学性质没有任何区别

蛋白质结构与功能是本章及后三章的主题，现在开始描述氨基酸、肽及蛋白质的基本化学性质。

Reading material

Amino acids, peptides, and proteins

1. Amino Acids

Proteins are polymers of amino acids, with each amino acid residue joined to its neighbor by a specific type of **covalent bond**. Proteins can be broken down (hydrolyzed) to their constituent amino acids by a variety of methods, and the earliest studies of proteins naturally **focused on** the free amino acids derived from them. Twenty different amino acids are commonly found in proteins. The first to be discovered was **asparagine**, in 1806. The last of the 20 to be found, **threonine,** was not identified until 1938. All the amino acids have **trivial** or common names, in some cases derived from the source from which they were first isolated. Asparagine was first found in **asparagus**, and **glutamate** in **wheat gluten**; **tyrosine** was first isolated from cheese (its name is derived from the Greek tyros, "cheese"); and **glycine** (Greek glykos, "sweet") was so named because of its sweet taste.

2. Peptides and Proteins

We now turn to polymers of amino acids, the peptides and proteins. Biologically occurring **polypeptides** range in size from small to very large, consisting of two or three to thousands of linked amino acid residues. Our focus is on the fundamental chemical properties of these polymers.

Two amino acid molecules can be covalently joined through a substituted amide linkage, termed a **peptide bond**, to yield a **dipeptide**. Such a linkage is formed by removal of the elements of water (dehydration) from the α-carboxyl group of one amino acid and the α-amino group of another .

Three amino acids can be joined by two peptide bonds to form a **tripeptide**; similarly, amino acids can be linked to form **tetrapeptides, pentapeptides, and so forth**. When a few amino acids are joined in this fashion, the structure is called an **oligopeptide**. When many amino acids are joined, the product is called a polypeptide.

Proteins may have thousands of amino acid residues. Although the **terms** "protein" and "polypeptide" are sometimes used interchangeably, molecules referred to as polypeptides generally have molecular weights below 10,000, and those called proteins have higher molecular weights.

Amino acids can be joined covalently through peptide bonds to form peptides and proteins. Cells generally contain thousands of different proteins, each with a different biological activity.

Proteins can be very long polypeptide chains of 100 to several thousand amino acid residues. However, some naturally occurring peptides have only a few amino acid residues. Some proteins **are composed of** several noncovalently associated polypeptide chains, called subunits. Simple proteins **yield** only amino acids on hydrolysis; **conjugated proteins** contain **in addition** some other component, such as a metal or organic **prosthetic group**.

The sequence of amino acids in a protein is Characteristic of that protein and is called its primary structure. This is one of four generally recognized levels of protein structure.

New Words

asparagine [əsˈpærədʒiːn] n.天冬氨酸
threonine [ˈθriːəniːn]n.苏氨酸
trivial [ˈtriviəl]adj. 通俗的
asparagus [əsˈpærəgəs]n. [植]芦笋
glutamate [ˈgluːtəmeit] n. 谷氨酸
tyrosine [ˈtirəsiːn]n. 酪氨酸
cheese [tʃiːz]n. 奶酪

glycine [ˈglaisiːn]n. 甘氨酸
polypeptide[ˌpɔliˈpeptaid]n. 多肽
dipeptide [diˈpeptaid]n. 二肽
dehydration [ˌdiːhaiˈdreiʃən] n. 脱水
tripeptide [traiˈpeptaid] n. 三肽
tetrapeptide [ˌtetrəˈpeptaid] n. 四肽
pentapeptide [ˌpentəˈpeptaid] n. 五肽

oligopeptide [ˌɔliˈgɔfəgəs] *n.* 寡肽
term [təːm] *n.* 专业术语

yield [jiːld] *v.* 产生

Expressions and Technical Terms

covalent bond 共价键
focused on 聚焦，集中于
wheat gluten 小麦面筋蛋白
peptide bond 肽键
and so forth 等等

composed of 由…组成
conjugated protein 结合蛋白质
in addition 另外
prosthetic group 酶活动基，辅基

Chapter 8　Enzymes

Many chemical **transformation** processes used in various industries have **inherent drawbacks** from a commercial and environmental point of view. **Non-specific** reactions may result in poor product yields. High temperatures and/or high pressures needed to drive reactions lead to high energy costs and may require large volumes of cooling water downstream. **Harsh** and hazardous processes involving high temperatures, pressures, acidity or **alkalinity** need high capital investment, and specially designed equipment and control systems. Unwanted by-products may prove difficult or costly to dispose of. High chemical and energy consumption as well as harmful by-products have a negative impact on the environment.

All of these drawbacks can be **virtually eliminated** by using ENZYMES. Enzyme reactions are carried out under mild conditions, they are highly specific, involve very fast reaction rates, and are carried out by numerous enzymes with different roles. Industrial enzymes **originate from** biological systems; they contribute to sustainable development through being isolated from microorganisms which are fermented using primarily renewable resources.

Table8-1　International Classification of Enzymes

No.	Class	Type of reaction catalyzed
1	Oxidoreductases	Transfer of electrons(hydride ions or H atoms)
2	Transferases	Group transfer reactions
3	Hydrolases	Hydrolysis reactions (transfer of functional groups to water)
4	Lyases	Addition of groups to double bonds, or formation of double bonds by removal of groups
5	lsomerases	Transfer of groups within molecules to yield isomeric forms
6	Ligases	Formation of C—C, C—S, C—O, and C—N bonds by condensation reactions coupled to ATP cleavage

Note: Most enzymes catalyze the transfer of elections, atoms, or functional groups, They are therefore classified, given code numbers, and assigned names according to the type of transfer reaction the group donor, and the group acceptor.

In addition, as only small amount of enzymes are required to carry out chemical reactions even on an industrial scale, both solid and liquid enzyme preparations take up very little storage space. Mild operating conditions enable uncomplicated and widely

Remarks Column

transformation [ˌtrænsfə'meiʃən] n.变化，转化 change

inherent [in'hiərənt] adj.固有的，内在的，与生俱来的 existing as an essential constituent or characteristic; intrinsic

drawback['drɔː,bæk]n.缺点，障碍 disadvantage

non-specific adj.非专一性的

harsh [hɑːʃ]adj.粗糙的；苛刻的，严厉的 coarse and rough; extremely severe

alkalinity [ˌælkə'liniti]n.碱性 base

virtually ['vɜːtjuəlɪ]adv.事实上，实质上 in fact

eliminate [i'limineit]v.排除，消除 to get rid of; remove

Profile ['prəufail] n. 轮廓,概要 an outline of an object.

oxidoreductase ['ɔksIdəurI'dʌkteIs] n.氧化还原酶

dehydrogenase [di:'haidrədʒə,neis] n.脱氢酶

transferase ['trænsfə,reis] n. 转移酶

alpha-keto-acid　n. α-酮酸

hydrolase ['haidrəleis] n.水解酶

cleavage ['kli:vidʒ] n. 劈开，分裂 division

lyase ['laiəs]n.裂解酶，裂合酶

pectate ['pekteit] n.果胶酸盐（或酯）

isomerase [ai'sɔməreis]n. 异构酶

ligase [li'geis] n.连接酶

available equipment to be used, and enzyme reactions are easily controlled and can be stopped when the desired degree of substrate conversion has been achieved. Enzymes also reduce the impact of manufacturing on the environment by reducing the consumption of chemicals and energy, and the subsequent generation of waste.

Developments in genetic and protein engineering have led to improvements in the stability, economy, specificity and overall application potential of industrial enzymes. When all the benefits of using enzymes are **taken into consideration**, it's not surprising that the number of commercial applications for enzymes is increasing every year.

Class of Enzyme Reaction Profile(table1)

1. Oxidoreductases

Oxidation reactions involve the movement of electrons from one molecule to another. In biological systems we usually see the removal of hydrogen from the substrate. Typical enzymes in this class are called **dehydrogenases.**

2. Transferases

This class of enzymes catalyses the transfer of groups of atoms (radicals) from one molecule to another. Aminotransferases or transaminases promote the transfer of an amino group from one amino acid to an **alpha-keto-acid**.

3. Hydrolases

Hydrolases catalyze reactions between a substrate and water, and bind water to certain molecules. In this way, larger molecules are broken up into smaller units. This class of enzymes catalyses the **cleavage** of peptide bonds in proteins, **glucosidic bonds** in carbohydrates, and ester bonds in lipids.

4. Lyases

Lyases catalyze the addition of groups to double bonds or the formation of double bonds through the removal of groups. Thus bonds are cleaved using a different principle to hydrolysis. **Pectate lyases**, for example, split the glycosidic linkages by beta-elimination.

5. Isomerases

Isomerases catalyze the transfer of groups from one position to another on the same molecule. In other words, these enzymes change the structure of a substrate by rearranging its atoms.

6. Ligases

Ligases join molecules together with **covalent bonds**. These enzymes participate in biosynthetic reactions where new groups of bonds are formed. Such reactions require the input of energy in the form of cofactors such as ATP.

Expressions and Technical Terms

product yield 产品收率
dispose of 处理
originate from 来源于，起源于
contribute to 对…贡献，有助于
take…into consideration 对…考虑
globular protein 球蛋白
as such 同样地
peptide bond 肽键
glucosidic bond 糖苷键
ester bond 酯键
covalent bond 共价键

Notes

[1] special background 酶（enzyme）是生物体活细胞产生的具有催化活性的蛋白质，是生物催化剂。酶具有催化效率高、专一性强、易失活、反应条件温和、酶活性可调控等特点，双成分酶的催化活性还与辅因子有关。根据酶蛋白分子结构不同，酶可分为单体酶、寡聚酶和多酶体系。近年来还发现了以 RNA 为主要成分，具催化活性的核酶。酶分为六大类，即氧化还原酶类、转移酶类、水解酶类、裂合酶类、异构酶类和合成酶（连接酶）类。酶有系统名和惯用名。酶与底物形成中间产物而使反应沿一个低活化能途径进行，酶活性中心的结合部位决定酶对底物的专一性，催化部位决定催化活性和效率。无催化活性的酶原经蛋白酶水解断裂几处肽键，并去除几个肽段后形成活性中心而具有了催化活性。

[2] Many chemical transformation processes used in various industries have inherent drawbacks from a commercial and environmental point of view. 从商业和环境角度看，在许多工业中使用的化学转变过程有着其本身固有的缺点。used 是过去分词，作定语修饰 processes.

[3] Unwanted by-products may prove difficult or costly to dispose of. 不需要的副产物很难处理或者是处理的成本高。这里 dispose of 的宾语是 by-products，costly 是形容词，表示成本昂贵。

Exercises

1. Put the following into Chinese

The isolation and crystallization of urease by James Sumner in 1926 provided a breakthrough in early enzyme studies. Sumner found that urease（脲酶）crystals consisted entirely of protein, and he postulated that all enzymes are proteins. In the absence of other examples, this idea remained controversial（争论） for some time. Only in the 1930s was Sumner's conclusion widely accepted, after John Northrop and Moses Kunitz crystallized pepsin, trypsin, and other digestive enzymes and found them also to be proteins. During this period, J. B. S. Haldane wrote a treatise entitled *Enzymes*. Although the molecular nature of enzymes was not yet fully appreciated, Haldane made the remarkable suggestion that weak bonding interactions between an enzyme and its substrate might be used to catalyze a reaction. This insight lies at the heart of our current understanding of enzymatic catalysis. Since the latter part of the twentieth century, research on enzymes has been intensive. It has led to the purification of thousands of enzymes, elucidation（说明，阐明）of the structure and chemical mechanism of many of them, and a general understanding of how enzymes work.

2. Put English sentences into Chinese

（1）Life depends on the existence of powerful and specific catalysts: the enzymes. Almost every biochemical reaction is catalyzed by an enzyme.

（2）With the exception of a few catalytic RNAs, all known enzymes are proteins. Many require nonprotein coenzymes or cofactors for their catalytic function.

（3）Enzymes are classified according to the type of reaction they catalyze. All enzymes have formal E.C. numbers and names, and most have trivial names.

3. Cloze

Many chemical transformation processes （1） in various industries have inherent drawbacks from a commercial and environmental point of view. Non-specific reactions may result （2） poor product yields. High temperatures and/or high pressures needed to drive reactions lead to high energy costs and may require large volumes of cooling water downstream. Harsh and hazardous processes （3） high temperatures, pressures, acidity or alkalinity need high capital investment, and specially designed equipment and control systems. Unwanted by-products may prove difficult or （4） to dispose （5）.High chemical and energy consumption as well as harmful by-products have a （6） impact on the environment.

All of these drawbacks can be virtually eliminated by using ENZYMES. Enzyme reactions are （7） out under mild conditions, they are highly specific, involve very fast reaction rates, and are carried out by numerous enzymes with different roles. Industrial enzymes originate （8） biological systems; they contribute （9） sustainable development through being isolated （10） microorganisms which are fermented using primarily renewable resources.

（1）A. using　　　B. used　　　C. uses　　　D. use　　　　　　（　　）
（2）A. in　　　　B. from　　　C. to　　　　D. down　　　　　（　　）
（3）A. involve　　B. involving　C. involved　D. have involved　（　　）
（4）A. cost　　　B. costly　　　C. easy　　　D. easily　　　　（　　）
（5）A. of　　　　B. for　　　　C. to　　　　D. up　　　　　　（　　）
（6）A. positive　　B. negative　　C. active　　D. creative　　　（　　）
（7）A. carried　　B. carrying　　C. carry　　　D. cared　　　　（　　）
（8）A. to　　　　B. from　　　　C. in　　　　D. by　　　　　（　　）
（9）A. on　　　　B. to　　　　　C. by　　　　D. for　　　　　（　　）
（10）A. by　　　　B. in　　　　　C. to　　　　D. from　　　　（　　）

4. Put the following into English

产品收率	处理	来源于	对…贡献	对…考虑
球蛋白	共价键	内能	活化能	活性部位
相当于	俗名	系统名	发酵培养基	操作参数

5. Writing

Write summary of this text (no more than 200 words).

参考译文

从商业和环境角度看，在许多工业中使用的化学转变过程有着其本身固有的缺点。非专一性的反应导致产率低。高温高压的反应带来高能耗，也需要大量的冷却水流出。涉及高温高压以及酸碱的工艺要求苛刻，具有危险性，需要高投资、特殊设计的设备和控制系统。不需要的副产物很难处理或者是处理的成本高。高化学能消耗和有毒的副产物会对环境产生负面影响。

所有这些缺点事实上可由酶来消除，酶反应是在温和的条件下进行的，专一性强，反应速率快，需要不同功能的许多酶来参与。工业用酶来源于生物系统，有利于可再生资源发酵微生物的可持续发展。

另外，由于仅需要少量的酶即可实现工业规模的化学反应，所以固液态酶的制备占用空间少。温和操作条件可使用不复杂和通用的设备。当获得底物转化率达到所需要的目标时，酶反应容易控制和停止。酶通过减少化学品和能量的消耗以及废物的产生，可减少对生产环境的影响。

遗传工程和蛋白质工程的发展，促进工业用酶稳定性、成本、专一性及应用潜力的改善。考虑到酶的这些优点，每年酶的商业应用数量一直增加就不觉得奇怪了。

表 8-1　酶的国际分类

序号	分　　类	催化反应类型
1	氧化还原酶类	电子的转移（氢离子或原子）
2	转移酶类	基团转移反应
3	水解酶类	水解反应
4	裂解酶类	双键的增加或基团消除双键的形成
5	异构酶类	分子类基团的转移成异构形式
6	连接酶类	与 ATP 偶联断裂反应形成 C—C,C—S,C—O,C—N 键

注：大多数酶催化电子、原子或者功能基团的转移。因此根据转移反应类型、基团供体以及基团受体，将它们分类、编号以及命名。

1. 氧化还原酶

氧化反应涉及电子的转移，生物体系中我们经常看到底物的脱氢。典型的这类酶是脱氢酶。

2. 转移酶

这类酶催化原子基团的转移，氨基转移酶或转氨酶促进氨基酸与 α-酮酸的转移。

3. 水解酶

水解酶催化底物与水之间的反应，连接水和某个底物分子。这种方式，大分子分解成小分子。这类酶催化蛋白质的肽键、糖的糖苷键、脂肪的酯键的断裂。

4. 裂解酶

裂解酶通过基团的消除催化双键的形成，这样运用不同水解原理断裂键。例如，果胶酸裂解酶（果胶酶）通过 β 消除断裂糖苷键。

5. 异构酶

异构酶催化同个分子内基团的转移，换句话说，这些酶通过原子重排改变底物结构。

6. 连接酶

连接酶通过共价键连接分子，这些酶参与新基团生成的生化合成反应，这些反应需要能量因子 ATP。

Reading material

Enzyme

1. introduction

Enzyme, biological catalyst. The term enzyme comes from zymosis, the Greek word for fermentation, a process accomplished by yeast cells and long known to the brewing industry, which occupied the attention of many 19th-century chemists.

Louis Pasteur recognized in 1860 that enzymes were essential to fermentation but assumed that their catalytic action was inextricably linked with the structure and life of the yeast cell. Not until 1897 was it shown by German chemist Edward Büchner that cell-free extracts of yeast could ferment sugars to alcohol and carbon dioxide; Büchner denoted his preparation zymase. This important achievement was the first indication that enzymes could function independently of the cell.

The first enzyme molecule to be isolated in pure crystalline form was urease, prepared from the jack bean in 1926 by American biochemist J. B. Sumner, who suggested, contrary to prevailing opinion, that the molecule was a protein. In the period from 1930 to 1936, pepsin, chymotrypsin, and trypsin were successfully crystallized; it was confirmed that the crystals were protein, and the protein nature of enzymes was thereby firmly established.

2. Enzymatic Action

Like all catalysts, enzymes accelerate the rates of reactions while experiencing no permanent chemical modification as a result of their participation. Enzymes can accelerate, often by several orders of magnitude, reactions that under the mild conditions of cellular concentrations, temperature, pH, and pressure would proceed imperceptibly (or not at all) in the absence of the enzyme. The efficiency of an enzyme's activity is often measured by the turnover rate, which measures the number of molecules of compound upon which the enzyme works per molecule of enzyme per second. Carbonic anhydrase, which removes carbon dioxide from the blood by binding it to water, has a turnover rate of 106. That means that one molecule of the enzyme can cause a million molecules of carbon dioxide to react in one second.

Most enzymatic reactions occur within a relatively narrow temperature range (usually from about 30℃ to 40℃), a feature that reflects their complexity as biological molecules. Each enzyme has an optimal range of pH for activity; for example, pepsin in the stomach has maximal reactivity under the extremely acid conditions of pH 1–3. Effective catalysis also depends crucially upon maintenance of the molecule's elaborate three-dimensional structure. Loss of structural integrity, which may result from such factors as changes in pH or high temperatures, almost always leads to a loss of enzymatic activity. An enzyme that has been so altered is said to be denatured.

Consonant with their role as biological catalysts, enzymes show considerable selectivity for the molecules upon which they act (called substrates). Most enzymes will react with only a small group of closely related chemical compounds; many demonstrate absolute specificity, having only one substrate molecule which is appropriate for reaction.

Numerous enzymes require for efficient catalytic function the presence of additional atoms of small nonprotein molecules. These include coenzyme molecules, many of which only transiently associate with the enzyme. Nonprotein components tightly bound to the protein are called prosthetic groups. The region on the enzyme molecule in close proximity to where the catalytic event takes place is known as the active site. Prosthetic groups necessary for catalysis are usually located there, and it is the place where the substrate (and coenzymes, if any) bind just before reaction takes place.

The side-chain groups of amino acid residues making up the enzyme molecule at or near the active site participate in the catalytic event. For example, in the enzyme trypsin, its complex tertiary structure brings together a histidine residue from one section of the molecule with glycine and serine residues from another. The side chains of the residues in this particular geometry produce the active site that accounts for the enzyme's reactivity.

3. Identification and Classification

More than 2,500 different enzymes have now been identified, and many have been isolated in pure form. Hundreds have been crystallized, and the amino acid sequences and three-dimensional structure of a significant number have been fully determined through the technique of X-ray crystallography. The knowledge gained has led to great progress in understanding the mechanisms of enzyme chemistry.

Biochemists categorize enzymes into six main classes, which are respectively Oxidoreductases, Transferases, Hydrolases, Lyases, Isomerases, Ligases and a number of subclasses, depending upon the type of reaction involved.

With the exception of ribonuclease, all enzymes are proteins. The 124-amino acid structure of ribonuclease was determined in 1967, and two years later the enzyme was synthesized independently at two laboratories in the United States.

4. Enzyme Deficiency

A variety of metabolic diseases are now known to be caused by deficiencies or malfunctions of enzymes. Albinism, for example, is often caused by the absence of tyrosinase, an enzyme essential for the production of cellular pigments. The hereditary lack of phenylalanine hydroxylase results in the disease phenylketonuria (PKU) which, if untreated, leads to severe mental retardation in children.

New Words

zymosis[zai'məusis]n.发酵，发酵作用　fermentation　n. 传染病　an infectious disease, especially one caused by a fungus

inextricably [in'ekstrikəbl]adv.不可避免地；无法逃离地　unavoidable; inescapable

denote[di'nəut]vt.指示，表示　indicate

zymase ['zaimeis]n. 酒化酶，酿酶

crystalline ['kristəlain] adj.晶体的

urease ['juəri,eis] n. 脲酶，尿素酶

pepsin ['pepsin]　n.胃蛋白酶，胃液素

chymotrypsin [,kaimə'tripsin] n.胰凝乳蛋白酶，糜蛋白酶

trypsin ['tripsin]n.胰蛋白酶

imperceptibly [,impə'septəbli] adv.察觉不到地，微细地

elaborate [i'læbərit]adj.精心制作的，详细阐述的，精细 v. 精心制作，详细阐述

specificity [,spesi'fisiti] n. 专一性

coenzyme [kəu'enzaim] n. 辅酶

histidine ['histidi:n]　n. 组氨酸

glycine ['glaisi:n] n.甘氨酸

crystallography [kristə'lɔgrəfɪ] n.结晶学

ribonuclease [,raibəu'nju:klieis]　n.核糖核酸酶

albinism ['ælbənizəm] n.白化病, 皮肤变白症

tyrosinase ['tairəsineis, tai'rɔsi,neis] n. 酪氨酸酶

phenylalanine [,fenəl'æləni:n] n.苯丙氨酸

hydroxylase [hai'drɔksileis] n.羟化酶

phenylketonuria(PKU)[,fi:nil ,ki:tə'njuəriə]n.苯丙酮酸尿症(一种先天性代谢异常)

Expressions and Technical Terms

catalytic action　催化（作用）

brewing industry　酿造工业，啤酒酿造工业

prosthetic group　辅基

order of magnitude　数量级

turnover rate　转换率

cellular pigment 细胞色素 （cytochrome）

mental retardation　智力迟钝

Chapter 9   Nucleotides and nucleic acids[1]

Nucleotides have **a variety of** roles in cellular **metabolism**. They are the energy **currency** in metabolic **transaction**s, the essential chemical links in the response of cells to hormones and other extracellular **stimuli**, and the structural components of **an array of** enzyme cofactors and metabolic **intermediate**s. And, **last but certainly not least**, they are the constituents of nucleic acids[2]: deoxyribonucleic acid (DNA) and ribonucleic acid (RNA), the **molecular repositories** of genetic information. The structure of every protein, and ultimately of every biomolecule and cellular component, is a product of information **programmed into** the nucleotide sequence of a cell's nucleic acids[3]. The ability to store and transmit genetic information from one generation to the next is a fundamental condition for life.

1.   Nucleotide——Building blocks of nucleic acids

The amino acid sequence of every protein in a cell, and the nucleotide sequence of every RNA, is **specified** by a nucleotide sequence in the cell's DNA. A **segment** of a DNA molecule that contains the information required for the synthesis of a functional biological product, whether protein or RNA, **is referred to as** a gene. A cell typically has many thousands of genes, and DNA molecules, not surprisingly, **tend to** be very large. The storage and transmission of biological information are the only known functions of DNA.

RNAs have a broader range of functions, and several classes are found in cells. Ribosomal RNAs (rRNAs) are components of ribosomes, the complexes that **carry out** the synthesis of proteins. Messenger RNAs (mRNAs) are **intermediarie**s, carrying genetic information from one or a few genes to a ribosome, where the corresponding proteins can be synthesized[4]. Transfer RNAs (tRNAs) are **adapter** molecules that faithfully translate the information in mRNA into a specific sequence of amino acids. In addition to these major classes there is a wide variety of RNAs with special functions, described in depth in Part III.

2.   Structure of nucleotides

Nucleotides have three characteristic components:(1) a nitrogenous (nitrogen-containing) base, (2) a pentose, and (3) a phosphate. The molecule without the phosphate group is called a nucleoside. The nitrogenous bases are **derivative**s of two parent

Remarks Column

metabolism [me'tæbəlizəm] n.新陈代谢，变形

currency ['kʌrənsi]n.货币；流通

transaction [træn'zækʃən]n.办理，处理，会报，学报，交易，事务，处理事务

stimuli['stimjuli]n.刺激物

intermediate [,intə'mi:djət] adj.中间的 n.媒介

ultimately ['ʌltɪmətlɪ] adv.最后，终于，根本，基本上

specify ['spesifai]   vt. 指定,详细说明，列入清单

intermediary[,intə'mi:diəri] n.仲裁者，调解者，中间物 adj.中间的，媒介的

adapter [ə'dæptə(r)] n.连接物；适配器；改编者

compounds, **pyrimidine** and **purine**. The bases and pentoses of the common nucleotides are **heterocyclic** compounds. The carbon and nitrogen atoms in the parent structures are conventionally numbered to **facilitate** the naming and identification of the many derivative compounds. The convention for the pentose ring follows rules outlined in Chapter 7, but in the pentoses of nucleotides and nucleosides the carbon numbers are given a prime(') designation to **distinguish** them **from** the numbered atoms of thc nitrogcnous bases[5].

heterocyclic[ˌhetərəu'saiklik]
adj. 杂环的，不同环式的
designation [ˌdezig'neiʃən]
n. 指示，指定，选派，名称
prime [praim] *n.* 符号 [']；初期，最初，开始；青春，全盛期；质数，素数

Expressions and Technical Terms
a variety of 种类多的，各种的
an array of 许多；一排；一批
last but certainly not least 最后但并非最不重要的
molecular repositories 分子库
programmed into 编码；编程
…is referred to as…被称为
tend to 往往会，往往是
carry out 执行，计划
distinguish…from 区别开

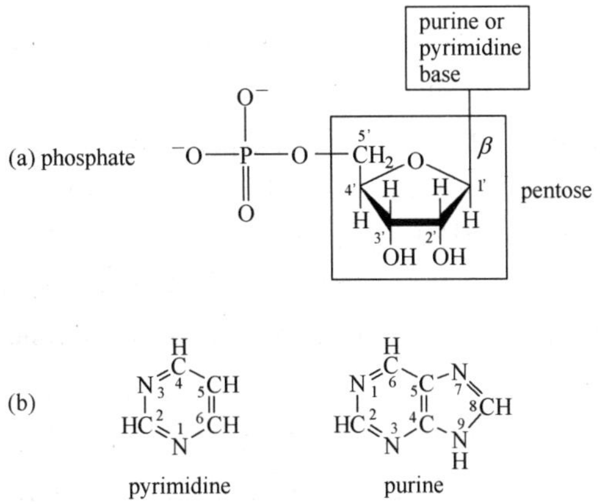

Fig. 9-1 Structure of nucleotides

(a) General structure showing the numbering convention for the pentose ring. This is a ribonucleotide. In deoxyribonucleotides the—OH group on the 2 carbon (in red) is replaced with H. (b)The parent compounds of the pyrimidine and purine bases of nucleotides and nucleic acids, showing the numbering conventions.

Notes

[1] special background 核酸是由许多核苷酸聚合而成的生物大分子化合物，为生命的最基本物质之一。最早由米歇尔于1868年在脓细胞中发现和分离出来。核酸广泛存在于所有动物、植物细胞、微生物体内，生物体内核酸常与蛋白质结合形成核蛋白。不同的核酸，其化学组成、核苷酸排列顺序等不同。根据化学组成不同，核酸可分为核糖核酸，简称RNA和脱氧核糖核酸，简称DNA。DNA是储存、复制和传递遗传信息的主要物质基础，RNA在蛋白质的合成过程中起着重要作用，其中转移核糖核酸，简称tRNA，起着携带和转移活化氨基酸的作用；信使核糖核酸，简称mRNA，是合成蛋白质的模板；核糖体的核糖核酸，简称rRNA，是细胞合成蛋白质的主要场所。核酸不仅是基本的遗传物质，而且在蛋白质的生物合成上也占有重要位置，因而在生长、遗传、变异等一系列重大生命现象中起决定性的作用。

[2] Nucleotides have **a variety of** roles in cellular **metabolism**. They are the energy **currency** in metabolic **transactions**, the essential chemical links in the response of cells to hormones and other extracellular **stimuli**, and the structural components of **an array of** enzyme cofactors and metabolic **intermediates**. And, **last but certainly not least**, they are the constituents of nucleic acids. 核苷酸在细

胞代谢中有各种作用，它们是代谢过程中的能量货币，是联系细胞应答与激素和胞外刺激物的必要化学物质，也是一系列酶辅因子和代谢中间产物的组成成分。最重要的是，它们是核酸的组成成分。这里 **last but certainly not least 表示** 最后但并非最不重要的意思，通常是作者就某个主题给出几点看法，最后一点用此短语。

[3] The structure of every protein, and ultimately of every biomolecule and cellular component, is a product of information **programmed into** the nucleotide sequence of a cell's nucleic acids. 每个蛋白质的结构及每个生物分子和细胞组分最终是细胞核苷酸序列编码成的信息产品。ultimately 与 of 之间省略了 the structure，**programmed into 过去分词短语，修饰** information。

[4] Messenger RNAs (mRNAs) are **intermediarie**s, carrying genetic information from one or a few genes to a ribosome, where the corresponding proteins can be synthesized. 信使 RNA(mRNAs)是中介物，起着把遗传信息传递给合成相应蛋白质核糖体的作用。Carrying 是现在分词，起着进一步补充说明的作用。Where 引导的是地点状语从句，修饰 ribosome。

[5] The convention for the pentose ring follows rules outlined in Chapter 7, but in the pentoses of nucleotides and nucleosides the carbon numbers are given a prime(') designation to **distinguish** them **from** the numbered atoms of the nitrogenous bases. 戊糖环遵循第七章列出的规则，核苷酸中的戊糖及核苷酸上的碳原子用引号（'）标号，以区别于含氮碱基上的标号原子。Outlined 是过去分词修饰的是 rules，are given a prime(') designation 是被动语态，to **distinguish** them **from** the numbered atoms of the nitrogenous bases 是目的不定式。

Exercises

1. Translate the following English into Chinese

（1）A nucleotide consists of a nitrogenous base (purine or pyrimidine), a pentose sugar, and one or more phosphate groups. Nucleic acids are polymers of nucleotides, joined together by phosphodiester linkages between the 5'-hydroxyl group of one pentose and the 3'-hydroxyl group of the next.

（2）There are two types of nucleic acid: RNA and DNA. The nucleotides in RNA contain ribose, and the common pyrimidine bases are uracil（尿嘧啶）and cytosine（胞嘧啶）. In DNA, the nucleotides contain 2-deoxyribose, and the common pyrimidine bases are thymine （胸腺嘧啶）and cytosine. The primary purines are adenine （腺嘌呤）and guanine（鸟嘌呤） in both RNA and DNA.

2. Cloze

The amino acid sequence of every protein in a cell, and the nucleotide sequence of every RNA, is specified （1） a nucleotide sequence in the cell's DNA. A segment of a DNA molecule that contains the information required for the synthesis of a functional biological product, whether protein （2） RNA, is referred （3） as a gene. A cell typically has many thousands of genes, and DNA molecules, not （4），tend to be very large. The storage and transmission of biological information are the only（5） functions of DNA.

RNAs have a broader（6）of functions, and several classes are found in cells. Ribosomal RNAs (rRNAs) are components of ribosomes, the complexes that carry（7）the synthesis of proteins. Messenger RNAs (mRNAs) are intermediaries, （8） genetic information from one or a few genes to a ribosome, where the corresponding proteins can be synthesized. Transfer RNAs (tRNAs) are adapter molecules that faithfully translate the information in mRNA （9） a specific sequence of amino acids. （10）these major classes there is a wide variety of RNAs with special functions, described in depth in Part III.

（1）A. by　　　　　B. to　　　　　　C. in　　　　　　　D. for　　　　　　　（　　　　）

（2）A. in　　　　　B. or　　　　　　C. for　　　　　　D. to　　　　　　　　（　　　　）

（3）A. for　　　　　B. in　　　　　　C. to　　　　　　D. of　　　　　　　　（　　　　）

（4）A. surprising　　B. surprised　　C. surprise　　　D. surprisingly　　（　　　　）

（5）A. known　　　　B. know　　　　C. knowing　　　D. knows　　　　　（　　　　）

（6）A. quantity　　　B. lot　　　　　C. range　　　　　D. much　　　　　（　　　　）

（7）A. of　　　　　B. for　　　　　C. in　　　　　　　D. out　　　　　　（　　　　）

（8）A. carrying　　　B. carried　　　C. carry　　　　　D. carries　　　　（　　　　）

（9）A. to　　　　　B. into　　　　　C. for　　　　　　D. by　　　　　　　（　　　　）

（10）A.Except　　　B. Except of　　　C. In addition to　D. In addition　　（　　　　）

3. Put the following into English

核苷酸　　遗传信息　　基因　　核糖体 RNA　　信使 RNA　　转运 RNA　　碱基

戊糖　　嘌呤碱　　嘧啶碱

4. Writing

Write summary of this text (no more than 200 words).

参考译文

核苷酸与核酸

核苷酸在细胞代谢中有各种作用，它们是代谢过程中的能量货币，是联系细胞应答与激素和胞外刺激物的必要化学物质，也是一系列酶辅因子和代谢中间产物的组成成分。最重要的是，它们是核酸-脱氧核糖核酸（DNA）和核糖核酸(RNA)的组成成分，是遗传信息的分子库。每个蛋白质的结构及每个生物分子和细胞组分最终是细胞核苷酸序列编码成的信息产品。储存和传递遗传信息给下一代是生命的基本条件。

1. 核苷酸-核酸的组件

每个细胞蛋白的氨基酸序列及每个核糖核酸的核苷酸序列由细胞 DNA 的核苷酸序列决定。含有生物功能产品（无论是蛋白质还是 RNA）的生物合成信息——DNA 片段称为基因。细胞含有成千上万个基因和 DNA 分子，很显然，是很大的。生物信息的储存和传递是 DNA 的已知功能之一。

RNA 有许多功能，细胞中发现的 RNA 有这几类，核糖体 RNA(rRNAs)，是核糖体的组成成分，执行生物合成的复合体；信使 RNA(mRNAs)是中介物，起着把遗传信息传递给合成相应蛋白质核糖体的作用；转运 RNA(tRNAs)是信使 RNA，信息忠诚翻译成特定氨基酸序列的连接分子。除了这几类，还有其他功能的 RNA，见文中第三部分详细描述。

2. 核苷酸的结构

核苷酸有三个特征组分：（1）一个氮碱基（含氮碱基）；（2）一个戊糖；（3）一个磷酸。不含磷酸基的分子称为核苷。含氮碱基是两个母体化合物——嘧啶和嘌呤，核苷酸中的碱基和戊糖是杂环化合物。母体结构中碳原子和氮原子一般编号，以便于许多衍生物的命名和鉴别。戊糖环遵循第七章列出的规则，核苷酸中的戊糖及核苷酸上的碳原子用引号（'）标号，以区别于含氮碱基上的标号原子。

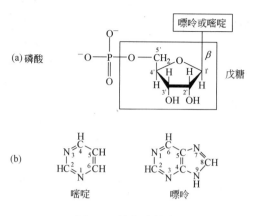

图 9-1 核苷酸的结构

（a）戊糖环结构的编号表示，这是一个核苷酸。在脱氧核苷酸中第 2 位碳原子上的—OH
被 H 取代；（b）核苷酸及核酸的嘌呤碱和嘧啶碱母体结构的编号表示

Nucleic Acid Structure

The discovery of the structure of DNA by Watson and Crick in 1953 was a **momentous** event in science, an event that gave rise to entirely new disciplines and influenced the course of many **established** ones. Our present understanding of the storage and utilization of a cell's genetic information is based on work made possible by this discovery, and an **outline** of how genetic information is processed by the cell is now a **prerequisite** for the discussion of any area of biochemistry. Here, we **concern** ourselves **with** DNA structure itself, the events that led to its discovery, and more recent **refinement**s in our understanding. RNA structure is also introduced. As in the case of protein structure (Chapter 4), it is sometimes useful to describe nucleic acid structure in terms of **hierarchical** levels of complexity (primary, secondary, tertiary). The primary structure of a nucleic acid is its covalent structure and nucleotide sequence. Any regular, stable structure taken up by some or all of the nucleotides in a nucleic acid can be referred to as secondary structure. All structures considered in the remainder of this chapter fall under the heading of secondary structure. The complex folding of large chromosomes within eukaryotic chromatin and bacterial nucleoids is generally considered tertiary structure; this is discussed in Chapter 24.

DNA Molecules Have Distinctive Base Compositions　A most important **clue** to the structure of DNA came from the work of Erwin Chargaff and his **colleague**s in the late 1940s. They found that the four nucleotide bases of DNA occur in different ratios in the DNAs of different organisms and that the amounts of certain bases are closely related. These data, collected from DNAs of a great many different species, led Chargaff to the following conclusions:

1. The base composition of DNA generally varies from one species to another.

2. DNA specimens isolated from different tissues of the same species have the same base composition.

3. The base composition of DNA in a given species does not change with an organism's age, nutritional state, or changing environment.

4. In all cellular DNAs, **regardless of** the species, the number of adenosine residues is equal to the number of thymidine residues (that is, A = T), and the number of guanosine residues is equal to the number of cytidine residues (G = C). From these relationships it follows that the sum of the purine residues equals the sum of the pyrimidine residues; that is, A +G =T + C.

These quantitative relationships, sometimes called "Chargaff's rules", were confirmed by many subsequent researchers. They were a key to establishing the three-dimensional structure of DNA and yielded clues to how genetic information is encoded in DNA and passed from one generation to the next.

New Words

momentous   [məu'mentəs]   *adj.*重大的，重要的
established   ['istæbliʃt]   *adj.* 已建立的，成形的
outline ['əutlain]   *n.*大纲，轮廓，略图，外形，要点，概要   *vt.*描画轮廓，略述
prerequisite ['pri:'rekwizit] *n.*先决条件 *adj.*首要必备的
refinement   [ri'fainmənt]   *n.*精致；（言谈，举止等的)文雅，精巧
hierarchical   [ˌhaiə'rɑ:kikəl]   *adj.*分等级的
clue [klu:]   *n.*线索
colleague   ['kɔli:g]   *n.*同事，同僚

Expressions and Technical Terms

concern with   关心，关注
regardless of   不管，不顾

Chapter 10   Fermentation and bioreactor

1. Fermentation

The origins of fermentation technology were largely with the use of **microorganism**s for the production of foods and beverages such as cheeses, yoghurts, alcoholic beverages, vinegar, Sauerkraut, fermented pickles and sausages, soya sauce and the products of many other Oriental fermentations (Table10-1).The present-day large scale production processes of these products are essentially scaled up versions of former domestic arts. Paralleling this development of product formation was the recognition of the role microorganisms could play in removing unpleasant wastes and this has resulted in massive world-wide service industries involved in water purification, effluent treatment and waste management. New dimensions in fermentation technology have made use of the ability of microorganisms (1) to overproduce specific essential primary metabolites such as glycerol, acetic acid, lactic acid, acetone, butyl alcohol, butane diol, organic acids, amino acids, vitamins, polysaccharides and xanthans; (2) to produce useful secondary metabolites (groups of metabolites that do not seem to play an immediate recognizable role in the life of the microorganism producing them) such as penicillin, streptomycin, oxytetracycline, cephalosporin, giberellins, alkaloids , actinomycin; and (3) to produce enzymes as the desired industrial product such as the exocellular enzymes amylases, proteases, pectinases or intracellular enzymes such as invertase, asparaginase, uric oxidase, restriction endonucleases and DNA ligase. More recently, fermentation technology has begun to use cells derived from higher plants and animals under conditions known as cell or tissue culture. Plant cell culture is mainly directed towards secondary product formation such as alkaloids, perfumes and flavours while animal cell culture has initially been mainly concerned with the formation of protein molecules such as interferons, monoclonal antibodies and many others.

Future markets are largely assured for fermentation products because, with limited exceptions, it is not possible to produce them economically by other chemical means. Furthermore economies in production will also occur by genetically engineering organisms to unique or higher productivities. The commercial market for products of fermentation technology is almost unlimited but will

Remarks Column

fermentation[ˌfəːmenˈteiʃən] *n.* 发酵

microorganism[maɪkrəʊˈɔːgenɪz(ə)m] *n.* [微生]微生物，微小动植物

giberellin *n.* 赤霉素

streptomycin[streptəˈmaɪsɪn] *n.* 链霉素

sauerkraut[ˈsauəkraut] *n.*<美> 德国泡菜的一种

dimension[diˈmenʃən] *n.*尺寸，尺度，维(数)，度(数)，元

overproduce[ˈəuvəprəˈdjuːs] *v.* 过度地生产

xanthan[ˈzænθən] *n.*黄原胶(用于食品工业，医学和药学作增稠剂和稳定剂)

ultimately depend on economics and safety considerations.

2. Bioreactor

The processes of commercial fermentation are in essence very similar no matter what organism is selected, what medium is used and what product formed. In all cases, large numbers of cells with uniform characteristics are grown under defined, controlled conditions. The same apparatus with minor modifications can be used to produce an enzyme, an antibiotic, an organic chemical or a single cell protein. In its simplest form fermentation processes can be just the mixing of microorganisms with a nutrient broth and allowing the components to react. More advanced and sophisticated large-scale processes require control of the entire environment so that the fermentation process can proceed efficiently and, what is more important, can be exactly repeated with the same amounts of raw materials, broth and cell inoculum producing precisely the same amount of product.

All biotechnological processes are carried out within a containment system or bioreactor. The physical form of most common bioreactors has not altered much over the past 30 years. Recently, however, many novel forms have been designed and they may play an increasingly active part in biotechnology. The main function of a bioreactor is to minimize the cost of producing a product or service while the driving force behind the continued improvement in design and function has been the need to increase the rate of product formation and the quality of the product or service. Studies have considered better aseptic design and operation, better process control including computer involvement, and how to obtain a better understanding of the rate-limiting steps of a system, especially heat and mass transfer.

Table 10-1　Fermentation products according to industrial sectors

Sector	Activities
Chemicals	
Organic (bulk)	Ethanol, acetone, butanol
	Organic acids (citric, itaconic)
Organic (fine)	Enzymes
	Perfumeries
	Polymers (mainly polysaccharides)
Inorganic	beneficiation, bioaccumulation and leaching(Cu, u)
Pharmaceuticals	Antibiotics
	Diagnostic agents (enzymes, monoclonal antibodies)
	Enzyme inhibitors
	Steroids
	Vaccines

exocellular ['eksə'seljulə] adj. 细胞外的

perfume['pə:fju:m] n. 香味，芳香，香水 vt. 使发香，洒香水于，发香味

inoculum[i'nɔkjuləm] n. 接种体

apparatus[,æpə'reitəs] n. 器械，设备，仪器

antibiotic[,æntibai'ɔtik] n. 抗生素 adj. 抗生的

contain[kən'tein] vt. 包含，容纳，容忍

bioreactor[,baiəuri(:)'æktə]n. 生物反应器

aseptic[æ'septik]n. 防腐剂 adj. 无菌的

Sector	Activities
Energy	Ethanol (gasohol)
	Methane (biogas)
	Biomass
Food	Dairy products (cheeses, yogurts, fish and meat products)
	Beverages (alcoholic, tea and coffee),
	Baker's yeast
	Food additives (antioxidants, colors, flavors, stabilizers)
	Novel foods (soy sauce, tempeh, miso)
	Mushroom products
	Amino acids, vitamins
	Starch products
	Glucose and high fructose syrups
	Functional modifications of proteins, pectins
Agriculture	Animal feedstuffs (SCP)
	Veterinary vaccines
	Ensilage and composting processes
	Microbial pesticides
	Rhizobium and other N-fixing,
	bacterial inoculants
	Mycorrhizal inoculants
	Plant cell and tissue culture (vegetative propagation, embryo production, genetic improvement)

In biotechnology, processes can be broadly considered to be either conversion cost intensive or recovery cost intensive. With conversion cost intensive processes the volumetric productivity, Q_p (kg of product $m^{-3} \cdot h^{-1}$), is of major importance while with recovery cost intensive processes the product concentration ($kg \cdot m^{-3}$), is the main criterion for the minimization of cost. Examples of the diverse product categories produced in bioreactors in the biochemical process industry are given in Table 10-2 while Table 10-3 identifies the various cultivation methods employed in biotechnology.

Table 10-2　Examples of products in different categories in biotechnological industries

Category	Example
Cell mass*	Baker's yeast, single cell protein
Cell components**	Intracellular proteins
Biosynthetic products **	Antibiotics, vitamins, amino and organic acids
Catabolic products*	Ethanol, methane, lactic acid
Bioconversion*	High-fructose corn syrup, 6-aminopenicillamc acid
Waste treatment	Activated sludge, anaerobic digestion

* Typically conversion of feedstock cost-intensive processes.

leach[li:tʃ]　v.滤去

monoclonal[ˌmɔnəˈkləunəl] adj.[生]单克隆的

steroid[ˈstiərɔid]　n.[生化]类固醇

vaccine[ˈvæksi:n] adj. 疫苗的，牛痘的 n.疫苗

starch[stɑ:tʃ]　n.淀粉

pectin[ˈpektin]　n.胶质

feedstuff[ˈfi:dstʌf]　n.饲料，饲料中营养成分

propagation[ˌprɔpəˈgeiʃən]　n.动植物，繁殖

volumetric[vɔljuˈmetrɪk]　adj.测定体积的

criterion[kraiˈtiəriən] n. （批评判断的）标准，准据，规范

intracellular[ˌintrəˈseljulə]·adj.细胞内的

There are three main operating types of bioreactors for biotechnological processes together with two forms of biocatalysts. Bioreactors can be operated on a batch, semi-continuous (fed-batch) or continuous basis. Reactions can occur in static or agitated cultures, in the presence or absence of oxygen, and in aqueous or low moisture conditions (solid substrate fermentations). The biological catalysts can be free or can be attached to surfaces by immobilization or by natural adherence. The biocatalysts can be cells in a growing or non-growing state or isolated enzymes used as soluble or immobilized catalysts. In general, the-reactions occurring in a bioreactor are conducted under moderate conditions of pH(near neutrality) and temperature (20 to 65 ℃). In most bioreactors the processes occur in an aqueous phase and product streams will be relatively dilute.

Table 10-3　Characteristics of cultivation methods

Type of culture	Operational characteristics	Application
Solid	Simple, cheap, selection of colonies from single cell possible; process control limited	Maintenance of strains, genetic studies; production of enzymes; composting
Film	Various types of bioreactors: trickling filter, rotating disc, packed bed, sponge reactor, rotating tube	Waste water treatment, monolayer culture (animal cells); bacterial leaching; vinegar production
Submerged homogeneous distribution of cells: batch	Spontaneous' reaction, various types of reactor: continuous stirred tank reactor, air lift, loop, deep shaft, etc. ; agitation by stirrers, liquid process control for physical parameters possible; less for chemical and biological parameters	Standard type of cultivation: antibiotics. solvents, acids , etc.
Fed-batch	Simple method for control of Regulatory effects , e. g. glucose repression	Production of baker's yeast
Continuous one-stage homogeneous	Proper control of reaction; excellent tool for kinetic and studies; higher costs for experiment; problem of aseptic operation, the need for highly trained operators	Few cases of application in industrial scale: production of single cell protein; waste water treatment

The optimization of a bioreactor process involves minimizing

syrup['sirəp]　*n.*糖浆，果汁

biocatalyst[,baiəu'kætəlist] *n.*[生化]生物催化剂

aqueous['eikwiəs]　*adj.*水的，水成的

dilute[dai'lju:t] *v.* 冲淡，变淡，变弱，稀释 *adj.* 淡的，弱的，稀释的

spontaneous[spɔn'teinjəs, -niəs] *adj.*自发的，自然产生的

homogeneous[,hɔməu'dʒi:njəs] *adj.* 同类的，相似的，均一的，均匀的

kinetic[kai'netik]　*adj.*(运)动的，动力(学)的

optimization[,ɔptimai'zeiʃən]　*n.*最佳化，最优化

regulatory['regjulətəri] *adj.*调整的

broth[brɔ(:)θ]　*n.*肉汤

the use of raw materials (e. g. nutrients, precursors, acid/base, air) and energy (the cost of energy since 1978 has risen at an annual rate of 16%), and maximizing product purity and quality in the broth before recovery. Process optimization is achieved by manipulation of both the physical and chemical parameters associated with the process. The range of process variables that are important to process development are listed in Table 10-4 and are discussed later.

Table 10-4 Process variables in fermentation processes

Temperature	pH	Respiratory quotient
Pressure	Oxidation reduction potential	Cell concentration
Agitation speed	Dissolved oxygen	Cellular composition:
Power input	Dissolved CO$_2$	protein (enzymes)
Air flow rate	Effluent oxygen	DNA
Feed rate of:	Effluent CO$_2$	RNA
nutrients	Dissolved concentrations of:	lipid and carbohydrate
precursors	carbohydrate	Specific activity of
inducers	nitrogen	enzyme
Weight of broth	mineral ions	Specific rates of:
Volume of liquid	precursor	product formation
Viscosity (apparent)	inducer	growth
Cumulative amount of:	product	oxygen uptake
acid	metabolites	precursor utilization
base	Broth rheology	nutrient uptake
antifoam	Power characteristics	CO$_2$ production
	Energy balance	Oxygen transfer rate

The remainder of this chapter will be concerned with the principles of organism growth in bioreactors and special attention is given to microbial to microbial cells used in product formation. The use of bioreactors for enzymic function either in soluble or immobilized form together with certain types of immobilized microbial cell systems will be considered in other chapter.

manipulation[mə,nipjuˈleiʃən] *n.* 处理，操作，操纵，被操纵

respiratory[risˈpaiərətəri] *adj.*呼吸的

antifoam[ˈæntifəum] *n.*防沫剂

precursor[pri(:)ˈkə:sə] *n.*先驱

utilization[,ju:tilaiˈzeiʃən] *n.*利用

Notes

[1] special background 发酵（fermentation）指微生物在无氧条件下，分解各种有机物质产生能量的一种方式。发酵工程泛指利用微生物制造或生产某些产品的过程，所利用的微生物主要是细菌、放线菌、酵母菌和霉菌。广义的发酵工程可分为产品发酵（上游）和产品提纯（下游）两大部分；狭义的发酵只是上游部分，主要包括：微生物菌种的特性和选育；培养基的特性；选择及其灭菌理论；发酵醪的特性；发酵机理；发酵过程控制（氧的传递、溶解、吸收；pH 控制；温度控制）；连续培养和分批发酵。目前发酵工业上的产品包括细胞代谢产物如菌体细胞、酒精、

有机酸、抗生素、干扰素、氨基酸、酶制剂等。

[2] Paralleling this development of product formation was the recognition of the role microorganisms could play in removing unpleasant wastes and this has resulted in massive world-wide service industries involved in water purification, effluent treatment and waste management. 随着（发酵）产品的发展，（人们）逐渐认识到微生物在消除讨厌的垃圾方面的作用，并因此形成了包括水的净化、污水与垃圾处理在内的大批世界性的服务行业。

[3] Future markets are largely assured for fermentation products because, with limited exceptions, it is not possible to produce them economically by other chemical means. 发酵产品将主导未来的市场，因为除了少量的特例（之外），不可能通过化学途径经济地生产这些产品。

[4] The processes of commercial fermentation are in essence very similar no matter what organism is selected, what medium is used and what product formed. 无论选择什么微生物，采用什么培养基，形成什么产品，商业发酵在工艺本质上是非常相似的。

[5] More advanced and sophisticated large-scale processes require control of the entire environment so that the fermentation process can proceed efficiently and, what is more important, can be exactly repeated with the same amounts of raw materials, broth and cell inoculum producing precisely the same amount of product. 更先进和经典的大规模化工艺需要控制整个（工艺）环境，这样可以确保发酵工艺能有效的进行，更重要的是，采用相同数量的粗原料、肉汤以及接种量精确地重复生产出相同数量的产品。

[6] Studies have considered better aseptic design and operation, better process control including computer involvement, and how to obtain a better understanding of the rate-limiting steps of a system, especially heat and mass transfer. （这些）研究考虑到了更好的无菌设计和操作，包括计算机在内的更好地工艺控制，以及如何更好地理解一个系统的限速步骤，特别是传质和传热。

[7] Process optimization is achieved by manipulation of both the physical and chemical parameters associated with the process. 工艺优化是通过对该工艺相关的物理与化学参数的控制得到的。

Exercises

1. Put the following into Chinese

This article is part Ⅰ of two reviews describing the process advantages in exploiting yeast cultures capable of retaining their metabolic activities at higher temperatures. Available literature shows the intensive and interesting work carried out by various researchers on different aspects related to properties and applications of thermotolerant(耐热的) yeast. Breakthroughs(突破) in obtaining such yeasts have mainly been achieved through fresh isolation programmes for new strains. Both temperature and ethanol tolerance appear to be heavily interrelated and progress in understanding this relationship has made significant advancement. Bioreactor configurations will play a major role in possible future commercial production strategies. Since this subject represents a topic of much industrial and biotechnological importance we concentrated our efforts on the isolation and characterization of a thermophilic(嗜热的)/thermotolerant(耐热的) yeast strains from samples exposed to higher temperature in natural environment. One of these isolates *Kluyveromyces marxianus* IMB3 has been most promising and details of progress in its potentials are described in Part Ⅱ of this review.

2. Put the following into English

发酵　　　生物反应器　　　抗生素　　　干扰素

好氧　　　厌氧　　　代谢　　　疫苗

3. Writing

Write summary of this text (no more than 150 words).

参考译文

发酵和生化反应器

1. 发酵

发酵技术的起源主要是由于微生物在食品和饮料产品中的应用，如奶酪、酸乳酪、酒精饮料、醋、泡菜、发酵的肉和香肠、大豆酱油以及一些东方的发酵产品（见表10-1）。现在的大规模的产品工艺实质上是以前家庭作坊式发酵的比例放大。随着（发酵）产品的发展，（人们）逐渐认识到微生物在消除讨厌的垃圾方面的作用，并因此形成了包括水的净化、污水与垃圾处理在内的大批世界性的服务行业。发酵工程的新型方向主要是充分利用微生物的能力：（1）高产特殊性质的初级代谢产物，如甘油、醋酸、乳酸、丙酮丁二醇、有机酸、氨基酸、维生素、多糖和黄原胶；（2）生产一些有用的次级代谢产物（指在微生物产生它们的过程中没有明确作用的一类代谢产物），如青霉素、链霉素、土霉素、头孢菌素、赤霉素、生物碱、放线菌素；（3）生产工业上需要的酶如胞外淀粉酶、蛋白酶、果胶酶或者胞内转移酶、天冬酰胺酶、氧化酶、限制性核酸内切酶和DNA连接酶。近来，发酵技术应用到一些从高等植物和动物体上得到的细胞，并在已知的培养条件下进行细胞或者组织培养。植物细胞培养主要是为了获得次级代谢产物，如生物碱、香料和香精，而动物细胞培养最初主要是为了获得相关的蛋白质，如干扰素、单克隆抗体以及其他的物质。

未来市场上将大量地出现发酵产品，因为除了少量特例（之外），不可能通过其他的化学途径如此经济地生产这些产品。而且这些产品的经济效益会通过遗传工程技术使细胞具有独特或者更高的生产能力来实现。依赖于发酵操作技术的产品市场将是不可限量的，但是根本上更依赖于经济和安全的考虑。

2. 生化反应器

无论你选择什么样的微生物、采用什么样的培养基以及最终形成什么样的产品，商业化发酵的过程在本质上是非常相似的。在所有的发酵过程中，具有相同特征的大量细胞生长在特定的控制条件下。通过小小的修改，相同设备能被用于生产酶、抗生素、有机化学物质或者单细胞蛋白。发酵工艺非常简单，可以仅仅把微生物细胞和营养肉汤混合，让各种组分在这个系统中发生反应。更先进和经典的大规模化工艺需要控制整个（工艺）环境，这样可以确保发酵工艺能有效的进行，更重要的是，采用相同数量的原料、肉汤以及接种量精确地重复生产出相同数量的产品。

所有的生化反应过程都是在一个封闭的反应系统或者生化反应器中进行的。大多数的生化反应器的外形在最近30年内没有什么改变。但是，最近设计了一些新式的生化反应器，可能在生物技术方面会产生越来越多的积极作用。生物反应器的主要功能是降低产品生产以及服务的消耗，同时在设计和功能上的不断提高背后的推动力可提高产品形成速率，产品以及服务的质量。（这些）研究考虑到了更好的无菌设计和操作，包括计算机在内的更好的工艺控制，以及如何更好地理解一个系统的限速步骤，特别是传质和传热。

表 10-1　工业生产部门的发酵产品

部　门	功能产品
化学制品 有机物（批量）	乙醇，丙酮，丁醇
	有机酸（柠檬酸，衣康酸）
	有机物（精细），酶
	香料
	聚合体（主要是多糖）
无机物	选矿，生物体内积累（如有毒化学物质）以及沥滤（铜，铀）
药品	抗生素
	诊断试剂（酶，单元隆抗体）
	酶抑制剂
	甾类化合物
	疫苗
能源	乙醇（如乙醇汽油）
	甲烷（沼气）
	生物质
食品	奶制品（奶酪，酸奶，鱼肉食品）
	饮料（酒精，茶和咖啡）
	面包酵母
食品	食品添加剂（抗氧化剂，色素，香料，稳定剂）
	新鲜食品（酱油，豆豉，日本豆面酱）
	菇类食品
	氨基酸，维生素
	淀粉类食品
	葡萄糖和高果糖浆
	功能蛋白，果胶
农业	动物饲料（SCP）
	禽兽疫苗
	青贮饲料堆肥
	微生物杀虫剂
	根瘤菌及其他固氮菌，细菌菌剂
	菌根菌剂
	植物细胞和组织培养（植物繁殖，胚胎生产，遗传改良）

　　生物技术的过程要更多地考虑到转化成本或者是回收成本，当转化成本促进体积生产力（提高）时，Q_p（千克每立方米每小时）具有相当的重要性；而当回收成本促进产品的浓度（千克每立方米）提高时，则是产品成本最小化的主要指标。生化工业中各种不同产品在生物反应器中的工艺的相关例子列举在表 10-2 中，同时表 10-3 列举出生物技术中使用的不同的培养方法。

表 10-2　生物技术行业中不同类产品实例

分　类	例　子
细胞菌体[①]	面包酵母，单细胞蛋白
胞内组分[②]	胞内蛋白
生物合成产品[②]	抗生素，维生素，氨基酸和有机酸

分　类	例　子
代谢产品	乙醇，甲烷，乳酸
生物转化	高果玉米糖浆，6-氨青霉烷酸（原英文名错误，应为 6-aminopenicillanic acid）
水处理	活性污泥，厌氧消化

① 典型高成本原料转化工艺。
② 典型高成本回收工艺。

表 10-3　培养方法特征

培养类型	操作特征	应用
固态	简单，便宜，可选择单细胞克隆酶的控制过程有限	菌株的保藏，遗传研究酶的生产；堆肥
薄膜	各种不同类型的反应器：滴滤器，转盘，填充床，海绵反应器；旋转列管	水处理，单层培养（动物细胞）；细菌浸出；醋的生产
深层液体分布	自发反应，各种不同类型的反应器；连续搅拌釜式反应器，气升式，环，深井等	标准培养类型；抗生素，溶剂，酸等
分批	搅拌器搅拌，液态过程物理参数可控制，生化参数少	
分批补料	调控作用的控制方法简单，如葡萄糖阻遏	面包酵母生产
连续单段均相	反应控制适当；具有好的动力学研究方法；实验成本高；操作的无菌问题，人才素质要求高	工业上应用少；单细胞蛋白生产；废水处理

　　生物反应器中的生化反应过程可以分为 3 种主要的操作方式，同时需要两种酶。生物反应器可以按照分批、半连续、连续发酵来进行。反应会在静态或者通气培养、好氧或者厌氧、液态或者低湿度（固体发酵）中进行。生物催化剂可以是自由分布或者是固定化或者是自然黏附吸附在表面。催化剂可以是正在生长或者是不在生长时期的细胞，或者是可溶的或固定化的酶。一般来说，生化反应器里发生的生化反应都是在温和 pH（中性）和温度 $20\sim65^{\circ}C$ 的条件下进行的。大多数生物反应器的生化反应过程是在液相中进行，产品浓度也很低。

　　生化反应器的优化包括降低原料（例如营养、前体、酸/碱、空气）和能量（从 1978 年每年能量的利用提高的年速率是 16%）用量，工艺的优化需要通过与物理和化学相关的参数的工艺操作来进行。提高工艺等重要参数的变化范围详见表 10-4，后面并有相关的讨论。

表 10-4　发酵过程的工艺变量

温　度	pH 值	呼　吸　商
压力	氧化还原电势	细胞浓度
搅拌速度	溶解氧	胞内组成：蛋白质（酶），DNA，RNA，脂类及糖类
输入功率	溶解二氧化碳	
空气流速	氧气排放量	
进料速率：营养，前体，诱导剂	CO_2 排放量	酶的比活力
发酵液重量	溶解浓度：糖类，氮，无机离子，前体，诱导剂，产物，代谢产物	比速率：产品生成，氧气吸收，前体，营养吸收
液体体积	发酵液流变性	CO_2 生成量
表观黏度	功率特性	氧的传递速率
累积量：酸，碱，消泡剂	能量平衡	

　　本章剩余部分与生化反应器中微生物生长相关的理论有关，特别是微生物细胞在产物形成方

面的作用会有特别的关注。关于生化反应器在特定的可溶的或者固定化细胞体系的应用将在其他章节讨论。

Reading material

Types of Fermentation Process

The fermentation unit in industrial microbiology is **analogous** to a chemical plant in the chemical industry. A fermentation process is a biological process and, therefore, has requirements of sterility and use of cellular enzymic reactions instead of chemical reactions aided by **inanimate** catalysts, sometimes operating at **elevated** temperature and pressure.

Industrial fermentation processes may be divided into two main types, with various combinations and modifications. These are batch fermentations and continuous fermentations.

Batch Fermentation Process

A tank of fermenter is filled with the prepared **mash** of raw materials to be fermented. The temperature and pH for microbial fermentation is properly adjusted, and occasionally nutritive **supplements** are added to the prepared mash. The mash is steam sterilized in a pure culture process. The **inoculum** of a pure culture is added to the fermenter, from a separate pure culture vessel.

Fermentation proceeds, and after the proper time the contents of the fermenter, are taken out for further processing. The fermenter is cleaned and the process is repeated. Thus each fermentation is a discontinuous process divided into batches.

Continuous Fermentation Process

Growth of microorganisms during batch fermentation confirms to the characteristic growth curve, with a lag phase followed by a **logarithmic** phase. This, in turn, is terminated by progressive **decrements** I in the rate of growth until the stationary phase is reached. This is because of limitation of one or more of the essential nutrients.

In continuous fermentation, the substrate is added to the fermenter continuously at, a fixed rate. This maintains the organisms in the logarithmic growth phase. The fermentation products are taken out continuously. The design and arrangements for continuous fermentation, are some what complex.

New Words

analogous[əˈnæləgəs] *adj.* 类似的，相似的，可比拟的
inanimat[inˈænimit] *adj.* 死气沉沉的，没有生命的，单调的
elevate[ˈeliveit] *vt.* 举起，提拔，振奋，提升…的职位
mash[mæʃ] *n.* 麦芽浆，浆状物 *v.* 捣碎
supplement[ˈsʌplimənt] *n.* 补遗，补充，附录，增刊
inoculum[iˈnɔkjuləm] *n.* 接种体
logarithmic[iˈɔgəˈriθmik] *adj.* 对数的
decrement[ˈdekrimənt] *n.* 消耗

Chapter 11　Downstream processing[1]

Downstream processing refers to the recovery and purification of biosynthetic products, particularly pharmaceuticals, from natural sources such as animal or plant tissue or fermentation broth, including the recycling of **salvageable** components and the proper treatment and disposal of waste[2]. It is an essential step in the manufacture of pharmaceuticals such as antibiotics, hormones (e.g. insulin and human growth hormone), antibodies (e.g. **infliximab** and **abciximab**) and vaccines; antibodies and enzymes used in diagnostics; industrial enzymes; and natural fragrance and flavor compounds. Downstream processing is usually considered a specialized field in biochemical engineering, itself a specialization within chemical engineering, though many of the key technologies were developed by chemists and biologists for laboratory-scale separation of biological products.

Downstream processing and analytical bioseparation both refer to the separation or purification of biological products, but at different scales of operation and for different purposes. Downstream processing **implies** manufacture of a purified product fit for a specific use, generally in marketable quantities, while analytical bioseparation refers to purification for the **sole** purpose of measuring a component or components of a mixture, and may deal with sample sizes as small as a single cell[3].

1. Stages in downstream processing

A widely recognized **heuristic** for **categorizing** downstream processing operations divides them into four groups which are applied in order to bring a product from its natural state as a component of a **tissue**, cell or **fermentation broth** through **progressive** improvements in purity and concentration [4].

Removal of insolubles is the first step and involves the capture of the product as a solute in a **particulate-free** liquid, for example the separation of cells, **cell debris** or other **particulate** matter from fermentation broth containing an antibiotic. Typical operations to achieve this are **filtration**, **centrifugation**, **sedimentation**, **flocculation**, **electro-precipitation**, and **gravity settling**. Additional operations such as **grinding**, **homogenization**, or **leaching**, required to recover products from solid sources such as plant and animal tissues, are usually included in this group.

Remarks Column

salvageable[ˈsælvɪdʒəbl] *adj.* 可用的，可挽救的，可挽回的；可抢救的，可打捞的

infliximab：译文因福利美，是一种细胞因子 TNF-α 的单克隆抗体，用于治疗类风湿性关节炎

abciximab：译文阿昔单抗，是一种抗血小板凝聚单克隆抗体，具有抑制血小板凝集的作用

imply [imˈplai] *vt.*暗示，意味

sole [səul] *adj.*单独的，唯一的

heuristic [hjuəˈristik] *adj.* 启发式的
categorize [ˈkætɪɡəraɪz] *v.*加以类别，分类
tissue [ˈtisjuː] *n.* [生]组织；薄的纱织品，薄纸，棉纸
progressive[prəˈgresiv] *adj.* 进步的，前进的
particulate [pəˈtikjulit, -leit] *n.*微粒 *adj.*微粒的
particulate-free 无颗粒的
filtration 过滤
centrifugation 离心
sedimentation 沉降
flocculation 絮凝，凝聚
electro-precipitation 凝聚
grinding 研磨
homogenization 匀浆化
leaching 沥滤

Product Isolation is the removal of those components whose properties vary markedly from that of the desired product. For most products, water is the chief impurity and isolation steps are designed to remove most of it, reducing the volume of material to be handled and concentrating the product[5]. Solvent extraction, adsorption, ultrafiltration, and precipitation are some of the unit operations involved.

Product Purification is done to separate those contaminants that resemble the product very closely in physical and chemical properties. Consequently steps in this stage are expensive to carry out and require sensitive and sophisticated equipment. This stage contributes a significant fraction of the entire downstream processing expenditure. Examples of operations include affinity, size exclusion, reversed phase chromatography, crystallization and fractional precipitation.

Product Polishing describes the final processing steps which end with packaging of the product in a form that is stable, easily **transportable** and **convenient**. **Crystallization**, **desiccation**, **lyophilization** and spray drying are typical unit operations[6]. Depending on the product and its intended use, polishing may also include operations to sterilize the product and remove or deactivate trace contaminants which might compromise product safety. Such operations might include the removal of viruses or **depyrogenation**.

A few product recovery methods may be considered to combine two or more stages. For example, expanded bed adsorption accomplishes removal of insolubles and product isolation in a single step. Affinity chromatography often isolates and purifies in a single step.

The various processes used for the actual recovery of useful products from a fermentation or any other industrial process is called downstream processing. The cost of downstream processing (DSP) is often more than 50% of the manufacturing cost, and there is product loss at each step of DSP.

Therefore, the DSP should be efficient, involve as few steps as possible (to avoid product loss), and be cost-effective. The various steps in DSP are as follows:

(i) separation of particles,

(ii) **disintegration** of cells,

(iii) extraction,

(iv) concentration,

(v) purification and

transportable[træns'pɔ:təbl] *adj.* 可运输的

convenient [kən'vi:njənt] *adj.* 便利的，方便的

crystallization['kristəlai'zeiʃən] *n.* 结晶

lyophilization[laɪ,ɔfɪlaɪ'zeɪʃən] *n.* 冻干法

depyrogenation[di,pairəudʒi'neiʃən] *n.* 去除热原

disintegration [dis,inti'greiʃən] *n.* 破碎；瓦解

(vi) drying.

2. Separation of particles

The first step in DSP is the separation of solids, usually cells, from the liquid medium. This is generally achieved as follows.

(1) Filtration

It is used for the separation of **filamentous** fungi and filamentous bacteria, e.g., **streptomycete**s, and often for yeast flocks. The various techniques of filtration employed are, surface filtration, depth filtration, centrifugal filtration, cross flow filtration, and rotary drum vacuum filtration.

(2) Centrifugation

It may be used to separate bacteria and usually protein precipitates. But difficulties arise due to small differences in the densities of the particles and the medium. In addition, equipment cost, power consumption, temperature, etc. are the other disadvantages.

(3) Flocculation and floatation

Flocculation, i.e., sticking together of cells, can be induced by inorganic salts, mineral **hydrocolloid**s are organic **polyelectrolyte**s. Since sedimentation rate of a particle increases with size, flocculated cells can be recovered by centrifugation.

In cases, where flocculation is not effective, very fine gas **bubble**s can be created by sparging, release of overpressure or electrolysis. The gas bubbles adsorb to and surround the cells, raising them to the surface of medium in form of foam (floatation); long chain fatty acids or amines promote stable foam formation.

The cells collected in the foam are **readily** recovered. Flocculation and floatation are used for the most efficient recovery of microbial biomass in some single cell protein production systems.

3. Disintegration of cells

Disruption of microbial cells is usually difficult due to their small size, strong cell wall and high osmotic pressure inside cells. Generally, cell disruption is achieved by mechanical means, **lysis** or drying.

(1) Mechanical cell disruption

This approach uses shear, e.g., grinding in a ball mill, colloid mill, etc., pressure and pressure release, e.g., homogenizer, and ultrasound. A widely used method is as follows: the cell suspension is forced through a fine nozzle; the cells disintegrate due to **hydrodyanamic** shear and **cavitation**.

filamentous [filə'mentəs] adj.细丝状的，纤维所成的，如丝的

streptomycete[ˌstreptəuˈmaɪsiːt] n.[微]链霉菌

floatation [fləuˈteiʃən] n.浮选

hydrocolloid[ˌhaidrəˈkɔlɔid] n.水状胶质，水状胶体

polyelectrolyte [ˌpɔliiˈlektrəuˌlait] n.[化]聚合(高分子)电解质

bubble ['bʌbl] n.泡沫；幻想的计划

readily ['redili] adv.乐意地，欣然地，容易地

lysis['laisis]n.(pl.-ses ['-siːz])[生化]细胞[菌]溶解

hydrodyanamic['haidrəudai'næmik] adj. 水力的

shear [ʃiə] n.剪切力

cavitation [ˌkæviˈteiʃən] n.空化作用

(2) Drying

The cells may be dried, e.g., by adding the cells into a large excess of cold acetone and subsequently extracted using **buffer** or salt solutions. Drying induces changes in cell wall structure, which facilitates extraction. This method is widely used.

(3) Lysis

Microbial cells may be lysed by chemical means, e.g., salts or **surfactants**, **osmotic shock**, freezing, or by lytic enzymes, e.g., **lysozyme**, etc.

4. Extraction process

The process of recovering a compound or a group of compounds from a mixture or from cells into a solvent phase is called extraction. Extraction usually achieves both separation as well as concentration of the product. It is especially useful for the recovery of **lipophilic** substances, and in antibiotic recovery; it is often an early step after cell separation.

(1) Liquid-liquid extraction

It employs two **immiscible** liquids into which the product is differentially soluble. Usually successively smaller volumes of the solvent are used for repeated extraction of a giver back-extraction also tends to increase the selectivity of extra extraction may be performed in a single step, by multi-stage **par** extraction, or by counter-current extraction (most complex effective).

(2) Whole broth (medium and cells) extraction

It should be used wherever possible since it reduces the number of steps as well as product loss. The effectiveness of extraction may, however, be reduced due to the presence of cells.

(3) Aqueous multiphase extraction

It is used for separation of enzymes from cells or cell debris. The enzymes are extracted in an aqueous polyethylene glycol-dextran mixture, which form separate phases. Recovery of enzymes from these phases is rather easy and free from some of the difficulties encountered in centrifugation.

5. Concentration of product

Some concentration of the product may occur during the extraction step. Further concentration may be achieved by

(i) **evaporation**,

(ii) membrane filtration,

(iii) ion exchange methods and

(iv) adsorption methods.

(1) Evaporation

It is generally used in cases of solvent extraction, and used

---

buffer ['bʌfə] n.缓冲溶液

surfactant [sə'fæktənt] n.& adj. [化]表面活性剂（的）

lysozyme ['laisəzaim]n.溶解酶

lipophilic [ˌlipə'filik]adj.亲脂性的

immiscible [i'misəbl] adj.不能混合的，不融合的

par [pɑ:] n.同等，(股票等)票面价值 adj.票面的，平价的，平均的，标准的

evaporation [i,væpə'reiʃən] n.蒸发(作用)

various devices, e.g., continuous flow evaporators, falling film evaporators, thin film evaporators, centrifugal thin film evaporators and spray dryers.

Efficient arrangements must be made for recovery of the evaporated solvent to reduce costs. For low grade products, often evaporation of the whole broth is undertaken using a spray-drier.

(2) Membrane filtration

It generally achieves both concentration and separation of the products usually based on the size of molecules. The different processes of membrane filtration are microfiltration, ultrafiltration, reverse osmosis and **electrodialysis**.

electrodialysis[ɪˌlektrəʊdaɪˈælɪsɪs] *n.*[化]电渗析

Micro and ultrafiltration work as sieves and separate molecules of different sizes, but reverse osmosis can separate molecules of similar size. Micro filtration can be used for cell separation as well.

(3) Ion exchange resins

These are polymers having firmly attached ionizable groups (**anion**s or **cation**s), which ionize under a suitable environment. These may be solid, e.g., dextran, **cellulose**, polyamine, **acrylate**, etc., or liquid, e.g., a solvent carrying a functional group like phosphoric acid mono or diester, etc. Solidion exchangers may be used in two ways:

anion [ˈænaiən] *n.*阴离子 cation [ˈkætaiən] *n.*[化]阳离子
cellulose [ˈseljuləus] *n.*纤维素
acrylate [ˈækrileit] *n.*[化]丙烯酸酯

(i) they may be packed in columns or

(ii) they may be added to the extract and removed by decantation.

Liquid ion exchangers dissolve only in nonaqueous solvent carrier and the separation is similar to liquid liquid extraction. Some antibiotics are recovered directly from the whole broth using ion exchange resins.

The product is recovered from the ion exchangers by ion displacement; this also regenerates the ion exchanger.

(4) Adsorption resins

These are **porous** polymers without ionization. Most compounds are adsorbed to the resins in nonionized state. The porosity of the resin determines the surface available for adsorption.

porous [ˈpɔːrəs] *adj.*多孔的

These resins may be apolar (e.g., styrene-divinyl beneze), polar (e.g., sulfoxide, amide, etc.), or semipolar (e.g., acrylic ester). The products are recovered from such resins by solvent (organic) extraction, changed pH, etc.

6. Purification of product

The final step in the recovery of a product is purification, which aims at obtaining the product in highly purified state. Purification is achieved by

(i) crystallization and

(ii) chromatographic procedures.

(1) Crystallization

It is mainly used for purification of low molecular weight compounds like antibiotics, e.g., penicillin G is usually extracted from fermentation broth in butyl acetate and crystallized by the addition of potassium acetate in ethanol solution. Crystallization is the final stage in purification of products like citric acid, sodium glutamate, etc.

(2) Chromatography methods

These are used for purification of low molecular weight compounds from mixtures of similar molecules, e.g., **homologous** antibiotics, and of macromolecules, especially enzymes, which are similar in properties. The materials used for chromatography are generally coated on particulate carriers, which are packed in columns through which the liquid containing the product is pumped either upward or downward.

The separated product is recovered in some sort of fraction collector. On a large scale, organic solvents are used for collection; therefore, the whole system has to be installed in a flame-proof and explosion-proof room.

The different chromatographic procedures are,

(i) adsorption,

(ii) **ion exchange,**

(iii) **gel filtratio**n,

(iv) **hydrophobic,**

(v) affinity,

(vi) covalent and

(vii) **partition chromatography**.

Adsorption chromatography separates molecules due to their differential affinities for the surface of a solid matrix, e.g., silica gel, **alumina**, **hydroxyapatite** (all inorganic) or an organic polymer.

In case of ion exchange chromatography, resins or **polysaccharide**s, e.g., cellulose, sepharose, having attached ionized functional groups are used for a high resolution separation of macromolecules, e.g., proteins.

Gel filtration uses molecular sieves, composed of neutral cross linked carriers (e.g., polymers like agarose, dextrans) of different pore sizes. Molecules smaller than the pore size enter the

homologous [hɔ'mɔləgəs] adj.相应的，类似的，一致的，[生物]同源的

hydrophobic [ˌhaɪdrəʊ'fəʊbɪk] adj.疏水的；狂犬病的，恐水病的，患恐水病的

alumina [ə'ljuːminə] n.[化]氧化铝(亦称矾土)

hydroxyapatite[hai,drɔksi'æpətait] n.[矿]羟磷灰石

polysaccharide[pɔlɪ'sækəraɪd] n.[生化]多糖，聚糖

antigen ['æntidʒən] n. [免疫]抗原

carrier and are retained; they are later eluted (in order of molecule size) and collected. Gel filtration is used in aqueous systems. Hydrophobic carriers are used for purification of hydrophobic molecules, e.g., many enzymes and other proteins.

Affinity chromatography uses molecules, called effectors, to which the product has high and specific affinity, e.g., using an antibody (effector) for the purification of the **antigen** to which it is specific.

The effector is immobilized on a water-insoluble carrier, which is packed in a column through which the mixture is passed. The effector binds only to the molecules for which it is specific and retains it in the column; it is later recovered by elution using a buffer solution of a specified pH.

For example, human **leucocyte** interferon is recovered in high yield and in high purity by affinity chromatography using **monoclonal antibody** immobilized on a sepharose column. Group specific affinity chromatography and covalent chromatography are based on chemical interactions between the carrier and the product molecules.

7. Drying of products

Drying makes the products suitable for handling and storage. It should be accomplished with a minimum rise in temperature due to heat sensitivity of most products. Addition of sugars or other stabilizers improves the heat tolerance of some products like enzymes and pharmaceutical preparations.

The most common approaches to drying are as follows:

(i) **vacuum drying**,

(ii) **spray drying**, and

(iii) **freeze drying**.

In spray drying, the solution or slurry to be dried is atomized by a nozzle or a rotating disc. A current of hot (150-250°C) air is passed; the drying is so rapid that the temperature of particles remains very low. Spray drying is used for enzymes, antibiotics and food products.

Vacuum drying uses both heat and vacuum for drying; it can be applied both in batch mode (e.g., chamber dryers) and in continuous mode (e.g., rotating drum vacuum dryers).

In freeze drying, the liquor to be dried is first frozen and the water is sublimed from the frozen mass. A very low pressure (partial vacuum) is maintained to promote sublimation of water. The energy needed for **sublimation** is provided by heated plates and radiation on to the surface. The temperature of solid is

leucocyte ['lju:kə,sait] n.[解]白细胞，白血球

sublimation [,sʌbli'meiʃən] n.升华

Expressions and Technical Terms

fermentation broth 发酵液
cell debris 细胞碎片
product polishing 精品;优质产品,抛光产品

gravity settling 重力沉降
osmotic shock 渗透压冲击
ion exchange 离子交换
gel filtration 凝胶过滤
partition chromatography 分配色谱
affinity chromatography 亲和色谱
monoclonal antibody 单克隆抗体
vacuum drying 真空干燥
spray drying 喷雾干燥
freeze drying 冷冻干燥

regulated by regulating the pressure in the drying chamber. This is the gentlest method of drying, and is used for many pharmaceutical products, e.g., viruses, vaccines, plasma fractions, enzymes, etc., and in food industries.

Notes

[1] special background　下游工程指从发酵液中分离和纯化产品的技术，包括固液分离技术（离心分离、过滤分离、沉淀分离等工艺）、细胞破壁技术（超声、高压剪切、渗透压、表面活性剂和溶壁酶等）、蛋白质纯化技术（沉淀法、色谱分离法和超滤法等），最后还有产品的包装处理技术（真空干燥和冰冻干燥等）。

生物下游加工过程的特点：① 操作条件应尽量减少生物物质的活性的丧失。② 除去影响目标产物稳定性的杂质,如蛋白酶等。③ 生物产物一般用作医药、食品和化妆品，需除去热原、具有免疫原性的异体蛋白等有害物质。④ 原料液中目标产物的浓度一般都很低,大多需浓缩。⑤ 纯化时注意分离与目标产物在结构与理化性质上相似的杂质。⑥ 获得高纯度的干燥产品。⑦ 分离过程精细，成本高。

[2] Downstream processing refers to the recovery and purification of biosynthetic products, particularly pharmaceuticals, from natural sources such as animal or plant tissue or fermentation broth, including the recycling of **salvageable** components and the proper treatment and disposal of waste. 下游过程指的是生物合成产品的回收与纯化，尤其是制药行业，包括从自然资源例如动植物组织或发酵液例如废物有用组分的回收和垃圾的处理。including 可以理解为现在分词，表示伴随状语。

[3] Downstream processing **implies** manufacture of a purified product fit for a specific use, generally in marketable quantities, while analytical bioseparation refers to purification for the **sole** purpose of measuring a component or components of a mixture, and may deal with sample sizes as small as a single cell. 下游过程指的是对有专门用途的产品纯化制造，一般是生产市场上所需要的量，而生物分析分离指的是以测量混合物中某一组分或多组分为单一目的的分离纯化，可处理如同单细胞大小的样品。这里 while 引导的是前后句的比较。

[4] A widely recognized **heuristic** for **categorizing** downstream processing operations divides them into four groups which are applied in order to bring a product from its natural state as a component of a **tissue**, cell or **fermentation broth** through **progressive** improvements in purity and concentration. 从自然资源例如组织、细胞或发酵液中通过进一步的分离纯化得到产品，将下游过程分成四个阶段，这种分类已得到广泛的认同。recognized 过去分词，修饰的是 downstream processing operations 。which 指的是 groups。

[5] Product Isolation is the removal of those components whose properties vary markedly from that of the desired product. For most products, water is the chief impurity and isolation steps are designed to remove most of it, reducing the volume of material to be handled and concentrating the product. 产品分离是除去那些与目的产物性质不同的组分。对于大多数产品来说，水是主要的杂质,需要设计分离步骤将其除去,减少处理的体积,浓缩产品。这里 that 指的是 property。reducing 是现在分词作状语，表示伴随状况。

[6] **Product Polishing** describes the final processing steps which end with packaging of the product in a form that is stable, easily **transportable** and **convenient**. **Crystallization, desiccation, lyophilization** and spray drying are typical unit operations. 成品化是使产品稳定，易于运输和方便

包装的最终步骤。结晶、干燥、冻干以及喷雾干燥是（该步骤中）典型的单元操作。which 指代的是 processing steps，这里 that 引导的是定语从句，指代的是 product。

Exercises

1. Put the following into English

过滤　离心　沉淀　絮凝　凝聚　研磨　匀浆　沥滤　吸附　超滤　亲和　浓缩　纯化　结晶　下游过程　重力沉降　溶剂萃取　分子排阻　反相色谱　分级沉淀　颗粒分离　细胞破碎　真空干燥　喷雾干燥　冷冻干燥

2. Cloze

Product Purification is done to separate those contaminants that resemble the product very （1） in physical and chemical properties. Consequently steps in this stage are expensive to carry （2） and require sensitive and （3） equipment. This stage contributes a significant fraction of the entire downstream processing expenditure. Examples of operations include affinity, size exclusion, reversed phase chromatography, crystallization and fractional precipitation.

Product Polishing describes the final processing steps which end （4） packaging of the product in a form that is stable, easily transportable and convenient. Crystallization, desiccation, lyophilization and spray drying are typical unit operations. Depending on the product and its intended use, （5） may also include operations to sterilize the product and remove or deactivate trace contaminants which might （6） product safety. Such operations might include the removal of viruses or depyrogenation.

A few product recovery methods may be considered to combine two or more stages. For example, expanded bed adsorption （7） removal of insolubles and product isolation in a single step. Affinity chromatography often isolates and purifies in a single step.

The various processes used for the actual recovery of useful products from a fermentation or any other industrial process is called （8） processing. The cost of downstream processing (DSP) is often （9） than 50% of the manufacturing cost, and there is product loss （10） each step of DSP.

（1）A. closely　　　B. close　　　　C. differently　　D. different　　　（　　）
（2）A. in　　　　　B. out　　　　　C. to　　　　　　D. for　　　　　（　　）
（3）A. complex　　　B. difficult　　　C. sophisticated　D. complicated　　（　　）
（4）A. of　　　　　B. into　　　　　C. in　　　　　　D. with　　　　　（　　）
（5）A. operation　　B. product　　　C. polishing　　　D. contaminant　　（　　）
（6）A. promote　　　B. comprise　　　C. promise　　　D. compromise　　（　　）
（7）A. reaches　　　B. accomplishes　C. finishes　　　D. arrives　　　　（　　）
（8）A. downstream　B. upstream　　　C. stream　　　　D. midstream　　　（　　）
（9）A. fewer　　　　B. greater　　　　C. less　　　　　D. more　　　　　（　　）
（10）A. in　　　　　B. of　　　　　　C. at　　　　　　D. for　　　　　（　　）

3. Translate the following English into Chinese

（1）Isolation and purification is done immediately after termination of fermentation in a manner that retains the enzyme activity. If the cells are to be used for immobilization, the biomass is isolated and treated to make it ready for use.

（2）The extracellular enzymes are recovered directly from broth, while enzymes localized within cells are isolated by rupturing the cells. Enzyme purification is based on various techniques whose efficacy（功效，效益）and cost differ widely; the process used will mainly depend on the purity needed and the cost, which is acceptable.

4. Writing

Write summary of this text (no more than 200 words).

参考译文

　　下游过程指的是生物合成产品的回收与纯化，尤其是制药行业，包括从自然资源例如动植物组织或发酵液例如废物有用组分的回收和垃圾的处理。它是制药过程中的必要步骤，像抗生素、激素（例如胰岛素和人生长激素）、抗体（例如细胞因子 TNF-α 的单克隆抗体和抗血小板凝聚）、疫苗、应用于诊断的抗体及酶、工业酶和天然芳香化合物。下游过程通常被认为是生化工程的专业领域，其本身属于化学工程专业领域，尽管化学家和生物学家在生物产品分离小试实验中开发出了许多关键技术。

　　下游过程和生物分析分离都指的是生物产品的分离与纯化，但是它们具有不同的规模和目的。下游过程指的是对有专门用途的产品纯化制造，一般是生产市场上所需要的量，而生物分析分离指的是以测量混合物中某一组分或多组分为单一目的的分离纯化，可处理如同单细胞大小的样品。

　　1. 下游过程步骤

　　从自然资源例如组织、细胞或发酵液中通过进一步的分离纯化得到产品，将下游过程分成四个阶段，这种分类已得到广泛的认同。

　　不溶物的去除是第一个步骤，可以得到非颗粒溶液的溶质产品。例如细胞，细胞碎片或含有抗生素的发酵液中颗粒物的沉淀。为此典型的操作方法是过滤、离心、沉淀、絮凝、凝聚以及重力沉降。还有其他的方法像研磨、匀浆、沥滤以及需要从动植物组织中回收产品通常属于这个阶段。

　　产品分离是除去那些与目的产物性质不同的组分。对于大多数产品来说，水是主要的杂质，需要设计分离步骤将其除去，减少处理的体积，浓缩产品。涉及该单元的步骤有溶剂萃取、吸附法、超滤和沉淀。

　　产品纯化是分离那些与产品理化性质相似的污染物。因此这阶段的步骤是昂贵的，需要灵敏和精密的设备。该阶段是整个下游工艺过程花费的重要部分。操作单元有亲和、分子排阻、反相色谱、结晶和分级沉淀。

　　成品化是使产品稳定，易于运输和方便包装的最终步骤。结晶、干燥、冻干以及喷雾干燥是（该步骤中）典型的单元操作。成品化取决于产品及其使用目的，也包括危及产品安全性的产品消毒及痕量污染物的去除或失活。这样的操作可能包括除去病毒或热原。

　　一些产品的回收方法需要由二步或更多步骤组成。例如，经过单步骤膨胀床吸附可除去不溶物，实现与产品的分离。再经过单步骤的亲和色谱分离和纯化。

　　用于从发酵液或任何工业工艺中回收有用产品的各种工艺方法称为下游过程。下游过程成本通常超过了生产成本 50% 以上，下游过程的每一步骤都有损失。

　　因此，下游过程应该是高效的、尽可能少的步骤（以防产品损失）和具有成本效益。下游过程的各种方法步骤如下：

　　（i）颗粒分离；

　　（ii）细胞破碎；

　　（iii）提取（萃取）；

（ⅳ）浓缩；

（ⅴ）纯化干燥。

2. 颗粒分离

下游过程的第一步是固体颗粒的分离，通常是从液体介质中分离出细胞，这主要有以下方法。

（1）过滤

过滤是用来对丝状真菌和丝状细菌的分离，例如链霉菌，也经常用来对酵母絮凝物的分离。利用到过滤的各种方法有表面过滤、深层过滤、离心过滤、错流过滤以及转鼓真空过滤。

（2）离心

离心是用来分离出细菌和一些蛋白质沉淀物。但由于颗粒及介质的密度差别小，困难性增大。而且还有一些不利的是装置成本、动力消耗及温度（的升高）。

（3）凝聚和浮选

凝聚（例如细胞黏合在一起）可由无机盐和矿物质胶体诱导，矿物质胶体是有机聚合电解质。由于颗粒沉降速率随颗粒尺寸增加而增加，细胞凝聚可以通过离心回收。

在多数情况下，凝聚不是有效的，通过喷射，高压的释放或电解形成小气泡，该气泡吸附并包围细胞，提升到泡沫介质的表面（浮选），长链脂肪酸或胺有助于泡沫的稳定性。

细胞很容易从泡沫中回收到。在一些单细胞蛋白生产体系中，使用凝聚和浮选是微生物菌体最有效的回收方法。

3. 细胞破碎

微生物细胞的破碎是困难的，因为它们的尺寸小，细胞壁坚韧和细胞内具有高渗透压。一般来说，细胞破碎可由机械法、溶解法或干燥法实现。

（1）机械破碎法

这种方法运用剪切力（例如球磨机、胶体磨的研磨等）、压力的释放（例如匀浆器或超声波）。一个广泛使用的方法如下：细胞悬浮液通过细小喷嘴在静水剪切力和空化作用下使细胞破碎。

（2）干燥法

细胞干燥后可向细胞中加入大量冷丙酮，然后运用缓冲液或盐溶液进行提取。干燥法诱导了细胞壁结构的改变，有助于提取，这种方法被广泛的使用。

（3）溶解

可由化学方法（例如盐，表面活性剂，渗透压冲击，冷冻）或由水解酶（如溶解酶）水解微生物细胞壁。

4. 萃取过程

回收混合物或细胞中的某个化合物或一组化合物成分进入有机相中的过程称为萃取。萃取可实现产品的分离和浓缩，尤其是亲脂性物质和抗生素的回收，也经常用在细胞分离后的步骤中。

（1）液-液萃取

液-液萃取是利用产品在两个互不相溶的液体中的溶解度不同。通常使用连续少量溶剂重复反萃取，通过多级平行萃取或逆流萃取（复杂而有效）也可增加单步骤萃取的选择性。

（2）全发酵液（培养基和细胞）萃取

该方法尽可能地被使用，因为它减少了分离步骤以及产品损失，尽管由于细胞的存在萃取效率降低。

（3）多相液体萃取

该方法通常适用于细胞或细胞碎片中酶的分离。在水相聚乙二醇-葡聚糖混合物中形成游离相。从这些相中分离回收酶是非常容易的，没有离心过程中遇到的困难。

5. 产品浓缩

在提取期间需要对产品进行浓缩，进一步的浓缩可以通过：

（i）蒸发；

（ii）膜过滤；

（iii）离子交换法；

（iv）吸附法。

（1）蒸发

蒸发一般在溶剂萃取的情况下用到各种装置，例如连续流动蒸发器、降膜蒸发器、薄膜蒸发器、离心薄膜蒸发器和喷雾干燥器。蒸发溶剂的回收可降低成本。对于低级产品，全发酵液的蒸发通常使用喷雾干燥。

（2）膜过滤

根据分子大小可获得产品的浓缩和分离。膜过滤的不同工艺过程有微滤、超滤、反渗透以及电渗析。

微滤和超滤如同筛子分离不同尺寸大小的物质，但是反渗透分离类似分子大小的物质。微滤也适用于细胞分离。

（3）离子交换树脂

这些树脂结合有离子基团（阴离子或阳离子），即在合适的环境下进行离子化。可以是固体（例如葡聚糖、纤维素、聚氨、丙烯等）或液体（如含有像磷酸单酯或二酯功能基团的溶剂），固体离子交换剂的使用有两种方法：

（i）它们被填充于柱中；

（ii）它们被加入到提取液中，然后通过倾倒除去。

液体离子交换剂仅溶解在非水溶剂载体上，该分离类似于液液萃取。一些抗生素就可利用离子交换树脂直接回收。

通过离子交换从离子交换剂上回收产品，这也是离子交换剂的再生。

（4）吸附树脂

吸附树脂是无离子化的多孔树脂。大多数化合物以非离子态被树脂吸附。树脂的多孔性决定了其可吸附表面积。

这些树脂可以是非极性（如苯乙烯-二乙烯苯）、极性（如亚砜、胺等）和中极性（如丙烯酸酯）。通过有机溶剂或改变 pH 值（洗脱）从树脂中回收产品。

6. 产品纯化

产品回收的最后步骤是纯化，目的是获得高纯度的产品。纯化可由结晶和层析法实现。

（1）结晶

结晶主要用于低分子量化合物的纯化，例如青霉素 G 是利用丁醇乙酯从发酵液中萃取得到的，将其在乙醇溶液中添加醋酸钾盐结晶。结晶是产品纯化的最后步骤，像柠檬酸、谷氨酸钠等。

（2）色谱法

该法用于相似分子量混合中低分子量化合物的分离纯化，例如同簇抗生素与大分子，特别是酶，具有相似性质的混合物中的分离。

用于色谱的材料一般结合于特殊的载体上，填充于色谱柱，含有产品的液体从上或下泵入色谱柱内。

用某种收集器回收分离的产品。要用大量有机溶剂收集洗脱，因此整个系统需要安置在防火和防爆的房间里。

不同的色谱法有：

（i）吸附色谱；

（ⅱ）离子交换色谱;

（ⅲ）凝胶过滤色谱;

（ⅳ）疏水色谱;

（ⅴ）亲和色谱;

（ⅵ）共价色谱;

（ⅶ）分配色谱。

吸附色谱分离的原理是待分离物与基质表面的亲和力不同，例如硅胶、氧化铝、羟基磷灰石（都是无机的）或者是有机聚合体。

对于离子交换色谱，树脂或多糖，例如纤维素、琼脂糖，与离子功能基团结合，可用来对大分子高分辨率的分离，例如蛋白质。

凝胶过滤运用分子筛，由不同孔径大小的中性交联载体（例如琼脂糖、葡聚糖）组成。比孔径小的分子进入到载体内，被延迟。因此它们较迟地被洗脱和收集。凝胶过滤使用在水相体系中。使用疏水载体可以进行纯化疏水性分子，例如许多酶和其他蛋白质。

亲和色谱运用分子（称为效因子）与产品具有高度专一的亲和性。例如抗原与抗体。

该效因子固定于不溶于水的载体上，填充于柱中，混合物流经该柱。效因子能特异性结合（流经）柱中的分子，而后通过特定 pH 值的缓冲溶液洗脱回收。

例如，人白细胞干扰素可通过亲和色谱运用固定于柱中琼脂糖载体上的单克隆抗体高产率高纯度地回收（得到）。基团特异亲和色谱和共价色谱是根据载体和产品分子的化学相互作用。

7. 产品干燥

干燥使得产品更适合于处理和储存。由于大多数生物产品的热敏性，干燥需要在最小温升速率下完成。在有些情况下，添加糖或其他的稳定剂可以改善一些产品的耐热性，例如酶或药物制备。

干燥最普通的方法有:

（ⅰ）真空干燥;

（ⅱ）喷雾干燥;

（ⅲ）冷冻干燥。

在喷雾干燥中，被干燥的料浆溶液通过喷嘴或圆盘喷成雾状。通过 150~250℃ 的热空气流。该干燥是如此迅速以致颗粒能维持低温。喷雾干燥可用于酶、抗生素和食品。

真空干燥运用热量和真空进行干燥。它既能分批操作（如干燥室），又能连续操作（转鼓真空干燥机）。

冷冻干燥中，液体首先冷冻，水被升华脱离冷冻体。维持低压促进水的升华。升华中通过搁热板及表面辐射提供热量。

通过调控干燥室内压力调节固体温度。这是最温和的干燥方法，用于许多制药产品，例如病毒、疫苗、血浆制品、酶和食品行业。

Reading material

Introduction of Downstream Processing

Downstream processing is a useful collective **term** for all the steps which are required in order actually to recover useful products from any kind of industrial process. It is particularly important, in biotechnology where the desired final forms of the products are usually quite far removed from the state in which they are first obtained in the bioreactor. For example, a typical fermentation process gives a mixture of a **dispersed** solid (the **cell mass**, perhaps with some components from the **nutrient medium**, etc.) and a **dilute** water solution; the **desired product** may be within the cells, as one constituent of a very complex mixture, or in the dilute aqueous medium, or even distributed between the two. **In any case** its recovery, concentration, and purification will require careful and effective operations which are also **constrain**ed by manufacturing economics. Any Special requirements, **such as** a need to **exclude** contaminants or to contain the process organism, will only **add to** the difficulties.

Many operations which are standard in the laboratory will become **impractical,** or uneconomic, on the process scale. Moreover, bioproducts are often very **labile** or sensitive compounds, whose active structures can survive only under defined and limited conditions of pH, temperature, **ionic strength**, etc. **Bearing in mind** such **restriction**s, much **ingenuity** is called for if the available **repertoire** of scientific methods is to be used to best effect. It will also be **apparent** that there is no one unique, ideal, or universal operation, or even sequence of operations, which can be **recommend**ed; individual unit operations must be combined in the most suitable way for a particular problem.

New Words

term [təːm] *n.* 学期，期限，期间，条款，条件，术语
disperse [disˈpəːs] *v.* （使）分散，（使）散开，疏散
dilute [daiˈljuːt, diˈl-] *v.* 冲淡，变淡，变弱，稀释 *adj.* 淡的，弱的，稀释的
constrain [kənˈstrein] *vt.* 强迫，抑制，拘束
exclude [iksˈkluːd] *vt.* 拒绝接纳，把…排除在外，排斥
impractical [imˈpræktikəl] *adj.* 不切实际的，违反实际的
labile [ˈleibail] *adj.* 不安定的，易发生变化的
restriction [risˈtrikʃən] *n.* 限制，约束
ingenuity [ˌindʒiˈnjuːiti] *n.* 机灵，独创性，精巧，灵活性
repertoire [ˈrepətwaː] *n.* （准备好演出的）节目，保留剧目；（计算机的）指令表，指令系统
apparent [əˈpærənt] *adj.* 显然的，外观上的
recommend [rekəˈmend] *vt.* 推荐，介绍，劝告，使受欢迎，托付，使…受欢迎

Expressions and Technical Terms

cell mass   细胞菌体
nutrient medium 营养培养基
desired product   目标产物
in any case   在任何情况下，无论如何
such as   例如
add to 增加
ionic strength 离子强度
bearing in mind 注意，小心

Chapter 12　Frontiers of biochemical engineering

12.1　Enzyme engineering

Enzyme engineering (or enzyme technology) is the application of **fermentation** process using **catalytic** activity of isolated enzymes, to produce new **metabolites** or to **convert** some compounds **into** another's **(biotransformation)**. These products will be useful as chemicals, **pharmaceutiacls**, **fuel**, food or agricultural **additives**. Enzyme **reactor consists of** a vessels, containing a reactional **medium,** used to perform a desired conversion by enzymatic means. Enzymes used in this process are free in the solution or **immobilized** in **particulate**, **membranous** or **fibrous** support.

A most exciting development over the last few years is the application genetic engineering techniques to enzyme technology. There are **a number of** properties which may be improved or altered by genetic engineering including the yield and kinetics of the enzyme, the ease of downstream processing and various safety aspects. Enzymes from dangerous or unapproved microorganisms and from slow growing or limited plant or animal tissue may be cloned into safe high-production microorganisms. In the future, enzymes may be redesigned to **fit** more appropriately **into** industrial processes; for example, making **glucose isomerase** less susceptible to inhibition by the Ca^{2+} present in the starch **saccharification** processing stream.

intact DNA ——→ cleaved DNA

The amount of enzyme produced by a microorganism may be increased by increasing **the number of** gene copies that code for it. This principle has been used to increase the activity of penicillin-G-amidase in Escherichia coli. The cellular DNA from a producing strain is selectively cleaved by the restriction **endonuclease** HindIII. This **hydrolyses** the DNA at relatively rare sites containing the 5'-AAGCTT-3' base sequence to give identical

Remarks Column

fermentation [ˌfə:men'teiʃən] n. 发酵
catalytic [ˌkætə'litik] adj.[化]催化剂的，起催化剂作用的
metabolite [mi'tæbəlait] n.代谢产物
convert [kən'və:t] v. 变换、转化 change the nature, purpose, or function of something
biotransformation [ˌbaiəu,trænsfə'meiʃən] n.生物转化，生物变（转）化
pharmaceutical [ˌfɑ:mə'sju:tikəl] adj. 制药的；配药的
fuel [fjuəl] n. 燃料，木炭
additive [ə'æditiv] n.（食品）添加剂
reactor [ri(:)'æktə] n.[电]电抗器；[物]反应堆；[化]反应器
medium ['mi:djəm] n. 介质,介体，中间的，培养基，培养基
immobilize [I'məubIlaIz] v.使不动；使固定 to hold fast or prevent from moving
particulate [pə'tikjulit, -leit] n.微粒子
membranous ['membrənəs, mem'breInəs] adj.膜的；膜状的
fibrous ['faibrəs] adj. 纤维的，纤维性的，具纤维的，纤维状的
unapproved ['ʌnə'pru:vd] adj. 未经批准的
susceptible [sə'septəbl] adj.敏感性，易感染的，易感的，易受影响的，易感者
saccharification [sækərifi'keiʃən] n. 糖化（作用）
endonuclease [ˌendə'nju:kli,eis] n. 核酸内切酶，内切核酸酶

"staggered" ends.

The total DNA is cleaved into about 10000 fragments, only one of which contains the required genetic information. These fragments are individual cloned into a **cosmid vector** and thereby returned to *E.coli*. These colonies containing the active gene are identified by their inhibition of a 6-amino-penicillanic acid-sensitive organism. Such colonies are isolated and the penicillin-G-amidase gene transferred on to pBR322 plasmids and recloned back into *E.coli*. The engineered cells, aided by the plasmid amplification at around 50 copies per cell, produce penicillin-G-amidase **constitutively** and in considerably higher quantities than does the fully induced parental strain. Such increased yields are economically relevant not just for the increased volumetric productivity but also because of reduced downstream processing costs, the resulting crude enzyme being that much purer.

hydrolyses *n.* （单 hydrolysis [haiˈdrɔlisis]）水解（作用）
constitutive [ˈkɔnstitjuːtiv] *adj.* 构成的，组成的

Expressions and Technical Terms

convert into （使）转而变为…
consist of 由…组成
a number of 许多的
in the future 今后，将来
fit into （使）适合，（使）合乎…的时间（空间）
susceptible to 易感的，敏感的
glucose isomerase 葡萄糖异构酶
the number of …的数量
cosmid vector 黏粒载体
staggered ends 黏性末端

Notes

[1] [special background] 酶工程（enzyme engineering）是生物工程的一个组成部分。利用酶、细胞器或细胞的特异催化功能，通过适当的反应器工业化生产人类所需产品或达到某种特殊目的的一门技术科学。它与微生物学、生物化学、化学和工程学等学科有着密切的联系，是一门综合性科学。

[2] Enzyme engineering (or enzyme technology) is the application of fermentation process using catalytic activity of isolated enzymes, to produce new metabolites or to convert some compounds into another's (biotransformation). 酶工程（酶技术）是指在发酵过程中利用分离出的酶的催化作用，生产新的代谢产物或进行物质转化（生物转化）的技术。using catalytic activity of isolated enzymes现在分词作方式状语，修饰 application。

[3] Enzymes used in this process are free in the solution or immobilized in particulate, membranous or fibrous support. 在这个过程中所使用的酶在溶液中是游离的，或固定在粒状、膜状、纤维状载体上。used in this process 作后置定语，修饰 enzymes。

[4] There are a number of properties which may be improved or altered by genetic engineering including the yield and kinetics of the enzyme, the ease of downstream processing and various safety aspects. 运用基因工程可以改善原有酶的各种性能，包括提高酶的产率、增加酶的稳定性、减轻下游加工和多方面的安全问题。a number of 的意思是"许多的"；而 the number of 的意思是"…的数量"。which 引导定语从句，修饰 properties。

[5] In the future, enzymes may be redesigned to fit more appropriately into industrial processes; for example, making glucose isomerase less susceptible to inhibition by the Ca^{2+} present in the starch saccharification processing stream. 今后，优化设计的酶可以更加适用于工业生产。例如，在淀粉糖化过程中有钙离子存在，葡萄糖异构酶不易受到抑制。susceptible to 的意思是"易感的，敏感的"；fit into 的意思是"（使）适合，（使）合乎…的时间（空间）"。

[6] The amount of enzyme produced by a microorganism may be increased by increasing the number of gene copies that code for it. 可以通过增加编码该酶的基因的拷贝数，来提高微生物产生的酶量。produced by a microorganism 过去分词作定语修饰 enzyme；the number of 的意思是 "…的数量"；that 引导定语从句，修饰 gene copies。

[7] The total DNA is cleaved into about 10000 fragments, only one of which contains the required genetic information. 总 DNA 水解为约 10000 个片段，其中只有一个载有所需的遗传信息。only one of which contains the required genetic information 是非限制性定语从句，其中 which 指代 fragments。

[8] Such increased yields are economically relevant not just for the increased volumetric productivity but also because of reduced downstream processing costs, the resulting crude enzyme being that much purer. 产量的增加与经济效益相关，不仅因为增加了产量，而且还减少了下游加工费用，使产生的天然酶更加纯净。not (only)…but also…的意思是 "不但…而且…"，because of reduced downstream processing costs,是插入语表原因。

Exercises

1. Put the following into Chinese

Enzymes are essential to life as we know it. These proteins serve as catalysts for nearly all the chemical reactions that define cellular metabolism（新陈代谢）. Their enormous rate accelerations and exacting selectivities also make them extremely valuable outside the cell. As a consequence, enzymes are being used increasingly in research, industry and medicine.

Nevertheless, our understanding of these biological macromolecules（大分子） lags far behind our understanding of small molecules. The properties of enzymes are determined by their precise three-dimensional（三维的，立体的） structures, but we don't know the detailed rules that govern protein folding and our knowledge of structure–function relationships in proteins is at best incomplete. Not surprisingly, then, the design of enzymes from first principles remains an unrealized dream.

Study of biomacromolecules, like many of today's most interesting scientific problems, demands a multidisciplinary（多准则性,多学科的） perspective. Enzyme engineering, in particular, has much to gain from an integration of chemistry, immunology, molecular biology and genetics. We may also be able to provide researchers of the future with useful catalysts for diverse applications.

['Enzyme Engineering' written by Donald Hilvert (THE DEPARTMENT OF CHEMISTRY, ETH ZÜRICH, IN THE NEW HÖNGGERBERG BUILDINGS, 2001)]

2. Put English sentences into Chinese

（1）Over the past three decades there have been serious attempts to improve the use of enzymes as catalyst for industrial, analytical and medical purposes by using new methods/techniques resulting in a new field of research called enzyme engineering.

（2）As there is a great number of parameters which influence the whole process performance, in the past enzyme reactors have been optimized empirically.

（3）Enzymes are biopolymers, which accelerate special biochemical reactions. Most of them act highly selectively, with great activity, at room temperature and normal pressure.

3. Cloze

Enzyme engineering (or enzyme technology) is the application of **fermentation** process __（1）__ **catalytic** activity of **isolated** enzymes, __（2）__ produce new **metabolites** or to __（3）__ some compounds into another's **(biotransformation)**. These products will be useful as chemicals, **pharmaceutiacls**, **fuel**, food or agricultural **additives**. Enzyme **reactor** consists （4） a vessels, （5） a reactional **medium**, used to perform a desired conversion by enzymatic means. Enzymes used in this process （6） free in the solution or **immobilized** in **particulate**, **membranous** or **fibrous** support.

A most exciting development over the last few years is the application genetic engineering techniques （7） enzyme technology. There are a number of properties （8） may be improved or altered by genetic engineering including the yield and kinetics of the enzyme, the ease of downstream processing and various safety aspects. Enzymes from dangerous or unapproved microorganisms and from slow growing or limited plant or animal tissue may be cloned into safe high-production microorganisms. In the future, enzymes may be （9） to fit more appropriately （10） industrial processes; for example, making glucose isomerase less susceptible to inhibition by the Ca^{2+} present in the starch **saccharification** processing stream.

（1）A. uses   B. used   C. using   D. use   （   ）
（2）A. in   B. from   C. for   D. to   （   ）
（3）A. convert   B. convene   C. covert   D. convenient   （   ）
（4）A. of   B. for   C. to   D. up   （   ）
（5）A. contain   B. have contained C. containing   D. contained   （   ）
（6）A. be   B. is   C. being   D. are   （   ）
（7）A. in   B. from   C. to   D. for   （   ）
（8）A. who   B. which   C. where   D. it   （   ）
（9）A. redesigned   B. redesigning   C. designing   D. designed   （   ）
（10）A. for   B. into   C. in   D. on   （   ）

4．Put the following into English

酶工程	酶反应器	（使）转而变为…	由…组成
许多的	今后，将来	（使）适合	易感的，敏感的
葡萄糖异构酶	…的数量	黏性末端	

5．Writing

Write summary of this text (no more than 200 words).

参考译文

酶工程（酶技术）是指在发酵过程中利用分离出的酶的催化作用，生产新的代谢产物或进行物质转化（生物转化）的技术。这些产品可应用于化学、医药、燃料、食品和农业添加剂方面。酶反应器是装有反应介质的管状容器，用来进行特定的酶转化反应。在这个过程中所使用的酶在溶液中是游离的，或固定在粒状、膜状、纤维状载体上。

基因工程技术在酶工程领域的成功应用，可以算是近年来酶工程最引人注目的发展之一。运用基因工程可以改善原有酶的各种性能，包括提高酶的产率、增加酶的稳定性、减轻下游加工和多方面的安全问题。可以将原来由有害的、未经批准的微生物产生的酶基因，或由生长缓慢的动植物产生的酶基因，克隆到生长迅速、安全高产的微生物体内进行生产。今后，优化设计的酶可以更加适用于工业生产。例如，在淀粉糖化过程中有钙离子存在，葡萄糖异构酶不易受到抑制。

$$\text{完整 DNA} \longrightarrow \text{裂解 DNA}$$

可以通过增加编码该酶的基因的拷贝数，来提高微生物产生的酶量。这一原理已成功地应用于提高大肠杆菌青霉素 G 酰胺酶的活性。限制性内切酶 *Hind*Ⅲ选择性酶切菌株获得细胞（宿主）DNA。*Hind*Ⅲ在包括了 5'-AAGCTT-3' 碱基序列的相关稀有位点上水解 DNA，使其水解为具有相同序列的黏性末端。

总 DNA 水解为约 10000 个片段，其中只有一个载有所需的遗传信息。这些片段克隆到（已酶切的）黏粒载体上，再转化到大肠杆菌中。可由带有 6-氨基青霉烷酸菌的抗生素筛选这些含有活性基因的菌落。筛选的（含有活性基因）菌落和青霉素 G 酰胺酶基因转染到 PBR322 质粒上并克隆回大肠杆菌。质粒扩增（速度）大约是 50 拷贝/细胞,含有该质粒的细胞生产的青霉素 G 酰胺酶比充分诱导亲本的菌株有更高的产量。产量的增加与经济效益相关，不仅因为增加了产量，而且还减少了下游加工费用，使产生的天然酶更加纯净。

Reading material

Restriction Endonucleases

Restriction endonucleases are possibly the most powerful tools in biotechnology. They allow scientists to precisely cut DNA in a predictable and reproducible manner. In the early 1950s, Salvador Luria and Giuseppe Bertani of the University of Illinois and Jean Weigle of the California Institute of Technology found evidence of a primitive immune system in bacteria. They observed that certain strains of the bacterium *Escherichia coli* are resistant to infection by various bacteriophages. The phenomenon seemed to be a properly of the bacterial cell, which is able to *restrict* the growth and replication of certain phages. In 1962, Werner Arber, at the University of Geneva, provided the first evidence that the resistant bacterium possesses an enzyme system that selectively recognizes and destroys foreign DNA while modifying its own chromosomal DNA to prevent self-destruction.

Several years later, Arber and his associate Stuart Linn, as well as Matthew Meselson and Robert Yuan at Harvard University, isolated *E.coli* extracts that efficiently cleaved phage DNA. These extracts contained the first known *restriction endonucleases*, enzymes that recognize and cut a specific sequence of DNA. Restriction endonucleases are members of a larger group of enzymes called nucleases, which generally break the phosphodiester bonds that link adjacent nucleotides in DNA. Endonucleases cleave DNA at internal positions, whereas exonucleases progressively digest from the ends of DNA molecules.

In addition to an endonuclease cutting activity, some of these enzymes also possess a modification activity that is protective to the host. It was later realized that the enzyme protects bacterial host DNA from digestion by adding methyl groups to a nucleotide within the sequence recognized by the restriction enzyme. This modification of the DNA blocks the restriction enzyme from recognizing its sequence-specific binding sites in the host. Although typically both strands of host DNA are methylated, bacterial DNA is protected from digestion even when only one strand is methylated (hemimethylated).This is important because following DNA replication , the newly synthesized DNA strand is not immediately methylated. Because hemimethylated DNA is protected, the methylated parertal strand protects the host chromosome while the new daughter strand becomes methylated.

The particular restriction enzymes isolated by Arber, Linn, Meselson, and Yuan were not of practical value as tools for manipulating DNA. Although these enzymes recognize specific nucleotide sequences, they cut the DNA molecule at positions that may be thousands of nucleotides distant from the recognition site. The phenomenon of restriction modification was therefore of little use as a tool until 1970, when Hamilton Smith and his student Kent Wilcox, at Johns Hopkins University, isolated a new restriction endonuclease from *Haemophilus influenzae*. The restriction activity of this enzyme, named *Hind*II, differed from previously discovered endonucleases in two important ways. First, the enzyme showed restriction activity but no modification activity. Second, *Hind*II cleaved DNA predictably by cutting at a precise position within its recognition sequence, not at a distance.

There are three major classes of restriction endonucleases: Types Ⅰ, Ⅱ, and Ⅲ. Type Ⅰ and Ⅲ enzymes have both restriction and modification activity, and they cut DNA at sites outside of their recognition sequences. Using ATP for energy, the enzymes move along the DNA molecule from recognition site to cleavage site. The lack of predict ability in cutting and the requirement of ATP make type Ⅰ and Ⅲ restriction enzymes of little practical use.

Type Ⅱ restriction endonucleases are ideal for several reasons:(1)each has restriction activity but no modification activity;(2)each cuts in a predictable and consistent manner ,at a site within or adjacent to the recognition sequence; and (3)type Ⅱ enzymes require only the magnesium ion（Mg^{2+}）as a cofactor; ATP is not needed. Type Ⅱ restriction enzymes have been isolated from a huge number of organisms. More than 200 restriction cnzymes are commercially available, enabling researchers to cut DNA at more than 100 different recognition sequences.

['DNA Science: A First Course' written by Micklos DA et al. (2003)]

New Words

reproducible [ˌriːprəˈdjuːsəbl] *adj.* 重现性的,可复现的,可再制的

bacteriophage [bækˈtiəriəfeidʒ] *n.* 噬菌体

phenomenon [fiˈnɔminən] *n.* 现象 any state or process known through the senses rather than by intuition or reasoning

self-destruction *n.* 自我毁灭

exonuclease [ˌeksəuˈnjuːklieis] *n.* 核酸外切酶,外切核酸酶

methylated[ˈmeθileitid]*adj.* 甲基化的

hemimethylated *adj.* 半甲基化的

synthesize [ˈsinθisaiz] *v.* 综合 combine so as to form a more complex product

adjacent [əˈdʒeisənt] *adj.* 毗连的, 邻近的, 接近的 nearest in space or position; immediately adjoining without intervening space

Expressions and Technical Terms

as well as 也，又

phosphodiester bond 磷酸二酯键

in addition 另外

at a distance 有相当距离

more than 比…多，超出预料，很

12.2　Genetic engineering

Genetic engineering, **recombinant** DNA technology, genetic **modification** /**manipulation** (GM) and gene **splicing** are terms that **apply to** the direct manipulation of an organism's genes. Genetic engineering is **different from** traditional breeding, where the organism's genes are manipulated indirectly; genetic engineering uses the techniques of molecular cloning and transformation to alter the structure and **characteristics** of genes directly. Genetic engineering techniques have found some successes in numerous applications. Some examples are in improving crop technology, the **manufacture** of **synthetic** human **insulin** through the use of modified bacteria, the manufacture of **erythropoietin** in hamster ovary cells, and the production of new types of experimental mice **such as** the oncomouse (cancer mouse) for research.

Genetic Engineering steps

There are a number of ways through which genetic engineering is accomplished. Essentially, the process has five main steps:

1. Isolation of the genes of interest;
2. **Insertion** of the genes into a transfer vector;
3. Transfer of the vector to the organism to be modified;
4. Transformation of the cells of the organism;
5. Separation of the **genetically modified organism** (GMO) from those that have not been successfully modified。

Isolation is achieved by identifying the gene of interest that the scientist wishes to **insert into** the organism, usually using existing knowledge of the various functions of genes. DNA information can be obtained from cDNA or gDNA libraries, and **amplified** using PCR techniques. If necessary, i.e. for insertion of **eukaryotic** genomic DNA into **prokaryotes**, further modification may be **carried out** such as **removal** of **introns** or **ligating** prokaryotic promoters.

Insertion of a gene into a vector such as a **plasmid** can be done once the gene of interest is isolated. Other vectors can also be used, such as **viral** vectors, and non-prokaryotic ones such as **liposomes**, or even direct insertion using DNA guns. Restriction enzymes and **ligases** are of great use in this crucial step if it is being inserted into prokaryotic or viral vectors. Daniel Nathans and Hamilton Smith received the 1978 Nobel Prize in **Physiology** or Medicine for their isolation of restriction **endonucleases**.

Once the vector is obtained, it can be used to transform the **target** organism. **Depending on** the vector used, it can be complex or simple. For example, using raw DNA with DNA guns is a fairly straightforward process but with low success rates, where the DNA is coated with molecules such as gold and fired directly into a cell. Other more complex methods, such as bacterial transformation or using viruses as vectors have higher success rates.

After transformation, the GMO can be isolated from those that have **failed to take up** the vector in various ways. One method is testing with DNA **probes** that can **stick to** the gene of interest that was supposed to have been transplanted, another would be to package resistance genes along with the vector, such that the resulting GMO is resistant to certain chemicals, and then they can be grown on agar dishes with the **herbicide**, to ensure only those that have taken up the vector will survive. Also those in the vector will only survive if the vector is not damaged.

physiology [ˌfizi'ɔlədʒi] *n.* 生理学
endonuclease [ˌendə'nju:kli,eis] *n.*核酸内切酶，内切核酸酶
target ['tɑ:git] *n.*目标，靶子

probe [prəub] *n.*探针
herbicide ['hə:bisaid] *n.*除草剂

Expressions and Technical Terms
apply to 适用于；运用；向…申请（要求）；致力于，专心于
be different from 异于…
such as 像，例如
genetically modified organism 转基因生物
insert into 把…插入（某处）
carry out 进行；完成，实现
depend on 依赖，依靠；相信；信赖；随…而定
fail to 未能…
take up 占去；接受（提议）
stick to 保留，保有；遵守，坚持；紧跟；粘住

Notes

[1] [special background] 基因工程（genetic engineering）是生物工程的一个重要分支，它和细胞工程、酶工程、蛋白质工程和微生物工程共同组成了生物工程。基因工程是在分子水平上对基因进行操作的复杂技术，是将外源基因通过体外重组后导入受体细胞内，使这个基因能在受体细胞内复制、转录、翻译表达的操作。它是用人为的方法将所需要的某一供体生物的遗传物质——DNA大分子提取出来，在离体条件下用适当的工具酶进行切割后，把它与作为载体的DNA分子连接起来，然后与载体一起导入某一更易生长、繁殖的受体细胞中，以让外源物质在其中"安家落户"，进行正常的复制和表达，从而获得新物种的一种崭新技术。

[2] Genetic engineering, recombinant DNA technology, genetic modification /manipulation (GM) and gene splicing are terms that apply to the direct manipulation of an organism's genes. 基因工程, 重

组 DNA 技术, 遗传学修饰/操作 (GM) 和基因剪接是适用于有机体基因直接操作的几种方式。recombinant DNA technology 作 Genetic engineering 的同位语；that 引导定语从句，修饰 terms。

[3]　Genetic engineering is different from traditional breeding, where the organism's genes are manipulated indirectly; genetic engineering uses the techniques of molecular cloning and transformation to alter the structure and characteristics of genes directly. 基因工程区别于传统繁殖技术（不是直接作用于基因），是使用分子克隆技术和转化技术，直接改变基因的结构和特征。where 引导非限制性定语从句。

[4]　Restriction enzymes and ligases are of great use in this crucial step if it is being inserted into prokaryotic or viral vectors. 在目的片段插入载体的过程中，限制性内切酶和连接酶至关重要。of +n.等同于 *adj*；if it is being inserted into prokaryotic or viral vectors 是条件状语从句，其中 is being inserted 是被动语态的现在进行时。

[5]　Once the vector is obtained, it can be used to transform the target organism. 一旦获得载体就可用于靶器官转化。once 表示"一旦"的意思。

[6]　One method is testing with DNA probes that can stick to the gene of interest that was supposed to have been transplanted, another would be to package resistance genes along with the vector, such that the resulting GMO is resistant to certain chemicals, and then they can be grown on agar dishes with the herbicide, to ensure only those that have taken up the vector will survive. 用 DNA 探针的方法可以调出已插入的目的片段。或者在载体中镶嵌抗性基因，例如已插入片段的转化子可以抵抗某种化合物，进而可以在涂有该化合物的琼脂板上生长，用这种方法确保载体连接有目的片段。to ensure only those that have taken up the vector will survive 作目的状语，其中 that 引导定语从句，修饰 those。

Exercises

1．Put the following into Chinese

Genetic engineering is a laboratory technique used by scientists to change the DNA of living organisms.

DNA is the blueprint（蓝图，设计图）for the individuality of an organism. The organism relies upon the information stored in its DNA for the management of every biochemical process. The life, growth and unique features of the organism depend on its DNA. The segments of DNA which have been associated with（与…交往，联系）specific features or functions of an organism are called genes.

Molecular biologists have discovered many enzymes which change the structure of DNA in living organisms. Some of these enzymes can cut and join strands of DNA. Using such enzymes, scientists learned to cut specific genes from DNA and to build customized DNA using these genes. They also learned about vectors, strands of DNA such as viruses, which can infect a cell and insert themselves into its DNA.

With this knowledge, scientists started to build vectors which incorporated genes of their choosing and used the new vectors to insert these genes into the DNA of living organisms. Genetic engineers believe they can improve the foods we eat by doing this. For example, tomatoes are sensitive to frost. This shortens their growing season. Fish, on the other hand, survive in very cold water. Scientists identified a particular gene which enables a flounder to resist cold and used the technology of genetic engineering to insert this "anti-freeze" gene into a tomato. This makes it possible to extend the growing season of the tomato.

At first glance, this might look exciting to some people. Deeper consideration reveals serious dangers.

2. Put English sentences into Chinese

（1）One of the best known applications of genetic engineering is the creation of genetically modified organisms (GMOs) such as foods and vegetables that resist pest and bacteria infection and have longer freshness than otherwise.

（2）The first genetically engineered medicine was synthetic human insulin, approved by the United States Food and Drug Administration in 1982.

（3）Human genetic engineering can be used to treat genetic disease, but there is a difference between treating the disease in an individual and changing the genome that gets passed down to that person's descendants.

3. Cloze

Genetic engineering, recombinant DNA technology, genetic modification /manipulation (GM) and gene splicing are terms that apply __(1)__ the direct manipulation of an organism's genes. Genetic engineering is different __(2)__ traditional breeding, where the organism's genes are manipulated indirectly; genetic engineering uses the techniques of molecular cloning and transformation __(3)__ alter the structure and characteristics of genes directly. Genetic engineering techniques __(4)__ some successes in numerous applications. Some examples are in __(5)__ crop technology, the manufacture of synthetic human insulin __(6)__ the use of modified bacteria, the manufacture of erythropoietin in hamster ovary cells, and the production of new types of experimental mice such __(7)__ the oncomouse (cancer mouse) __(8)__ research.

Genetic Engineering steps

There are a number of ways through __(9)__ genetic engineering is accomplished. Essentially, the process has five main steps:

（i）Isolation of the genes of interest

（ii）__(10)__ of the genes into a transfer vector

（iii）Transfer of the vector to the organism to be modified

（iv）Transformation of the cells of the organism

（v）Separation of the genetically modified organism (GMO) from those that have not been successfully modified

（1）A. in	B. from	C. to	D. into	（　）
（2）A. to	B. from	C. by	D. in	（　）
（3）A. to	B. on	C. for	D. in	（　）
（4）A. have found	B. find	C. found	D. finding	（　）
（5）A. have improved	B. improved	C. improved	D. improving	（　）
（6）A. to	B. through	C. on	D. from	（　）
（7）A. as	B. for	C. that	D. in	（　）
（8）A. to	B. for	C. in	D. of	（　）
（9）A. what	B. as	C. that	D. which	（　）
（10）A. Insertion	B. Isolatio	C. Separation	D. Transformation	（　）

4. Put the following into English

基因工程	重组 DNA 技术	适用于	异于…
像，例如	转基因生物	把…插入（某处）	进行；完成，实现
依赖，依靠	未能…	占去；接受（提议）	保留，保有

5. Writing

Write summary of this text (no more than 200 words).

参考译文

基因工程,重组 DNA 技术,遗传学修饰/操纵(GM)和基因剪接是适用于有机体基因直接操作的几种方式。基因工程区别于传统繁殖技术（不是直接作用于基因），是使用分子克隆技术和转化技术，直接改变基因的结构和特征。基因工程技术已经有许多成功应用的例子。例如一些提高产量的技术,通过使用修饰细菌合成人胰岛素,在仓鼠卵巢细胞制造红细胞生成素和生产新型的用于研究的实验鼠，如 oncomouse（癌症鼠）。

基因工程的步骤

基因工程有多种方法已经成熟。基本上此过程分为五步:

1. 获取目的基因;
2. 将目的基因插入到载体当中;
3. 把目的 DNA 导入受体细胞;
4. 细胞转化;
5. 筛除没有转化的转基因生物（把目的基因能表达的受体细胞挑选出来）。

分离指科学家常通过现存的若干功能基因寻找欲插入的目的基因。DNA 信息可从 cDNA 或 gDNA 文库中获得或使用 PCR 技术进行扩增。对于真核生物的 DNA 插入到原核生物里的片段，需要进一步修饰才能进行，例如去除内含子或连接启动子。

分离出目的片段后就可插入到质粒载体。其他载体有病毒载体和非原核载体脂质体或直接用基因枪插入。在目的片段插入载体的过程中，限制性内切酶和连接酶至关重要。Daniel Nathans 和 Hamilton Smith 因成功分离限制性核酸内切酶，在 1978 年获得了诺贝尔医学生理学奖。

一旦获得载体就可用于靶器官转化。这个过程或简单或复杂取决于载体的应用。举例来说，用基因枪将初始 DNA 插入是一个简单的过程，在此过程中 DNA 被黄金标记后再注入细胞之中，但其成功率低。还有更复杂的技术，例如细菌转化或使用病毒载体可以获得高转化率。

转化后，可通过多种方式将 GMO 转基因体与未插入片段的载体相区分。用 DNA 探针的方法可以调出已插入的目的片段。或者在载体中镶嵌抗性基因，例如已插入片段的转化子可以抵抗某种化合物，进而可以在涂有该化合物的琼脂板上生长，用这种方法确保载体连接有目的片段。如果载体没有改变，那些载体也不能生长。

Reading material

Genetically modified food

Genetically modified (GM) foods are food items that have had their DNA changed through genetic engineering. Unlike conventional genetic modification that is carried out through conventional breeding and that have been consumed for thousands of years, GM foods were first put on the market in the early 1990s. The most common modified foods are derived from plants: soybean, corn, canola, and cotton seed oil. For example, a typical GM Food could be a strawberry that has to survive in cold climates. Therefore, the farmer would get its DNA altered so it could survive in the frost. They would take DNA from a frost resistant cell, and transfer it into the strawberry cells genes. Therefore, the cells of the strawberry are now frost resistant and will survive the frost, so the farmer does not lose money.

Many major controversies surround genetically engineered crops and foods. These commonly focus on the long-term health effects for anyone eating them, environmental safety, labeling and consumer choice, intellectual property rights, ethics, food security, poverty reduction, environmental conservation, and potential disruption or even possible destruction of the food chain. Proponents claim the technology to be a boon for the human race, while critics believe it to be a potential or actual health or ecological disaster.

Kenyans examining insect-resistant transgenic Bt corn.

Development

The first commercially grown genetically modified whole food crop was the tomato (called Flavr Savr), which was made more resistant to rotting by Californian company Calgene. Calgene was allowed to release the tomatoes into the market in 1994 without any special labeling. It was welcomed by consumers who purchased the fruit at two to five times the price of regular tomatoes. However, production problems and competition from a conventionally bred, longer shelf-life variety prevented the product from becoming profitable. A variant of the Flavr Savr was used by Zeneca to produce tomato paste which was sold in Europe during the summer of 1996. The labeling and pricing were designed as a marketing experiment, which proved, at the time, that European consumers would accept genetically engineered foods. However with news that Dr. Árpád Pusztai a leading UK scientist who had been hired by the Rowett Institute to develop the new safety protocol for genetically modified foods in Europe. He found that the rats in his study had developed potentially precancerous cell growth in the digestive tract, inhibited development of their brains, livers, and testicles, partial atrophy of the liver, enlarged pancreases and intestine, and immune system damage. He concluded that it was not the insecticide gene that was inserted, but was the process of genetic engineering itself. Upon appearing on television where he said he expressed his concerns that the government and companies were using the population as Guinea pigs. Europeans were outraged, and within a week every major food company on the continent including McDonalds, Nestlé and Burger King, all committed to not purchase GM foods. To date this remains one of the best designed and carefully controlled feeding studies of genetically engineered foods on mammals.

The attitude towards GM foods only got worse after outbreaks of Mad Cow Disease weakened consumer trust in government regulators, and protesters rallied against the introduction of Monsanto's "Roundup Ready" soybeans. The next GM crops included insect-resistant cotton and herbicide-tolerant soybeans both of which were commercially released in 1996. GM crops have been widely adopted in the United States. They have also been extensively planted in several other countries (Argentina, Brazil, South Africa, India, and China) where the agriculture is a major part of the total economy. Other GM crops include insect-resistant maize and herbicide-tolerant maize, cotton, and rapeseed varieties.

New Words

conventional [kən'venʃənl] *adj.* 常规的，惯例的，一般的 following accepted customs and proprieties

consume [kən'sju:m] *v.* 耗尽，消费，用光 spend extravagantly; destroy completely

soybean ['sɔɪbi:n] *n.* 大豆

strawberry ['strɔ:bəri] *n.* 草莓

resistant [ri'zistənt] *adj.* 抵抗的，抗(耐)…的，有抵抗力的，抵抗力的，抵抗的，抗性的 able to tolerate environmental conditions or physiological stress; incapable of absorbing or mixing with

controversy ['kɔntrəvə:si] *n.* 论争，辩论论战，争论 a contentious speech act; a dispute where there is strong disagreement

label ['leibl] *n.* 标签，签条，商标 a brief description given for purposes of identification *v.* 贴标签于，指…为，分类，标签费，标贴，标志 attach a tag or label to

ethics ['eθiks] *n.* 伦理学

potential [pə'tenʃ(ə)l] *adj.* 有潜力的，可能的，潜在的 existing in possibility

proponent [prə'pəunənt] *n.* 建议者，支持者

ecological [ˌekə'lɔdʒikəl] *adj.* 生态学的； *n..* 生态学

precancerous ['pri:'kænsərəs] *adj.* 癌前期的，癌变前的 of or relating to a growth that is not malignant but is likely to become so if not treated

testicle ['testikl] *n.* 睾丸

atrophy ['ætrəfi] *n.* 萎缩，萎缩症

pancrea *n.* 胰，胰腺

intestine [in'testin] *n.* 肠

immune [i'mju:n] *adj.* 免疫，有免疫应答的，免疫系统的 secure against;not affected by a given influence

rapeseed ['reipsi:d] *n.* 油菜籽

Expressions and Technical Terms

carry out 执行，贯彻；完成，实现；进行

put on 穿上，戴上；把…放在…上；展览

be derived from 源自于

transfer into 搬进，转到

focus on 致力于；对（某事或做某事）予以注意；使聚焦于

at the time 当时，那时

shelf life （包装食品的）货架期，保存限期

12.3　The Human Genome Project

The Human Genome Project (HGP) was an international scientific research project with a primary goal to determine the sequence of chemical base pairs which **make up** DNA and to identify the **approximately** 20000-25000 genes of the human genome from both a physical and functional **standpoint**.

The project began in 1990 **initially** headed by James D. Watson at the U.S. National Institutes of Health. A working draft of the genome was released in 2000 and a complete one in 2003, with further analysis still being published. A **parallel** project was conducted outside of government by the Celera Corporation. Most of the government-sponsored sequencing was performed in universities and research centers from the United States, Canada, New Zealand and Britain. The mapping of human genes is an important step in the development of medicines and other aspects of health care.

While the objective of the Human Genome Project is to understand the genetic makeup of the human species, the project also has **focused on** several other nonhuman organisms such as *E. coli*, the **fruit fly**, and the laboratory mouse. It remains one of the largest single investigational projects in modern science.[citation needed]

The HGP originally aimed to map the nucleotides contained in a **haploid** reference human genome (**more than** three billion). Several groups have announced efforts to extend this to **diploid** human genomes including the International HapMap Project, Applied **Biosystems**, Perlegen, Illumina, JCVI, Personal Genome Project, and Roche-454.

The "genome" of any given individual (except for identical twins and cloned animals) is unique; mapping "the human genome" involves sequencing **multiple** variations of each gene. The project did not study the entire DNA found in human cells; some **heterochromatic** areas (about 8% of the total) remain un-sequenced.

Although the working draft was announced in June 2000, it was not until February 2001 that Celera and the HGP scientists published details of their drafts. Special issues of *Nature* (which published the publicly funded project's scientific paper) and *Science* (which published Celera's paper) described the methods used to produce the draft sequence and offered analysis of the sequence.

These drafts covered about 83% of the genome (90% of the **euchromatic** regions with 150000 gaps and the order and **orientation** of many segments not yet established). In February 2001, at the time of the joint publications, press releases announced that the project had been completed by both groups. Improved drafts were announced in 2003 and 2005, **filling in** to ~92% of the sequence currently.

In 2004, researchers from the International Human Genome Sequencing Consortium (IHGSC) of the HGP announced a new estimate of 20000 to 25000 genes in the human genome. Previously 30000 to 40000 had been predicted, while estimates at the start of the project reached up to as high as 2000000. The number continues to **fluctuate** and it is now expected that it will take many years to **agree on** a precise value for the number of genes in the human genome.

euchromatic *adj.*常染色质的
orientation [ˌɔ(ː)rienˈteiʃən] *n.*取向，定位，定向，归巢本领，方向　the act of orienting; an integrated set of attitudes and beliefs
fluctuate [ˈflʌktjueit] *v.*波动，起伏　cause to fluctuate or move in a wavelike pattern; move or sway in a rising and falling or wavelike pattern

Expressions and Technical Terms

the Human Genome Project 人类基因组计划
make up 组成，构成
focus on 致力于；对（某事或做某事）予以注意；使聚焦于
fruit fly 果蝇
more than 超过
fill in 填平，填满
agree on 对某事（物）有同样看法，商定（同意）某事，商定做某事

Notes

[1]　[special background]　人类基因组计划（The Human Genome Project ）与曼哈顿"原子弹"计划、"阿波罗"登月计划，并称为自然科学史上的"三计划"，但它对人类自身的影响，将远远超过另两项。HGP 是由美国科学家 1985 年首先提出，1990 年正式启动的全球合作项目，我国于 1999 年加入该计划，在中科院遗传研究所杨焕明教授带领下完成人类基因组全部序列的 1%。该计划旨在阐明人类基因组 3.2×10^9 个核苷酸的序列，发现所有人类约 3 万～4 万个基因并阐明其在染色体上的位置，破译人类全部遗传信息，使得人类第一次从分子水平全面地认识自我。

[2]　The Human Genome Project (HGP) was an international scientific research project with a primary goal to determine the sequence of chemical base pairs which make up DNA and to identify the approximately 20000～25000 genes of the human genome from both a physical and functional standpoint. 人类基因组计划（HGP）是一个国际科学研究项目，其主要目的是确定构成 DNA 的化学碱基对序列，并从物理与功能的角度识别鉴定组成人类基因的人类基因组的大约 20000～25000 个遗传因子（遗传基因）。which 引导定语从句。

[3]　The project began in 1990 initially headed by James D. Watson at the U.S. National Institutes of Health. 该项目始于 1990 年，最初是由美国国立卫生研究院詹姆斯 D 沃森领头进行的。headed 前面省略 which was，修饰 project。

[4]　While the objective of the Human Genome Project is to understand the genetic makeup of the human species, the project also has focused on several other nonhuman organisms such as *E.coli*, the

fruit fly, and the laboratory mouse. 虽然这项人类基因组计划的目标是了解人类的基因构成，但该项目也一直关注一些其他的非人类生物，如大肠杆菌、果蝇、实验用鼠。while 的意思是"尽管"，可用 although 代替；这里 to 引导动词不定式作表语。

[5] It remains one of the largest single investigational projects in modern science. [citation needed] 在现代科学领域，它仍是最大的单项调查项目之一[据需要引用]。one of 的意思是"…之一"，作主语时谓语用单数形式。

[6] Although the working draft was announced in June 2000, it was not until February 2001 that Celera and the HGP scientists published details of their drafts. 虽然工作草案在 2000 年 6 月宣布，但直到 2001 年的 2 月 Celera 和 HGP 的科学家才出版了他们的基因组图谱的细节。it was… that…是强调句型，正常顺序是 Celera and the HGP scientists did not publish details of their drafts until February 2001.

[7] Previously 30000 to 40000 had been predicted, while estimates at the start of the project reached up to as high as 2000000. 先前的人类基因组有 30000～40000 个基因被证明正确，而这个估计在此项目一开始时是 2000000。while 的意思是"而"，表示转折。

Exercises

1. Put the following into Chinese

The analysis of similarities between DNA sequences from different organisms is also opening new avenues（途径，手段） in the study of evolution（进化）. In many cases, evolutionary questions can now be framed in terms of molecular biology; indeed, many major evolutionary milestones（里程碑）[the emergence of the ribosome（核糖体） and organelles, the development of embryos with body plans, the vertebrate immune system（脊椎动物免疫系统）] can be related to the molecular level. Many questions about the similarities and differences between humans and our closest relatives [the primates, and indeed the other mammals] are expected to be illuminated by the data from this project.

The Human Genome Diversity Project (HGDP), spinoff research aimed at mapping the DNA that varies between human ethnic groups, which was rumored to have been halted, actually did continue and to date has yielded new conclusions. In the future, HGDP could possibly expose new data in disease surveillance, human development and anthropology（人类学）. HGDP could unlock secrets behind and create new strategies for managing the vulnerability of ethnic groups to certain diseases (see race in biomedicine). It could also show how human populations have adapted to these vulnerabilities.

2. Put English sentences into Chinese

（1）There are multiple definitions of the "complete sequence of the human genome".

（2）A graphical history of the human genome project shows that most of the human genome was complete by the end of 2003. However, there are a number of regions of the human genome that can be considered unfinished.

（3）The process of identifying the boundaries between genes and other features in raw DNA sequence is called genome annotation and is the domain of bioinformatics.

3. Cloze

The Human Genome Project (HGP) was an international scientific research project __(1)__ a primary goal to determine the sequence of chemical base pairs __(2)__ make up DNA and to __(3)__ the **approximately** 20000-25000 genes of the human genome from __(4)__ a physical and functional **standpoint**.

The project began in 1990 **initially** headed by James D. Watson at the U.S. National Institutes of

Health. A working draft of the genome （5） in 2000 and a complete one in 2003, （6） further analysis still being published. A **parallel** project was conducted outside of government by the Celera Corporation. Most of the government-sponsored sequencing （7） in universities and research centers from the United States, Canada, New Zealand and Britain. The mapping of human genes is an important step in the development of medicines and other aspects of health care.

While the objective of the Human Genome Project is to understand the genetic makeup of the human species, the project also has focused （8） several other nonhuman organisms such as *E.coli*, the fruit fly, and the laboratory mouse. It （9） one of the largest single investigational projects in modern science.[citation needed]

The HGP originally aimed to map the nucleotides contained in a **haploid** reference human genome (more than three billion). Several groups have announced efforts to extend this to （10） human genomes including the International HapMap Project, Applied **Biosystems**, Perlegen, Illumina, JCVI, Personal Genome Project, and Roche-454.

（1） A. with B. of C. for D. in （ ）
（2） A. what B. which C. it D. who （ ）
（3） A. identify B. indeed C. identity D. identical （ ）
（4） A. double B. one C. all D. both （ ）
（5） A. released B. was released C. release D. releasing （ ）
（6） A. for B. to C. with D. of （ ）
（7） A. performe B. performing C. was performed D. performed （ ）
（8） A. to B. though C. on D. of （ ）
（9） A. remarks B. remains C. removals D. removes （ ）
（10） A. double B. one C. diploid D. haploid （ ）

4．Put the following into English

人类基因组计划　　组成，构成　　　致力于　　　　果蝇
超过　　　　　　　填平，填满　　　商定做某事　　单倍体
二倍体

5．Writing

Write summary of this text (no more than 200 words).

参考译文

人类基因组计划

　　人类基因组计划（HGP）是一个国际科学研究项目，其主要目的是确定构成 DNA 的化学碱基对序列，并从物理与功能的角度识别鉴定组成人类基因的人类基因组的大约 20000～25000 个遗传因子（遗传基因）。

　　该项目始于 1990 年，最初是由美国国立卫生研究院詹姆斯 D 沃森领头进行的。基因组项目的工作草案于 2000 年公布，根据进一步研究而成的完整版于 2003 年发布，更多的分析仍在发行中。除政府以外，还有一个与之并行的项目是由瑟雷拉公司在进行。大部分由政府赞助（发起）的测序是在美国、加拿大、新西兰和英国的大学和研究中心执行。绘制人类基因图谱在药物以及其他医疗方面发展是极为重要的一步。

　　虽然这项人类基因组计划的目标是了解人类的基因构成，但该项目也一直关注一些其他的非

人类生物，如大肠杆菌、果蝇、实验用鼠。在现代科学领域，它仍是最大的单项调查项目之一 [据需要引用]。

国际人类基因组计划最初的目标是绘出人类基因组（超过 30 亿）单倍染色体中所含的核苷酸。包括国际人类基因组单体型图计划、美国应用生物系统公司、Perlegen（佩尔金基因研究公司）、Illumina、JCVI（美国克雷格·文特尔研究所）、个人基因组项目以及罗氏-454 在内的几个组织已宣布将努力把此项目扩展到二倍体人类基因组范畴。

任何特定个体的"基因组"（除同卵双胞胎和克隆动物）都是独一无二的；绘制"人类基因组"涉及对每个基因各种多倍体的测序工作。该项目并未对人类细胞中发现的整个 DNA 进行研究，一些异染色质区（约占总数的 8%）仍然未进行测序。

虽然工作草案在 2000 年 6 月宣布，但直到 2001 年的 2 月 Celera 和 HGP 的科学家才出版了他们的基因组图谱的细节。自然杂志（出版政府资助项目的科学论文）和科学（出版了 Celera 公司的论文）描述了基因草图测序使用的方法并对序列进行了分析。

这些基因草稿覆盖了大约 83% 的基因组（90% 染色区与 150000 个非编码区和编码区对应，仍有许多区段不能确定）。2001 年 2 月的联合出版物中，新闻发布署宣布项目由两个小组完成了。优化的草图在 2003 年和 2005 年被宣布，目前已填写了 92% 序列。

在 2004 年，国际人类基因组测序组织(IHGSC)的研究员宣布了最新发现，人的基因组预计有 20000~25000 个基因。先前的人类基因组有 30000~40000 个基因被证明正确，而这个估计在此项目一开始时是 2000000。这个数字仍在变动，并且将需要许多年去确定人类基因组基因的精确数目。

Reading material

A History of the Human Genome Project

Science's News staff tells the history of the quest to sequence the human genome, from Watson and Crick's discovery of the double helical structure of DNA to today's publication of the draft sequence. A graphical, interactive versiony of this timeline, containing links to some classic *Science* articles and news coverage from the early genomics era, is also available on *Science*'s Functional Genomics Web site.

1953

(April) **James Watson** and **Francis Crick** discover the double helical structure of DNA (*Nature*).

Credit: A. Barrington Brown/Science Photo Library

1985

(May) **Robert Sinsheimer** hosts a meeting at the University of California (UC), Santa Cruz, to discuss the feasibility of sequencing the human genome.

(December) **Kary Mullis** and colleagues at Cetus Corp. develop PCR, a technique to replicate vast amounts of DNA (*Science*).

1990

Three groups develop capillary electrophoresis, one team led by **Lloyd Smith** (*Nucleic Acids Research*, August), the second by **Barry Karger** (*Analytical Chemistry*, January), and the third by **Norman Dovichi** (*Journal of Chromatography*, September).

(April) NIH and DOE publish a 5-year plan. Goals include a complete genetic map, a physical map with markers every 100 kb, and sequencing of an aggregate of 20 Mb of DNA in model organisms by 2005.

(October) **David Lipman**, **Eugene Myers**, and colleagues at the National Center for Biotechnology Information (NCBI) publish the BLAST algorithm for aligning sequences (*Journal of Molecular Biology*).

1991

(June) NIH biologist **J. Craig Venter** announces a strategy to find expressed genes, using ESTs (*Science*). A fight erupts at a congressional hearing 1 month later, when **Venter** reveals that NIH is filing patent applications on thousands of these partial genes.

(December) **Edward Uberbacher** of Oak Ridge National Laboratory in Tennessee develops GRAIL, the first of many gene-finding programs (*PNAS*).

1992

(June) **Venter** leaves NIH to set up The Institute for Genomic Research (TIGR), a nonprofit in Rockville, Maryland. **William Haseltine** heads its sister company, Human Genome Sciences, to commercialize TIGR products.

(October) U.S. and French teams complete the first physical maps of chromosomes.

(December) U.S. and French teams complete genetic maps of mouse and human (*Genetics*, June; *Nature*, October).

1993

(October) NIH and DOE publish a revised plan for 1993-98. The goals include sequencing 80 Mb of DNA by the end of 1998 and completing the human genome by 2005.

(October) The GenBank database officially moves from Los Alamos to NCBI, ending NIH's and DOE's tussle over control.

1994

(September) **Jeffrey Murray** of the University of Iowa, **Cohen** of Généthon, and colleagues publish a complete genetic linkage map of the human genome, with an average marker spacing of 0.7 cM (*Science*).

1995

(May to August) **Richard Mathies** and colleagues at UC Berkeley and Amersham develop improved sequencing dyes (*PNAS*, May); **Michael Reeve** and **Carl Fuller** at Amersham develop thermostable polymerase (*Nature*, August).

(December) Researchers at Whitehead and Généthon (led by **Lander** and **Thomas Hudson** at

Whitehead) publish a physical map of the human genome containing 15000 markers (*Science*).

1996

(April) NIH funds six groups to attempt large-scale sequencing of the human genome.

(April) Affymetrix makes DNA chips commercially available.

(November) **Yoshihide Hayashizaki's** group at RIKEN completes the first set of full-length mouse cDNAs.

1997

(September) **Fred Blattner**, **Guy Plunkett**, and University of Wisconsin, Madison, colleagues complete the DNA sequence of *E. coli*, 5 Mb (*Science*).

1998

(February) Representatives of Japan, the U.S., the E.U., China, and South Korea meet in Tsukuba, Japan, to establish guidelines for an international collaboration to sequence the rice genome.

(March) **Phil Green** (pictured) and **Brent Ewing** of Washington University and colleagues publish a program called phred for automatically interpreting sequencer data (*Genetic Research*). Both phred and its sister program phrap (used for assembling sequences) had been in wide use since 1995.

(October) NIH and DOE throw HGP into overdrive with a new goal of creating a "working draft" of the human genome by 2001, and they move the completion date for the finished draft from 2005 to 2003.

1999

(March) NIH again moves up the completion date for the rough draft, to spring 2000. Large-scale sequencing efforts are concentrated in centers at Whitehead, Washington University, Baylor, Sanger, and DOE's Joint Genome Institute.

(April) Ten companies and the Wellcome Trust launch the SNP consortium, with plans to publicly release data quarterly.

(December) British, Japanese, and U.S. researchers complete the first sequence of a human chromosome, number 22 (*Nature*).

2000

(March) Celera and academic collaborators sequence the 180-Mb genome of the fruit fly *Drosophila melanogaster* (under), the largest genome yet sequenced and a validation of **Venter's** controversial whole-genome shotgun method (*Science*).

Credit: Adams *et al.*

(March) Because of disagreement over a data-release policy, plans for HGP and Celera to collaborate disintegrate amid considerable sniping.

(May) HGP consortium led by German and Japanese researchers publishes the complete sequence of chromosome 21 (*Nature*).

(June) At a White House ceremony, HGP and Celera jointly announce working drafts of the human genome sequence, declare their feud at an end, and promise simultaneous publication.

(December) HGP and Celera's plans for joint publication in *Science* collapse; HGP sends its paper to *Nature*.

2001

(February) The HGP consortium publishes its working draft in *Nature* (15 February), and Celera publishes its draft in *Science* (16 February).

'A History of the Human Genome Project' written by Roberts et al. (*Science* 9 February 2001)

New Words

graphical ['græfikəl]   *adj.* 图的，图解的 relating to or presented by a graph; written or drawn or engraved

interactive [ˌintər'æktiv] *adj.*相互作用的，活性的 used especially of drugs or muscles that work together so the total effect is greater than the sum of the two (or more); capable of acting on or influencing each other

feasibility *n.* 可行性，可能性 the quality of being doable

strategy ['strætidʒi] *n.*策略，战略 an elaborate and systematic plan of action

erupt [i'rʌpt] *v.* 爆发 break out

congressional [kən'greʃə nəl] *adj.* 会议的，议会的，国会的 of or relating to congress

chromosomes *n.* 同原染色体

thermostable [ˌθəː'məu'steibəl] *adj.*耐热的，热稳定的

representative [ˌrepri'zentətiv] *n.* 代表，众议员，典型 a person who represents others *adj.* 代表性的， 代议制的，典型的 serving to represent or typify

guideline *n.* 指导方针

concentrate ['kɔnsentreit] *n.* 浓缩，精选 a concentrated example *v.* 集中，专心，浓缩 direct one's attention on something; compress or concentrate

Expressions and Technical Terms

links to   与…连接；联系
the double helical structure of DNA   DNA 双螺旋结构
capillary electrophoresis   毛细管电泳
set up   建立，创立，竖立；准备；安排
by the end of   到…为止
take on   承担
move up   （使）升级，提升

Unit **4** Pharmaceutical engineering

Chapter 13 Introduction to drugs

13.1 What is a drug

A drug is any natural or **synthetic** substance that alters the **physiological** state of a living organism. Drugs can be divided into two groups:

1. Medicinal drugs are substances used for the treatment, prevention, and diagnosis of disease.

2. Non-medicinal drugs, or social drugs, are substances used for recreational purposes. Non-medicinal drugs include illegal mood-altering substances such as **cannabis**, heroin, and cocaine as well as everyday substances such as caffeine, nicotine, and alcohol.

Although drugs are intended to have a selective action, this is rarely achieved. There is always a risk of adverse effects associated with the use of any drug. No drug is without side effects, although the severity and frequency of these will vary from drug to drug and from person to person. Those who are more prone to the adverse effects of drugs include:

1. Pregnant women, who must be careful about taking drugs as certain drugs cause **fetal malformations**.

2. Breast-feeding women, who must also be careful about which drugs they take, as many drugs can be passed on in the breast milk and consumed by the developing infant.

3. Patients with liver or kidney disease. These illnesses will result in decreased **metabolism** and **excretion** of the drug and will produce the side effects of an increased dose of the same drug.

4. The elderly, who tend to take a large number of drugs, greatly increasing the risk of drug interactions and the associated side effects. In addition, elderly patients have a reduced renal clearance,

and a nervous system that is more sensitive to drugs. The dose of drug initially given is usually 50% of the adult dose, and certain drugs are **contraindicated**.

contraindicate [kɔntrə'indikeit]
v. [医学] 禁忌（某种疗法等）

Drug names and classification

A single drug can have a variety of names and belong to many classes. Factors used for classifying drugs include their pharmacotherapeutic actions, **pharmacological** actions, molecular actions, and chemical nature. The generic name of a drug is that which appears in official national **pharmacopoeias**. All drugs available on prescription or sold over the counter have a generic name that may vary from country to country. Newly patented drugs usually have one generic name and one brand name. However, once the patent expires, the marketing of the drug is open to any number of manufacturers and, although the generic name is retained, the variety of brand names inevitably increases.

pharmacological [,fɑːməkə`lɔdʒ
Ikəl] adj. 药理学的
pharmacopoeia [,fɑːməkə'piːə]
n. 药典

How do drugs work?

A drug causes a change of physiological function by interacting with the organism at the chemical level.

Certain drugs work by means of their physicochemical properties and are said to have a non-specific mechanism of action. For this reason, these drugs must be given in much higher doses (mg-g) than the more specific drugs.

Most drugs produce their effects by targeting specific cellular macromolecules. This may involve modification of DNA or RNA function, inhibition of transport system or enzymes or, more commonly, action on receptors.

Notes

[1] special background 药物指能影响机体生理、生化和病理过程，用以预防、诊断、治疗疾病和计划生育的化学物质。药物包括有利于健康的催眠药、感冒药、退烧药、胃药、泻药等各种药品。药物分类可以根据药物的治疗作用、药理作用、分子作用和化学性质来划分。药物与生物机体在化学水平上的相互作用改变其生理功能。

Exercises

1. Put the following into Chinese

Drugs are essentially pain-killers. They cover up emotional and physical pain, providing the user with a temporary and illusionary escape from life. When a person is unable to cope with some aspect of their reality and is introduced to drugs, they feel they have perhaps solved the problem itself. The more a person uses drugs or alcohol, the more inflated the problem becomes. More problems are created by their use.

2．Put the following words into English

胎儿畸形　诊断疾病　　哺乳妇女　副作用

肾结石　成人剂量　　学名　　修改 DNA

3．Cloze

The person tries to escape some physical or emotional pain by （1） drugs. This could be a physical or （2） pain, or the discomfort of boredom, peer pressure, lack of social skills.

The person finds that the drugs offer temporary relief, so continues to abuse them. When the person uses the drugs it seems to handle their immediate problem.

With continued use of the drug, the body's ability to produce certain chemicals is diminished because these chemicals are replaced by the drug. The body uses the drug as a substitute for its own natural chemicals.

Deprived 　（3） its own resources (and the ability to create them the body perceives that it needs the drug to function and demands the drug, through physical cravings. The cravings are a way of making the person 　（4） more drugs to be able to function at all.

Drug cravings become so severe that the addict will do almost anything (in many cases, abandoning all previous moral teachings) to get more of the drug. People who are addicted will find themselves 　（5） things they would never have contemplated before.

（1）A. taking　　　　B. having　　　C. using　　　　D. eating　　　　　（　　）

（2）A. psychological　B. emotional　C. psychic　　　D. mental　　　　　（　　）

（3）A. by　　　　　　B. with　　　　C. of　　　　　　D. in　　　　　　　（　　）

（4）A. to get　　　　B. getting　　　C. get　　　　　D. got　　　　　　　（　　）

（5）A. doing　　　　B. to do　　　　C. do　　　　　D done　　　　　　　（　　）

参考译文

什么是药物

药物是能改变生物机体生理状态的天然或合成物质。药物可以分成两类。

1．用于治疗、预防、诊断疾病的药用物质。

2．用于娱乐的非药用物质，包括一些非法的、用以兴奋情绪的物质，如大麻、海洛因、可卡因，还有日常生活中常见的东西，如咖啡因、烟碱和酒精。

尽管人们期望药物有选择性作用，但这一点很难达到。任何药物在使用时都存在毒副作用。没有副作用的药物是不存在的，不同的只是在药物与药物之间以及人与人之间毒副作用的严重程度和发生概率不一样。容易受毒副作用伤害的有以下几类人员。

1．孕妇：应慎重服用药物，因某些药物会导致婴儿畸形。

2．哺乳期妇女：应慎重服用药物，因为很多药物会传递到乳汁，从而进入婴儿体内。

3．肝、肾病患者：这些疾病会使药物的代谢和排泄减慢（导致体内药物浓度增加），从而产生相当于药物过量而带来的副作用。

4．老年人：这类人群通常吃很多药，极大增加了药物之间相互作用的可能性，从而产生相关副作用。另外，老年患者肾清除能力下降，神经系统对药物敏感度增加，药物的初始剂量通常只有成年人的一半，有些药物根本不能给老年人服用。

药物的名称与分类

一个药物可以有很多名称并隶属许多门类。划分药物类别的因素包括药物的治疗作用、药理作用、分子作用和化学性质。官方国家药典中出现的是药物的正式名称。不同国家，不管是处方药或非处方药，其正式名称不尽相同。新注册专利的药物通常有一个正式名称和一个商品名称。然而，一旦专利过期，任何商家都可以营销该药品，在正式名称保留下来的同时，将不可避免地涌现出大量商品名称。

药物如何起作用？

药物通过与生物体在化学水平上的相互作用改变其生理功能。

某些药物借助它们的物理化学性质起作用，即所谓的非特异性功能药。由于没有特定的作用机制，这类药的给药剂量要比特异性功能药大很多（从毫克到克）。大多数药物通过作用于细胞上的大分子团起作用。这些作用包括修改 DNA、RNA 的功能，抑制（细胞）传输系统或酶系统，或者更普遍的情况——结合到受体上产生作用。

13.2 Drug absorption

Drug absorption is process of drug movement from the **administration** site to the systemic circulation. Drug absorption is determined by physicochemical properties of drugs, their **formulations**, and routes of administration. Drug products——the actual dosage forms（eg, tablets, capsules, solutions）, consisting of the drug **plus** other ingredients——are formulated to be administered by various routes, including **oral**, **buccal**, **sublingual**, **rectal**, **parenteral**, **topical**, and **inhalational**. A prerequisite to absorption is drug dissolution. Solid drug products （e.g., tablets） disintegrate and deaggregate, but absorption can occur only after drugs enter solution.

1．Transport across cell membranes

When given by most routes （excluding IV[1]）, a drug must **traverse** several semipermeable cell membranes before reaching the systemic circulation. These membranes are biologic barriers that selectively inhibit the passage of drug molecules and are composed primarily of a bimolecular lipid matrix, containing mostly **cholesterol** and **phospholipid**s. The lipids provide stability to the membrane and determine its permeability characteristics. Globular proteins of various sizes and composition are embedded in the matrix; they are involved in transport and function as receptors for cellular regulation. Drugs may cross a biologic barrier by passive diffusion, facilitated passive diffusion, active transport, or **pinocytosis**.

Remarks Column

administration [ədminis'treiʃən] n.给药；经营,管理

formulation [,fɔːmju'leiʃən] n. 配方；用公式表示；表达, 陈述

plus [plʌs] prep. 加上

oral ['ɔːrəl] adj. 口服的；口头的

buccal ['bʌkəl] adj. 口腔的

sublingual [sʌb'liŋwəl] adj. 舌下的

rectal ['rekt(ə)l] adj. 直肠的

parenteral [pæ'rentərəl] adj. 肠胃外的,非肠道的

topical ['tɔpikəl] adj. 局部的；论题的, 题目的

traverse ['trævə(ː)s] vt. 横过,穿过

cholesterol [kə'lestərəul] n. 胆固醇

phospholipid [,fɔsfəu'lipid] n. 磷脂

pinocytosis [,painəusai'təusis] n. 胞饮作用

2. Passive diffusion

In this process, transport across a cell membrane depends on the concentration gradient of the solute. Most drug molecules are transported across a membrane by simple diffusion from a region of high concentration （e.g., GI fluids[2]） to one of low concentration （e.g., blood）. Because drug molecules are rapidly removed by the systemic circulation and distributed into a large volume of body fluids and tissues, drug concentration in blood is initially low compared with that at the administration site, producing a large gradient.

3. Facilitated passive diffusion

For certain molecules （e.g., glucose）, the rate of membrane **penetration** is greater than expected from their low lipid solubility. One theory is that a carrier component combines reversibly with the substrate molecule at the cell membrane exterior, and the carrier-substrate complex diffuses rapidly across the membrane, releasing the substrate at the interior surface. Carrier-mediated diffusion is characterized by selectivity and **saturability**: The carrier transports only substrates with a relatively specific molecular configuration, and the process is limited by the availability of carriers. The process does not require energy expenditure, and transport against a concentration gradient does not occur.

4. Active transport

This process is characterized by selectivity and saturability and requires energy expenditure by the cell. Substrates may accumulate intracellularly against a concentration gradient. Active transport appears to be limited to drugs structurally similar to **endogenous** substances. These drugs are usually absorbed from sites in the small **intestine**. Active transport processes have been identified for various ions, vitamins, sugars, and amino acids.

5. Pinocytosis

Fluid or particles are **engulf**ed by a cell. The cell membrane **invaginate**s, encloses the fluid or particles, then fuses again, forming a **vesicle** that later detaches and moves to the cell interior. This mechanism also requires energy expenditure. Pinocytosis probably plays a minor role in drug transport, except for protein drugs.

penetration [peni'treiʃən] n.渗透, 穿过

saturability [,sætʃərə'biliti] n. 饱和性

endogenous [en'dɔdʒənəs] adj. 内长的, 内生的
intestine [in'testin] n. 肠

engulf [in'gʌlf] vt. 卷入, 吞没, 狼吞虎咽
invaginate [in'vædʒineit] v. 内陷; 收进鞘中, 套进内部
vesicle ['vesikl] n.囊, 泡

Notes

[1]　intravenous injection　静脉注射

[2]　gastrointestinal fluid　胃肠液

[3]　special background　药物进入机体后，一方面作用于机体引起某些组织器官机能的改变，另一方面药物在机体的影响下发生一系列的转运和转化。自给药部位吸收（静脉注射除外）进入血液循环，然后随血液循环向全身分布，在肝脏等组织发生化学变化（生物转化），最后药物通过肾脏等多种途径排出体外（排泄）。药物的体内过程就是药物在体内的吸收、分布、代谢和排泄过程，是一个动态的变化过程。

Exercises

1．Put the following into Chinese

Absorption affects bioavailability——how quickly and how much of a drug reaches its intended target (site) of action. Factors that affect absorption (and therefore bioavailability) include the way a drug product is designed and manufactured, its physical and chemical properties, and the physiologic characteristics of the person taking the drug. Physiologic characteristics that may affect the absorption of drugs taken by mouth include how long the stomach takes to empty, what the acidity (pH) of the stomach is, and how quickly the drug is moved through the digestive tract.

2．Put the following words into English

片剂　胃肠液　胶囊剂　溶液剂　跨膜转运　被动扩散　易化被动扩散　主动转运　胞饮作用　静脉注射

3．Cloze

A drug product is the actual dosage form of a drug——a tablet, capsule, suppository, transdermal patch, or solution. It consists　（1）　the drug (active ingredient) and additives (inactive ingredients). For example, tablets are a mixture of drug and diluents, stabilizers, disintegrants, and lubricants. The mixture is granulated and compressed　（2）　a tablet. The type and　（3）　of additives and the degree of compression　（4）　how quickly the tablet disintegrates and how quickly the drug is absorbed. Drug manufacturers　（5）　these variables to optimize absorption.

（1）A. with	B. of	C. by	D. in	（　）
（2）A. in	B. to	C. into	D. out	（　）
（3）A. amount	B. number	C. quantity	D. quality	（　）
（4）A. affect	B. affects	C. effects	D. effect	（　）
（5）A. change	B. vary	C. adjust	D adapt	（　）

参考译文

药物吸收

药物吸收是指药物由用药部位进入体循环的转运过程。药物的吸收是由药物的理化性质、药剂的配方及给药途径所决定的。药物制品，即一种药物的实际剂型（如片剂、胶囊剂、溶液剂），包含了药物本身及其他成分，配制后经不同途径服用，如口服、口腔、舌下、直肠、非肠道、局部和吸入等。吸收的先决条件是药物溶解。固体药物制品（如片剂）需经崩解和解聚，但其吸收则要等进入溶液后才能发生。

1. 跨膜转运

采用大多数给药途径给药（静脉注射除外）的药物在进入体循环之前必须通过数层半渗透性细胞膜。这些细胞膜起着生物屏障的作用，有选择地抑制某些药物分子的通过。细胞膜主要由双分子的脂质基质构成，主要成分是胆固醇和磷脂。膜脂质使细胞膜具有稳定性，决定着细胞膜的渗透性特点。大小及组成各异的球形蛋白质就埋嵌在基质中，参与转运过程，发挥细胞调节受体的作用。药物可通过被动扩散、易化被动扩散、主动转运或胞饮作用等方式穿越生物屏障。

2. 被动扩散

在被动扩散过程中，跨细胞转运依赖于溶质浓度梯度。大多数药物分子以简单扩散方式从高浓度区（如胃肠液）透膜进入低浓度区（如血液）。由于药物分子是经体循环快速转运并分布到大容积体液和组织中去的，所以开始时，血液中的药物浓度低于给药部位的药物浓度，形成大的浓度梯度。

3. 易于被动扩散

某些分子（如葡萄糖）虽然脂溶性低，但透过细胞膜的速率却比预料的快，其中一个说法就是，有一种载体成分可以与底物分子在细胞膜外面进行可逆性结合，这种载体-底物复合物迅速扩散通过细胞膜，将底物释放在细胞膜内面。这种载体介导扩散具有选择性和饱和性特征。载体只转运那些具有特异性分子构型的底物。转运过程受有效载体数量控制。这种转运过程不消耗能量，也不会导致逆浓度梯度转运的发生。

4. 主动转运

这种转运过程的特征是选择性和饱和性，需要细胞的能量消耗。底物可以逆浓度梯度积聚于细胞内。主动转运似乎只限于其结构类似于机体内源性物质的那些药物。它们通常经小肠特殊部位被吸收。现已确认，多种离子、维生素类、糖类和氨基酸类都采取这种主动转运方式。

5. 胞饮作用

胞饮指细胞吞入液体或微粒。细胞膜先内陷关住液体或微粒，然后再次加以融合，形成小泡，小泡随后脱离细胞膜进入细胞内。这种机制也需要消耗能量。除蛋白质类药物外，胞饮在药物转运过程中作用不大。

13.3　The history of pharmacopoeia

The term **pharmacopeia** comes from the Greek, *pharmakon*, meaning "drug," and *poiein*, meaning "make," and the combination indicates any **recipe** or formula or other standards required to make or prepare a drug. The term was first used in 1580 in connection with a local book of drug standards in Bergamo[1], Italy. From that time on there were countless city, state, and national pharmacopeias published by various European pharmaceutical societies. As time passed, the value of a uniform set of national drug standards became apparent. In England, for example, three city pharmacopeias——the London, the Edinburgh, and the Dublin——were official throughout the kingdom until 1864, when they were replaced by the British Pharmacopoeia (BP).

In the United States, drug standards were first provided on a national basis in 1820, when the first United States Pharmacopeia

Remarks Column

pharmacopoeia [ˌfɑːməkəˈpiːə] *n.*药典
recipe [ˈresipi] *n.* 处方，制法

(USP) was published. However, the need for drug standards was recognized in this country long before the first USP was published. For convenience and because of their familiarity with them, colonial physicians and **apothecaries** used the pharmacopeias and other references of their various homelands. The first American pharmacopeia was the so-called "Lititz Pharmacopeia", published in 1778 at Lititz[2], Pennsylvania, for use by the Military Hospital of the United States Army. It was a 32-page booklet containing information on 84 internal and 16 external drugs and **preparations**.

During the last decade of the 18th century, several attempts were made by various local medical societies to collate drug information, set appropriate standards, and prepare an extensive American pharmacopeia of the drugs in use at that time. In 1808, the Massachusetts Medical Society published a 272-page pharmacopeia containing information or **monographs** on 536 drugs and pharmaceutical preparations. Included were monographs on many drugs **indigenous** to America, which were not described in the European pharmacopeias of the day.

On January 6, 1817, Dr. Lyman Spalding, a physician from New York City, submitted a plan to the Medical Society of the County of New York for the creation of a national pharmacopeia. Dr. Spalding's efforts were later to result in his being recognized as the "Father of the United States Pharmacopeia". He proposed dividing the United States as then known into four **geographic** districts——Northern, Middle, Southern, and Western. The plan provided for a convention in each of these districts, to be composed of delegates from all medical societies and medical school, voluntary associations of physicians and surgeons were invited to assist in the **undertaking**. Each district's convention was to draft a pharmacopeia and appoint delegates to a general convention to be held later in Washington, D.C. At the general convention, the four district pharmacopeias were to be **compiled** into a single national pharmacopeia.

Draft pharmacopeias were submitted to the convention by only the Northern and Middle districts. These were reviewed, **consolidated**, and adopted by the first United States Pharmacopeial Convention assembled in Washington, D.C., on January 1, 1820. The first United States Pharmacopeia (USP) was published on December 15, 1820, in English and also in Latin, then the international language of medicine, to render the book more intelligible to physicians and pharmacists of any nationality. Within its 272 pages were listed 217 drugs considered worthy of

apothecary [ə'pɒθikəri] n. 药剂师

preparation [ˌprepə'reiʃən] n. 药剂，制备

monograph ['mɒnəugrɑːf] n. 专门描述，专题

indigenous [in'didʒinəs] adj.本土的，本地的

geographic [ˌdʒiə'græfik] adj.地理的，地理学的

undertaking [ˌʌndə'teikiŋ] n. 事业

compile [kəm'pail] vt.编译，编辑，汇编

consolidate [kən'sɔlideit] v. 使联合，统一

recognition; many of them were taken from the Massachusetts Pharmacopeia, which is considered by some to be the **precursor** to the USP.

> precursor [pri(:)'kə:sə] *n.* 先驱，前导

Notes

[1] Bergamo，地名，位于意大利北部阿尔卑斯山脉的南方山麓小丘中。

[2] Lititz，地名，距离美国宾州首府哈利斯堡市东南约 30 英里（1 英里=1.609 千米）。

Exercises

1．Put the following into Chinese

Increased facilities for travel have brought into greater prominence the importance of an approach to uniformity in the formulae of the more powerful remedies, in order to avoid danger to patients when a prescription is dispensed in a different country from that in which it was written. Attempts have been made by international pharmaceutical and medical conferences to settle a basis on which an international pharmacopoeia could be prepared, but due to national jealousies and the attempt to include too many preparations nothing has yet been achieved.

2．Put the following words into English

内用药　外用药　药剂师　药典　地理区域
医学协会　编纂　外科医生　内科医生

3．Cloze

The rapid increase in （1） and pharmaceutical knowledge renders necessary frequent new （2） of the national pharmacopoeias, the office of which is to furnish definite formulae for preparations that have already come into extensive use in medical （3）, so as to ensure uniformity of strength, and to give the characters and tests by which their purity and potency may be determined. But each new edition （4） several years to carry out numerous （5） for devising suitable formulae, so that the current Pharmacopoeia can never be quite up to date.

（1）A. physical　　　B. surgical　　　C. mental　　　D. medical　　　（　　）
（2）A. copies　　　　B. editions　　　C. books　　　　D. periodicals　　（　　）
（3）A. use　　　　　B. examination　C. practice　　　D. treatment　　（　　）
（4）A. requests　　　B. asks　　　　　C. wants　　　　D. requires　　　（　　）
（5）A. tests　　　　　B. trial　　　　　C. experiments　D. examination　（　　）

参考译文

药典的历史

药典一词来源于希腊文，"pharmakon" 和 "poiein"，前者含义为药物，后者为制造，二者合起来表示制备某种药物的配方、过程或其他一些标准。1580 年，药典一词首次用于意大利贝加莫

的一本地方药物标准。从那以后，欧洲不同的制药组织出版了各种城市、州和国家药典。随着时间的推移，人们越来越认识到需要有一套统一的国家药物标准。比如，在英格兰，伦敦、爱丁堡和都柏林这三个城市的地方药典一度在全国通用，1864年以后全部统一为英国国家药典（BP）。

在美国，作为国家药物标准的第一部药典于1820年颁布。其实，在此以前很久，这块土地上的人们就已经意识到药物标准的必要性。那时，殖民时期的医生和药剂师使用的是他们自己祖国的药典或标准，一是为了方便，二是他们也不熟悉其他药典。1778年，在宾夕法尼亚州的李提兹城，美国人出版了第一部药典（并不作为国家药典），称为《李提兹药典》，主要用于美国的军队医院。这是一本32页的小册子，记录了84种内用和16种外用药物及剂型。

18世纪的最后十年，一些地方的医药组织曾几次对那个时期使用的药物进行数据的收集整理工作，并对此制定适当的标准，编撰能够广泛适用的药典。1808年，密西西比医药协会曾出版了一本272页的药典，包含有532种药物和制备剂型的有关信息，其中有很多美国当地产药物，这些药物在那时的欧洲药典中没有记载。

1817年1月6日，来自纽约城的医生，莱曼·斯波尔丁向纽约郡医药协会提交了一份计划，建议编撰一本国家药典。这份计划使斯波尔丁医生后来得到了"美国药典之父"之名。斯波尔丁医生建议按照当时的地理划分将美国分为四个区域——北部地区、中部地区、南部地区和西部地区，在每个地区都成立一个委员会，代表来自该地区的所有医药协会和医学院，同时邀请一些自发的医生协会或外科医生协会出席。每个地区委员会都要完成一部药典草案，并指派代表参加此后在华盛顿特区举办的全国委员会。全国委员会将根据各个地区委员会提交的药典草案编撰完成一部统一的国家药典。

1820年1月1日，第一届美国药典委员会在华盛顿特区召开。在这次会议上，只有北部地区和中部地区提交了药典草案，会议审阅了这两部草案，并将其合为一部药典通过。1820年12月15日，第一部美国国家药典（USP）以英语和拉丁语同时出版。此后，为了方便其他国籍的药师和医生使用，出版了其他语言版本。这部药典共272页，收录了217种当时认为有记载价值的药物，其中很多收录来自密西西比药典。因此，有人认为密西西比药典是美国国家药典的前身。

13.4　Good Manufacturing Practices （GMP）

GMP refers to the Good Manufacturing Practice **Regulations promulgated** by the US Food and Drug Administration under the authority of the Federal Food, Drug, and Cosmetic Act. These regulations, which have the force of law, require that manufacturers, processors, and packagers of drugs, medical devices, some food, and blood take **proactive** steps to ensure that their products are safe, pure, and effective. GMP regulations require a quality approach to manufacturing, enabling companies to minimize or eliminate instances of **contamination**, mixups, and errors. This in turn, protects the consumer from purchasing a product which is not effective or even dangerous. Failure of firms to **comply** with GMP regulations can result in very serious consequences including recall, seizure, fines, and jail time.

GMP regulations address issues including recordkeeping, personnel qualifications, **sanitation**, cleanliness, equipment

Remarks Column
regulation [regju'leiʃən] *n.* 规章，管理
promulgate ['prɔməlgeit] *v.* 发布，传播
proactive [,prəu'æktiv] *adj.*预防性的
contamination [kən,tæmi'neiʃən] *n.* 污染，污染物
comply [kəm'plai] *v.* 遵守，顺从
sanitation [sæni'teiʃən] *n.* 卫生，

verification, process **validation**, and complaint handling. Most GMP requirements are very general and open-ended, allowing each manufacturer to decide individually how to best **implement** the necessary controls. This provides much flexibility, but also requires that the manufacturer interpret the requirements in a manner which makes sense for each individual business.

GMP is also sometimes referred to as "cGMP". The "c" stands for "current", reminding manufacturers that they must employ technologies and systems which are up-to-date in order to comply with the regulation. Systems and equipment used to prevent contamination, mixups, and errors, which may have been "top-of-the-line" 20 years ago, may be less than adequate by today's standards.

GMP is believed to be a good business tool which will help to refine both compliance and performance at your company. GMP requirements are largely common sense practices which will help your company better itself as it moves toward a quality approach using continuous improvement. Fig.13-1 illustrates how a company approaches creating and maintaining a GMP lifestyle in the company.

Fig. 13-1 Creating and maintaining a GMP lifestyle

First, set standards of performance. These include GMP regulations and other standards which are necessary for the

卫生设施
verification [ˌverifiˈkeiʃən] n. 认证，验证
validation [væliˈdeiʃən] n. 批准，确认
implement [ˈimplimənt] v. 贯彻，执行

company. Then, train to those standards. All departments in the company should be trained (to varying degrees) on GMP and other standards. The diagram lists four types of employees which are especially critical to train: top management, managers and supervisors, operators and technicians, and support staff. Because training is such an important part of maintaining a GMP Lifestyle, the company focuses heavily on training.

The next step in the GMP Lifestyle is to **reinforce** what was learned in training. This falls on the managers and supervisors in a plant. Therefore, it is important that managers and supervisors be involved in training, so that they can support it through reinforcement. The same four job categories are listed as being the most critical in promoting and receiving reinforcement.

The third stage is to **audit** to ensure that your efforts have provided adequate controls by auditing. Audits fall in the following three categories: personal, whereby every individual does a self-check to make sure that he/she is complying with all appropriate standards; internal audit, which should be performed by the quality assurance department as required by GMP, and external audits, which can consist of an FDA audit, a consultant checking your compliance status, or you performing a supplier audit.

Finally, the results of audits will help you to know if you need to **modify** your standards of performance. Of course, no procedures should be changed without appropriate change control and approval from quality assurance. The glue that sticks the whole process together is commitment. **Commitment** to GMP and quality is critical at all levels of the organization, starting with top management.

reinforce [ˌriːinˈfɔːs] v. 加固，强化，加深

audit [ˈɔːdit] v. 检验，查账

modify [ˈmɔdifai] v. 修改，更改

commitment [kəˈmitmənt] n. 承诺，托付

Notes

[1]　GMP 是英文 Good Manufacturing Practice 的缩写，中文的意思是"良好作业规范"，或是"优良制造标准"，是一种特别注重在生产过程中实施对产品质量与卫生安全的自主性管理制度。它是一套适用于制药、食品等行业的强制性标准，要求企业从原料、人员、设施设备、生产过程、包装运输、质量控制等方面按国家有关法规达到卫生质量要求，形成一套可操作的作业规范，帮助企业改善自身卫生环境，及时发现生产过程中存在的问题，加以改善。简要地说，GMP 要求食品生产企业应具备良好的生产设备，合理的生产过程，完善的质量管理和严格的检测系统，确保最终产品的质量（包括食品安全卫生）符合法规要求。

Exercises

1. Put the following into Chinese

Since sampling product will statistically only ensure that the samples themselves (and perhaps the areas adjacent to where the samples were taken) are suitable for use, and end-point testing relies on sampling, GMP takes the holistic approach of regulating the manufacturing and laboratory testing environment itself. An extremely important part of GMP is documentation of every aspect of the process, activities, and operations involved with drug and medical device manufacture.

2. Put the following words into English

法律效力　　医疗设备　　预防措施　　　设备认证　　　防止污染

处理投诉　　高级管理层　　遵守状况

3. Cloze

The World Health Organization (WHO) version of GMP is used by pharmaceutical regulators and the pharmaceutical industry in （1）one hundred countries worldwide, primarily in the developing world. The European Union's GMP (EU-GMP)　（2）　 more compliance requirements than the WHO GMP, as （3）　 the Food and Drug Administration's version in the US. Similar GMPs are used in other countries, with Australia, Canada, Japan, Singapore and others having highly developed/sophisticated GMP requirements. In the United Kingdom, the Medicines Act (1968) covers most 　（4）　 of GMP in what is commonly referred to as "The Orange Guide", because of the colour of its cover, is （5）　 known as The Rules and Guidance for Pharmaceutical Manufacturers and Distributors.

（1）A. over　　　　　B. more　　　　　C. less　　　　　D. fewer　　　　　（　　）

（2）A. implements　　B. forces　　　　C. enforces　　　D. impose　　　　（　　）

（3）A. does　　　　　B. do　　　　　　C. did　　　　　D. done　　　　　（　　）

（4）A items　　　　　B. conditions　　C. aspects　　　D. clauses　　　　（　　）

（5）A. formal　　　　B. informally　　C. privately　　D. officially　　　（　　）

参考译文

GMP

　　GMP 指美国食品药品管理局根据联邦食品、药品和化妆品法案公布的良好生产规范章程。这些章程具有法律效力，要求药品、医疗器械、某些食品和血液制品的生产者、加工者、包装者采取预防性的措施确保他们的产品安全、纯净和有效。GMP 章程要求一个质量解决方案应用于加工过程，使各公司尽量减少或者消除生产过程中的污染、混杂和错误。这些措施起到保护消费者的作用，确保不使他们购买到无效甚至危险的产品。不遵守 GMP 规章会给企业带来严重的后果，包括产品召回、查封资产、罚款、甚至坐牢。

　　GMP 规章涉及的方面包括生产纪录、人员要求、卫生、洁净、设备验证、工艺认证和投诉处理。大部分的 GMP 规定是一般性的和开放的，允许企业自行决定如何最好地贯彻执行这些规定。这无疑给企业提供了很大的灵活性，但是，GMP 还要求：企业对这些规定的解释必须是合理和符合逻辑的，能够被同行认可和接受。

有时 GMP 被说成是 "cGMP"。 这里的 "c" 代表 "现行（current）"，它提醒生产者要符合 GMP 的规定，必须使用最新的技术和装备。使用 20 年前的 "最先进" 设备和技术来预防产品污染、混杂及错误可能不符合现行的标准。

GMP 被认为是一个非常好的商业手段，它可以帮助你的企业提高标准化程度，提升企业的表现。GMP 的规定大部分符合常理且切实可行，遵循这些规定并进行不断的改善最终会形成一个质量解决方案，从而帮助你的企业进行自身完善。图 13-1 展示了一个企业怎样才能在内部营造一个 GMP 文化并使其长盛不衰。

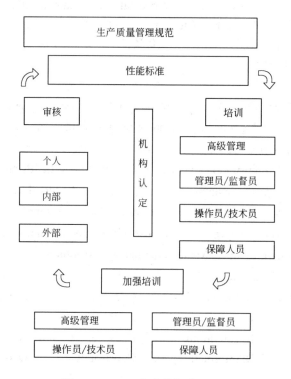

图 13-1　GMP 方式的创建和运行

首先，制订工作标准。这些标准包括 GMP 的规定和公司认为必要的其他一些制度。然后，对这些标准进行培训。公司所有部门应该对 GMP 和其他一些标准进行培训（程度不同）。图 13-1 中列出了四种员工，对他们的培训十分关键：最高层管理人员，经理和检查人员，操作工和技术人员，支持人员。因为培训是公司 GMP 文化中很重要的一个部分，所以这个企业很重视培训。

其次，加强和深化培训内容。这个任务由经理和检查人员按照预先设定的方案进行。因此，经理和检查人员参与培训很重要，这样他们可以在整个加强和深化过程中唱主角。与上述相同的四类人员列入了参加人员名单，因为他们在促进和接受强化培训中是最关键的力量。

第三步是考核，目的是确保以上努力产生了充分的管理效果。考核分为三类：员工考核，即每个员工进行一个自查，确保自己符合所有有关标准；公司内部考核，这类考核应由公司的质量管理部门按照 GMP 的要求进行；外部考核，这些考核包括一次 FDA 的考核，一次专家团对公司标准化程度的检查，或者进行一次供应商考核。

最后，考核的结果将有助于确定是否需要修改工作标准。当然，任何的修改动作需要按照一定的管理程序并经过质量管理部门的批准。将以上整个过程连接在一起的是承诺。对 GMP 和质量的承诺在整个公司，从最高管理层到各级部门都至关重要。

A Brief History of FDA

1800s

Federal controls over the US drug supply began in 1848 with the Drug Importation Act, which required US Customs to stop the importation of adulterated drugs. Due to the growing necessity for safe food and drug products, in 1862 President Abraham Lincoln appointed chemist Charles M. Wetherill to head the chemical division in the newly created Department of Agriculture. This division conducted numerous food adulteration studies. Late in the 1800s, more than 100 food and drug bills[1] were introduced in Congress.

Early 1900s

In 1902, the Biologics Control Act was passed to ensure purity and safety of serums, vaccines, and similar products used to prevent or treat diseases in humans. Shocking disclosures of insanitary conditions in meatpacking plants, the use of poisonous preservatives and dyes in foods, and cure-all claims for worthless and dangerous patent medicines[2] prompted Congress to pass the Food and Drugs Act in 1906. This federal law prohibited interstate commerce in misbranded and adulterated foods, drinks, and drugs. In 1930, what had become the Food, Drug, and Insecticide Administration was renamed the Food and Drug Administration (FDA).

1938

FDA was involved in a five-year legislative struggle to completely revise the Food and Drugs Act. Following the death of 107 persons, mostly children, who took a poisonous Elixir of Sulfanilamide, Congress greatly strengthened the public health protection by passing the Federal Food, Drug, and Cosmetic Act (FD&C Act). This new Act: extended FDA's control to cosmetics and therapeutic devices; required new drugs to be proven safe before marketing; authorized standards of identity, quality, and fill-of-container for foods; authorized factory inspections; and increased the legal tools available to enforce provisions of the Act.

Mid 1900s

After the passage of the FD&C Act, numerous amendments, standards, and laws were passed, and court cases set precedents to further define FDA's role in protecting the public health. These covered areas such as food sanitation standards, prosecution for violations, drug labeling and effectiveness, pesticide residues, biologics, food additives, packaging and labeling, low-acid canned foods, medical devices, infant formula[3], nutrition labeling, and dietary supplements. In 1949, FDA published its first guidance to industry.

1997

The Food and Drug Administration Modernization Act (FDAMA) mandated the most wide-ranging reforms in Agency practices since 1938. In FDAMA, Congress recognized that the protection of public health is a responsibility shared by the entire health care community. The law directs the Agency to carry out its mission in consultation and cooperation with all FDA stakeholders, including consumer and patient groups, the regulated industry, healthcare professionals, and FDA's regulatory counterparts abroad. Provisions of FDAMA include measures to accelerate review of devices, regulate advertising of unapproved uses of approved drugs and devices, and regulate health claims for foods.

FDA today

With a more than 80% favorable rating in public opinion polls, the Agency is cooperating with its stakeholders in the US and abroad to continue protecting consumers and the public health in the new era of technological and scientific advances.

In the wake of the terrorist attacks on September 11, 2001, FDA has also been entrusted with two critical functions in the nation's war on terrorism:

To prevent the willful contamination of all regulated products, including food.

To improve the availability of medications to prevent or treat injuries caused by biological, chemical, or nuclear agents.

Notes

[1] bill, 这里指法律草案, 还没有通过的法律提案。

[2] patent medicine: a packaged nonprescription drug which is protected by a trademark and whose contents are incompletely disclosed. 即带有商标, 包装好的一种非处方药, 这种药的成分保密。

[3] formula: mixture fed to a baby in place of mother's milk. 在这里指某种婴儿代用品。

New Words

adulterate [ə'dʌltəreit] v. 掺杂, 掺假
vaccine ['væksiːn] n. 疫苗
shocking ['ʃɔkiŋ] adj. 令人震惊的
disclosure [dis'kləuʒə] adj. 曝光, 揭露
insanitary [in'sænitəri] adj. 不卫生的
meatpacking ['miːt,pækiŋ] v. 肉类加工业
preservative [pri'zəːvətiv] n. 防腐剂
prompt [prɔmpt] v. 促使, 鼓动
interstate [,intə(ː)'steit] adj. 州 (美国) 际的
misbrand ['mis'brænd] v. 冒牌, 贴假商标于
insecticide [in'sektisaid] n. 杀虫剂
legislative ['ledʒis,leitiv] adj. 立法的, 立法机关的
authorize ['ɔːθəraiz] n. 批准, 许可
identity [ai'dentiti] n. 身份, 一致
inspection [in'spekʃən] n. 检查, 视察

provision [prə'viʒən] v. 强迫, 执行
amendment [ə'mendmənt] n. 修正案
precedent [pri'siːdənt] n. 案例, 先例
prosecution [,prɔsi'kjuːʃən] n. 起诉
violation [,vaiə'leiʃən] n. 违反, 违背
canned [kænd] adj. 罐装的, 罐头装的
nutrition [njuː'triʃən] n. 营养, 营养学
dietary ['daiətəri] adj. 饮食的
guidance ['gaidəns] n.. 指导
mandate ['mændeit] v. 使…成为必需, 给…权威性
stakeholder ['steikhəuldə(r)] n. 利益攸关者
counterpart ['kauntəpɑːt] n. 同行, 合作者
terrorist ['terərist] adj. 恐怖主义的, n. 恐怖分子

Chapter 14   Synthesis of drug

1. Introduction

Since ancient times, the peoples of the world have used a wide range of natural products for medicinal purposes. These products, obtained from animal, vegetable and mineral sources, were sometimes very effective. However, many of the products were very toxic. Information about these ancient remedies was not readily available to users until the invention of the printing press in the 15th century. This information led to the widespread publication and circulation of herbals and pharmacopoeias. This resulted in a rapid increase in the use, and misuse, of herbal and other remedies. However, improved communications between practitioners in the 18th and 19th centuries resulted in the progressive removal of preparations that were either ineffective or too toxic from herbals and pharmacopoeias. It also led to a more rational development of new drugs. Initially this development was centered around the natural products isolated from plant and animal material, but as knowledge increased a wider range of pharmaceutically active compounds were used as the starting point for the development of drugs. The compounds on which a development is based are now known as lead compounds, which the synthetic compounds developed from a lead are referred to as its analogues.

In the total synthesis of a complex product it may take multiple steps to synthesize the product of interest, and inordinate amounts of time. Skill in organic synthesis is prized among chemists and the synthesis of exceptionally valuable or difficult compounds has won chemists such as Robert Burns Woodward the Nobel Prize for Chemistry. If a chemical synthesis starts from basic laboratory compounds and yields something new, it is a purely synthetic process. If it starts from a product isolated from plants or animals and then proceeds to a new compound, the synthesis is described as a semisynthetic process.

2. Total synthesis

In principle a total synthesis is the complete chemical synthesis of complex organic molecules from simpler pieces, usually without the aid of biological processes.

Remarks Column

New words

remedy ['remidi]   *n.* 治疗(法); 药物; 补救(法), 纠正(法)

herbal ['hə:bəl] *adj.* 草本植物的

pharmacopoeia [ˌfɑːməkə'piːə] *n.* 处方书, 药典

practitioner [præk'tiʃənə] *n.* 习艺者, 实习者, 从业者(尤指医师)

rational ['ræʃənl] *adj.* 神智清楚的; 理性的; 理智的; 合理的; 出于理性的

pharmaceutically [ˌfɑːmə'sjuːtikəli] *adv.* 药物地, 药用地, 制药（学）上地

analogue ['ænəlɔg] *n.* 相似物, 类似物

inordinate [i'nɔːdinit] *adj.* 过度的, 过量的

yield [jiːld] *vt.* & *vi.* 生出, 出产; 产生

semisynthetic ['semisin'θetik] *adj.* [化]半合成的

precursor [pri'kəːsə] *n.* 先驱; 先行者; 先兆, 前兆; 初期形式

In practice, these simpler pieces are commercially available in bulk and semi-bulk quantities, and are often petrochemical precursors. Sometimes bulk natural products (e.g. sugars) are used as starting materials and it is assumed that these have or can be synthesized from their constituent elements. The target molecules can be natural products, medicinally important active ingredients, or organic compounds of theoretical interest in chemistry or biology. A new route for synthesis is developed in the course of the investigation, and the route may be the first one to be developed for the substance.

The first demonstration of organic total synthesis was Friedrich Wöhler's synthesis of urea in 1828, which demonstrated that organic molecules can be produced from inorganic precursors, and the first commercialized total synthesis was Gustaf Komppa's synthesis and industrial production of camphor in 1903. Early efforts focused on building chemicals which were extracted from biological sources, and using them to verify their biological activities—in this fashion, total synthesis was associated with disproving the existence of a vital force. As biology and chemistry became more sophisticated, the primary purpose for total synthesis changed, although some total synthesis continues to be a tool for biological verification, for example if a compound contains ambiguous stereochemistry or to create analogs ("chemical mutations") to directly assess or improve the mechanism of biological activity.

Today, total synthesis is often justified as a playground for the development of new chemical reactions and routes, and highlights the sophistication of modern synthetic organic chemistry. Sometimes total synthesis inspires the development of novel mechanisms, catalysts, or techniques. Finally since a total synthesis project will often span a variety of reactions; it serves to prepare chemists for pursuits in process chemistry, where encyclopedic knowledge of chemical reactions and a strong and accurate sense of chemical intuition are necessary.

Classical examples are the total syntheses of cholesterol, cortisone, strychnine, lysergic acid, reserpine, chlorophyll, colchicine, vitamin B_{12} and prostaglandin F-2a by the Nobel Prize winner Robert Burns Woodward between 1945 and 1976. Another classic is quinine total synthesis that has a history spanning 150 years. In some cases the structures of the molecules assigned by spectroscopic methods have been shown to be wrong, when synthesized.

constituent [kən'stitjuənt] adj. & n. 构成的；组成的；成分，构成部分，要素

ingredient [in'gri:diənt] n. (混合物的)组成部分；[化]拼份，拼料，组分，配料；成分，要素

urea ['juəriə] n. 尿素

camphor ['kæmfə] n. 樟脑

ambiguous [.æm'bigjuəs] adj. 引起歧义的；模棱两可的，含糊不清的

stereochemistry [.stiəriə'kemistri] n. 立体化学

mutation [mju(:)'teiʃ(ə)n] n. 变异，变化，更换；[生]突变；突变种

span [spæn] vt. 跨越，穿越，贯穿

pursuit [pə'sju:t] n. 追求，寻求

encyclopedic [in'saiklə'pi:dik] adj. 百科全书般的；学识渊博的

intuition [.intju(:)'iʃ(ə)n] n. 直感，直觉知识[事物]，直觉力

cholesterol [kə'lestərɔl] n. [生化]胆固醇，胆甾醇，异辛甾烯醇

cortisone ['kɔ:tisəun] n. (肾上腺)皮质酮[素]；[药]可的松

strychnine ['strikni:n] n. 士的宁，番木鳖碱

lysergic acid [lai'sə:dʒik'æsid] n. 麦角酸；

reserpine [ri'sə:pin] n. 利血平

chlorophyll ['klôrə,fil] n. 叶绿素

colchicine ['kɔltʃisi:n] n. 秋水仙碱

prostaglandin [.prɔstə'glændin] n. 前列腺素 (缩 PG)

quinine [kwi'ni:n] n. [化] 奎宁；金鸡纳碱；金鸡纳霜

spectroscopic [.spektrə'skɔpik] adj. 分光镜的, 光谱学的

Elias James Corey won the Nobel Prize in Chemistry in 1990 for lifetime achievement in total synthesis and the development of retrosynthetic analysis. In 2005 the group of Corey published an Aflatoxin total synthesis and in 2006 an oseltamivir total synthesis.

Among many groups who have made great strides in advancing the art and science of total synthesis, Kyriacos Costa Nicolaou at the Scripps Research Institute has also produced a number of review articles and books that highlight some of the accomplishments of the field. One example of his work is his contribution to Taxol total synthesis.

3. Semisynthesis

"Semisynthesis" or partial chemical synthesis is a type of chemical synthesis that uses compounds isolated from natural sources (e.g. plant material or bacterial or cell cultures) as starting materials. These natural biomolecules are usually large and complex molecules. This is opposed to a total synthesis where large molecules are synthesized from a stepwise combination of small and cheap (petrochemical) building blocks. Semisynthesis is usually used when the precursor molecule is too structurally complex, too costly or too inefficient to be produced by total synthesis. It is also possible that the semisynthetic derivative outperforms the original biomolecule itself with respect to potency, stability or safety.

Drugs derived from natural sources are usually produced by harvesting the natural source or through semisynthetic methods: one example is the semisynthesis of LSD from ergotamine, which is isolated from ergot fungus cultures. The commercial production of paclitaxel is also based on semisynthesis.

The antimalarial drug artemether (a component of Coartem) is a semisynthetic derived from naturally occurring artemisinin. The latter is unstable due to the presence of a lactone group and therefore this group is replaced by an acetal through organic reduction with potassium borohydride and methoxylation.

retro-表示 "向后", "倒退", "追溯"
aflatoxin [ˌæfləˈtɔksin] n. 黄曲霉毒素
oseltamivir 奥司他韦
stride [straid] n. 大步，阔步
Taxol 紫杉酚泰素
derivative [diˈrivətiv] n. [化]衍生物
outperform [ˌautpəˈfɔːm] vt. (机器等)性能比…好，在使用上胜过；超额完成
LSD 迷幻药 (摇头丸)
ergotamine[əˈgɔtəmiːn] n. 麦角胺
ergot [ˈəːgət] n. 麦角，麦角碱，麦角菌
paclitaxel 紫杉醇
antimalarial [ˌæntiməˈlɛəriəl] n. 抗疟药
artemether 蒿甲醚
Coartem 蒿甲醚-苯芴醇
artemisinin 青蒿素
lactone [ˈlæktəun] n. [化] 内酯
acetal [ˈæsitæl] n. 乙缩醛；乙醛缩二乙醇
potassium borohydride 硼氢化钾
methoxylation 甲氧基化

Expressions and Technical Terms

natural products 天然产物
lead compound 先导化合物
derive from 得自，衍生
derivative 衍生物
retrosynthetic analysis 逆向合成分析
stereochemistry 立体化学
chemical mutations 化学变化
vital force 生命力

Notes

[1] special background **Robert Burns Woodward**，美国有机化学家。1917 年 4 月 10 日生于美国马萨诸塞州波士顿。1937 年获博士学位，当时年仅 20 岁。毕业后在哈佛大学任教，1950 年为教授，终生在该校任教。伍德沃德一生主要从事天然有机化合物生物碱和甾族化合物结构与合成的研究。1945~1947 年间，伍德沃德测定了青霉素、土霉素、士的宁等 12 种天然有机化合物的结构。1944~1975 年间，他合成了奎宁、胆固醇、肾上腺皮质激素可的松和利血平、叶绿素、羊毛甾醇、维生素 B 等 20 余种复杂的有机化合物，并用于生产，具有现代合成化学的最高水平，从而伍德沃德被尊称为现代有机合成大师。伍德沃德还善于从实践中总结并提高理论，在大量合成研究过程中，他观察到分子轨道对称性，而且发现其对反应的难易和产物的构型起决定作用。由此，他于 1965 年与量子化学专家 R.霍夫曼合作提出了分子轨道对称性守恒原理，通常称为伍德沃德-霍夫曼规则。1965 年由于他在天然有机化合物结构和合成方面的研究成果，获得了诺贝尔化学奖。

[2] **Quinine** 奎宁是喹啉类衍生物，金鸡纳的树皮和根皮含有 30 多种生物碱，其中以奎宁最多，正是奎宁具有抗疟疾的药效。18 世纪中叶，欧洲的化学家们相信金鸡纳树皮里含有一种化学物质具有真正的疗效。直到 1820 年，这种神奇的化合物才被两名法国药学家培尔艾迪（Pierre-Joseph Pelletier）和卡芳杜（Joseph-Bienaime Caventou）分离出来，他们把这种生物碱命名为奎宁（Quinine）。"奎宁"这个词在秘鲁文字中是树皮的意思。19 世纪末，奎宁由欧洲传入我国，被称为"金鸡纳霜"，当时是非常罕见的药。奎宁的正确的经验分子式直到 1854 年才得到。人工合成奎宁到 1944 年才取得了重大突破。为了解决第二次世界大战造成的奎宁短缺，哈佛大学的化学家伍德沃德（Robert B. Woodward）和德林（William von E. Doering）成功地合成了奎宁毒（D-quinotoxin）。一种被认为可以转化成奎宁的中间体。因为这个合成的精巧设计，伍德沃德的这个合成被有机化学界认为是一个有机合成史上里程碑式的成就。直到 1970 年，奎宁的全合成才被新泽西的霍夫曼-罗斯（Hoffman-La Roche）制药公司的化学家乌斯可可维奇（Milan R. Uskokovic）实现，这被认为是第一个真正意义的奎宁合成。但是这一条合成路线仍然没有实现对立体化学的控制。完全立体选择的奎宁全合成直到 2001 年才由哥伦比亚大学的斯托克教授（Gilbert Stork）小组完成。

[3] **Elias James Corey**，美国有机化学家，生于 1928 年 7 月 12 日，科里从 20 世纪 50 年代后期开始从事有机合成的研究工作，30 多年来他和他的同事们共同合成了几百个重要天然化合物。这些天然化合物的结构都比较复杂，合成难度很大。按照科里和他的学生成学敏在 1989 年出版的专著《化学合成的逻辑》一书的分类，他的合成工作主要包括：①大环结构，如红霉素大环内酯；②杂环结构，如翼萼藤碱；③倍半萜类化合物，如长叶烯；④多环异戊二烯类化合物，如银杏内酯；⑤前列腺素类化合物，如前列腺素 E_1；⑥白三烯类化合物，如白三烯 A 等。科里不仅在有机合成研究方面显示出他的天才，而且他还总结出重要理论。1967 年他提出了具有严格逻辑性的"逆合成分析原理"，以及合成过程中的有关原则和方法。科里还开创了运用计算机技术进行有机合成设计。由于科里提出有机合成的"逆合成分析方法"并成功地合成出 50 多种药剂和百余种天然化合物，对有机合成有重大贡献，获得了 1990 年的诺贝尔化学奖。

Exercises

1．Put the following into Chinese

At the dawn of the twenty-first century, the state of the art and science of total synthesis is as healthy and vigorous as ever. The birth of this exhilarating, multifaceted, and boundless science is marked by Wohler's synthesis of urea in 1828. This milestone event as trivial as it may seem by today's standards—contributed to a "demystification of nature" and illuminated the entrance to a path which subsequently led to great heights and countless rich dividends for humankind. Being both a precise science and a fine art, this discipline has been driven by the constant flow of beautiful molecular architectures from nature and serves as the engine that drives the more general field of organic synthesis forward. Organic synthesis is considered, to a large extent, to be responsible for some of the most exciting and important discoveries of the twentieth century in chemistry, biology, and medicine, and continues to fuel the drug discovery and development process with myriad processes and compounds for new biomedical breakthroughs and applications. In this review, we will chronicle the past, evaluate the present, and project to the future of the art and science of total synthesis.

2．Put English sentences into Chinese

(1) Today, natural product total synthesis is associated with prudent and tasteful selection of challenging and preferably biologically important target molecules; the discovery and invention of new synthetic strategies and technologies; and explorations in chemical biology through molecular design and mechanistic studies.

(2) Future strides in the field are likely to be aided by advances in the isolation and characterization of novel molecular targets from nature, the availability of new reagents and synthetic methods, and information and automation technologies.

(3) Such advances are destined to bring the power of organic synthesis closer to, or even beyond, the boundaries defined by nature, which, at present, and despite our many advantages, still look so far away.

3．Cloze

The twentieth century has been an age of enormous scientific advancement and technological progress. To be sure, we now stand ___(1)___ the highest point of human accomplishment in science and technology, and the twenty-first century promises to be even more revealing and rewarding. Advances in medicine, computer science, communication, and transportation ___(2)___ dramatically changed the way we live and the way we interact with the world around us. An enormous amount of wealth has been created and opportunities for new enterprises abound. It is clear that at the heart of this technological revolution ___(3)___ science, and one cannot deny that basic research has ___(4)___ the foundation for this to occur.

Chemistry has ___(5)___ a central and decisive role in shaping the twentieth century. Oil, for example, has reached its potential only after chemistry allowed its analysis, fractionation, and transformation into myriad of useful products such ___(6)___ kerosene and other fuels. Synthetic organic chemistry is perhaps the most expressive branch of the science of chemistry in view of its creative power and unlimited scope. To appreciate its impact on modern humanity one only has to look ___(7)___ and recognize that this science is a pillar ___(8)___ pharmaceuticals, high-tech materials, polymers, fertilizers, pesticides, cosmetics, and clothing. The engine that ___(9)___ forward and sharpens our ability to create such molecules through chemical synthesis (from which we can pick and choose the most appropriate for each application) is total synthesis. In its ___(10)___ to construct the most complex and challenging of natures products, this endeavor-perhaps more that any other-becomes the prime driving force for the advancement of the art and science of organic synthesis. Thus, its value as a research discipline extends beyond providing a test for the state-of-the-art. It offers the opportunity to discover and invent new science in chemistry and related disciplines, as well as to train, in a most rigorous way, young practitioners whose expertise may feed many peripheral areas of science and technology.

（1）A. at　　　　　　B. in　　　　　C. to　　　　　　D. of　　　　　　（　　　）

（2）A. have　　　　　B. has　　　　　C. had　　　　　D. have had　　　（　　　）

（3）A. has been　　　　B. was　　　　　C. had　　　　　D. is　　　　　　（　　　）

（4）A. been provided　B. provided　　　C. contributed　　D. surpported　　（　　　）

（5）A. acted　　　　　B. played　　　　C. held　　　　　D. possessed　　（　　　）

（6）A. as　　　　　　B. for　　　　　C. to　　　　　　D. that　　　　　（　　　）

（7）A. for　　　　　　B. at　　　　　C. around　　　　D. upon　　　　　（　　　）

（8）A. after　　　　　B. before　　　　C. beyond　　　　D. behind　　　　（　　　）

（9）A. improves　　　B. increases　　　C. drives　　　　D. enhances　　　（　　　）

（10）A. quest　　　　　B. pursuit　　　　C. seek　　　　　D. hanker　　　　（　　　）

4．Put the following into English

全合成　　半合成　　得自　　　　处方　　　药典　　　天然产物

前体　　　先导化合物　逆向合成分析　立体化学　化学变化

衍生物　　光谱学　　类似物　　　　生命力　　石化产品

内酯　　　甲氧基化　　还原反应

5．Writing

Write summary of this text (no more than 200 words).

参考译文

药物合成

1. 介绍

从古代起，人类已经广泛应用天然产物用于医疗目的。这些从动物、蔬菜和矿物资源中得到的产品有时候是非常有效的。然而，这些天然产物大多数是有很大的毒性的。由于信息的不畅通，使用者并不能知道这些有用的信息，直到15世纪印刷机的发明，直接促进了草本植物和处方的广泛印刷和流通。同时这也导致了使用和滥用草本植物和其他药物的快速增加。然而，随着18世纪和19世纪医师之间交流的增多，在配制药品时，一些无用的或者毒性太大的成分就从本草书或者处方书中剔除了，同时也引导了新药更理性的发展。最初新药的发展以从植物和动物中分离出来的天然产物为中心，但是随着知识的增加，更广泛的具有药物活性的化合物开始作为药物发展的起始物。这些化合物就是先导化合物，从先导化合物合成出来就是它的类似物。

一个结构复杂的产品的全合成需要多步反应得到所需要的产物，而且需要花费大量的时间。化学家重视的是有机合成技巧，特别有价值的或者复杂化合物的合成为一些化学家赢得了诺贝尔化学奖，Robert Burns Woodward 就是一个例子。如果一个化学合成从基本的实验室化合物开始，到产生新的物质，那就是一个纯正的合成过程。如果化学合成是从植物或者动物中分离得到的产品开始，然后产生一个新的化合物，这个合成就被称作是半合成过程。

2. 全合成

原则上全合成是指从比较简单的分子到复杂的有机分子的全化学合成过程，通常没有生物学过程。实际上,这些简单的化合物是商业上大批量的或者散装的，而且通常是石油化学制品的初级产物。有时候大量的天然产物（例如糖）被用作初始原料，并且认为已经或者能够从它们的构成元素合成出目标分子。目标分子可以是天然产物，医学上重要的活性组分，或者是在化学或者生物学中能够使人从理论上感兴趣的有机化合物。一条新的合成路线总是在调查研究中发现的，这条路线也可能是某种物质的第一条合成路线。

第一个有机全合成的例子是Friedrich Wöhler在1828年合成尿素，说明了有机分子可以从无机前体得到，第一个商业和工业化的全合成产品是Gustaf Komppa在1903年合成的樟脑。早期研究的重点是从生物资源中提取得到的化学品，并且利用它们去证实得到的化学品的生物活性。这样，全合成就与否定生命力存在有关。随着化学和生物学的深入发展，尽管一些全合成仍继续作为生物学上的验证工具，但是全合成的主要目的已经改变了，比方说如果一个化合物有含糊不清的立体化学结构，或者合成了类似物（化学变化），则直接测定或改进其生物活性机制。

通常，全合成是为新化学反应和路线的发展提供依据，突出现代合成有机化学的复杂性。有时候，全合成启发新颖的反应机制、催化剂或者技术的发展。最后，由于一个全合成计划往往会包含各种类型的反应，化学家追求合成过程，不仅需要渊博的化学反应知识，而且需要具备强烈而精准的化学直觉。

全合成的经典例子胆固醇、可的松、士的宁、麦角酸、利血平、叶绿素、秋水仙碱、维生素 B_{12} 和前列腺素 F-2a，这些都是诺贝尔化学奖获得者 Robert Burns Woodward 在 1945~1976 年间合成出来的。另一个经典的例子是奎宁的全合成花费了 150 年的时间。在某些情况下合成出来的分子结构经光谱法确定是错误的。

Elias James Corey 因为在全合成和逆向合成分析的发展方面做出了毕生的贡献在 1990 年荣获诺贝尔化学奖。Corey 的研究团队在 2005 年公开发表了黄曲霉毒素的全合成，在 2006 年公布了奥司他韦的全合成。在提升全合成的科学和艺术的很多研究小组里面,斯克里普斯研究所的 Kyriacos Costa Nicolaou 取得了很大的成就，出版了很多综述文章和专注，突出了在这一领域的研究成果。他的其中一项突出的成就是对泰素全合成的贡献。

3. 半合成

半合成或者部分化学合成是一种使用从天然资源中分离出来的化合物作为起始物的化学合成,这些天然资源可以是植物、细菌或者细胞培养。所以天然的生物分子通常是复杂的大分子。这就和全合成形成对比，全合成里的大分子是通过价廉易得的小分子石化产品逐步反应化合得到的。

当前体分子结构太复杂,使用全合成成本太高或者效率太低时，通常使用半合成。也可能是通过半合成得到的衍生物在效力、稳定性或安全性方面比原来的生物分子本身要好。

如果药物是从自然资源得到的，通常是通过收割自然资源或者半合成的方法进行生产，其中一个例子是从麦角菌培养基分离得到的麦角胺半合成生产迷幻药 LSD。紫杉醇的商业生产同样是半合成过程。

　　抗疟药物蒿甲醚(蒿甲醚-苯芴醇复方药的一种成分)是通过天然存在的青蒿素半合成得到的,青蒿素分子中存在内酯基团, 不稳定, 因此内酯基团经硼氢化钾还原和甲氧基化, 用乙缩醛取代得到蒿甲醚。

Reading material

The Art and Science of Total Synthesis at the Dawn of the Twenty-First Century

In our days, the chemistry of natural products attracts a very lively interest. New substances, more or less complicated, more or less useful, are constantly discovered and investigated. For the determination of the structure, the architecture of the molecule, we have today very powerful tools, often borrowed from Physical Chemistry. The organic chemists of the year 1900 would have been greatly amazed if they had heard of the methods now at hand. However, one cannot say that the work is easier; the steadily improving methods make it possible to attack more and more difficult problems and the ability of Nature to build up complicated substances has, as it seems, no limits.

In the course of the investigation of a complicated substance, the investigator is sooner or later confronted by the problem of synthesis, of the preparation of the substance by chemical methods. He can have various motives. Perhaps he wants to check the correctness of the structure he has found. Perhaps he wants to improve our knowledge of the reactions and the chemical properties of the molecule. If the substance is of practical importance, he may hope that the synthetic compound will be less expensive or more easily accessible than the natural product. It can also be desirable to modify some details in the molecular structure. An antibiotic substance of medical importance is often first isolated from a microorganism, perhaps a mould or a germ. There ought to exist a number of related compounds with similar effects; they may be more or less potent， some may perhaps have undesirable secondary effects. It is by no means, or even probable, that the compound produced by the microorganism-most likely as a weapon in the struggle for existence-is the very best from the medicinal point of view. If it is possible to synthesize the compound, it will also be possible to modify the details of the structure and to find the most effective remedies.

The synthesis of a complicated molecule is, however, a very difficult task; every group, every atom must be placed in its proper position and this should be taken in its most literal sense. It is sometimes said that organic synthesis is at the same time an exact science and a fine art. Here nature is the uncontested master, but I dare say that the prize-winner of this year, Professor Woodward, is a good second.

New Words

architecture ['aːkitektʃə] n. 建筑学, 建筑艺术; 建筑(样式、风格); 建筑物; 构造, 结构
confront [kən'frʌnt] vt. 使面对, 对抗, 遭遇, 使对质, 比较
mould [məuld] 霉菌; 模; 样板
uncontested ['ʌnkən'testid] adj. 无竞争的, 无人争夺的; 无异议的

Chapter 15   Pharmaceutical production

15.1   Clarification and filtration

The preparation of **pharmaceutical dosage** forms frequently requires the separation of particles from a fluid. The usual objective is a sparkling liquid[1] that is free of **amorphous** or **crystalline** precipitates, **colloidal** hazes, or insoluble liquid drops. Sterility specifications may expand the objective to include removal of microorganisms.

Filtration is defined as the process in which particles are separated from a liquid by passing the liquid through a **permeable** material. The porous **filter** medium[2] is the permeable material that separates particles from the liquid passing through it and is known as a *filter*. Thus, filtration is a unit operation in which a mixture of solids and liquid, the *feed, suspension, dispersion, influent* or *slurry*, is forced through a porous medium, in which the solids are deposited or entrapped. The solids retained on a filter are known as the *residue*. The solids form a cake on the surface of the medium, and the clarified liquid known as *effluent* or *filtrate* is discharged from the filter. If recovery of solids is desired, the process is called cake filtration[3]. The term *clarification* is applied when the solids do not exceed 1.0% and filtrate is the primary product.

Filtration is frequently the method of choice for sterilization of solutions that are chemically or physically unstable under heating conditions. In many applications, **sterile filtration** is an ideal technique. Sterile filtration of liquids and gases is commonly used in the pharmaceutical industry. Final product solutions or vehicles for suspensions are sterile-filtered prior to an aseptic filling process. Sterile filtration of bulk drug solution[4] **prior to** an aseptic crystallization process eliminates the possibility of organisms being **occluded** within crystals.

The broad **span** of pharmaceutical requirements cannot be met by a single type of filter. The industrial pharmacist must achieve a balance between filter media and equipment capabilities, slurry characteristics, and quality specifications for the final product. The choice is usually a batch pressure filter, which uses either surface or depth principles.

Remarks Column

filtration [fil'treiʃən] *n.* 过滤, 筛选

pharmaceutical [ˌfɑːmə'sjuːtikl] *n.* 药物; *adj.* 制药(学)上的

dosage ['dəusidʒ] *n.* 剂量, 配药

amorphous [ə'mɔːfəs] *adj.* 无定形的, 无组织的

colloidal [kə'lɔidl] *adj.* 胶状的, 胶质的

permeable ['pəːmiəbl] *adj.* 有浸透性的, 能透过的

filter ['filtə] *n.* 过滤器, 筛选 *vt.* 过滤, 渗透 *vi.* 滤过, 渗入

suspension [səs'penʃən] *n.* 吊, 悬浮, 悬浮液, 暂停

slurry ['sləːri] *n.* 泥浆, 浆

effluent ['efluənt] *adj.* 发出的, 流出的 *n.* 流出物, 排水道, 污水

filtrate ['filtreit] *v.* 过滤, 筛选; *n.* 滤出液

sterile filtration *n.* 无菌过滤

prior to *adv.* 在前, 居先

occlude [ɔ'kluːd] *v.* 使闭塞, 使堵塞

span [spæn] *n.* 广度, 范围; 跨度, 跨距 *v.* 横越

Surface filtration is a screening action by which pores or holes in the medium prevent the passage of solids. The depth filter permits slurry to **penetrate** to a point where the diameter of a solid particle is greater than the diameter of a **tortuous** void or channel. The solids are retained within a gradient density structure[5] by physical restriction or by absorption properties of the medium.

penetrate
['penitreit] *vt.* 穿透, 渗透, 看穿, 洞察 *vi.* 刺入, 看穿, 渗透, 弥漫
tortuous ['tɔ:tjuəs] *adj.* 曲折的, 转弯抹角的

Notes

[1] sparkling liquid, 晶莹透亮的液体。
[2] porous filter medium, 多孔的过滤介质（滤布、滤纸等）。
[3] cake filtration, 滤饼过滤, 是固体堆积在介质上并架桥形成饼层的过滤方式。
[4] 整批的药物溶液。
[5] gradient density structure, 密度梯度结构。

参考译文

过滤和净化

在药物剂型的制备过程中常常需要从液体中将微小颗粒分离出去。通常情况下, 这样做的目的是除去液体中结晶或非结晶形态的固体沉淀、胶体物质或不互溶的液滴, 以得到澄清闪亮的液体。如果要求无菌, 需要除去的固体颗粒还要包括微生物。

过滤可定义为使液体通过可渗透材料从而除去其中微小颗粒的过程。这种可渗透材料是一种多孔物质, 称为过滤介质（滤布、滤纸等）, 液体通过它后固体颗粒被截留下来。因此, 过滤是一个单元操作, 固液混合物（原料, 悬浮液, 分散液, 过滤液或浆液）被强制通过多孔介质, 其中的固体沉积或截留在多孔介质上。沉积或截留的固体叫做滤渣。滤渣在介质表面形成滤饼, 流过介质的澄清液叫做滤出液或滤液。如果固体是所需要的产品, 则过滤过程称为滤饼过滤。如果滤液是所要的产品, 并且过滤液中固体含量不超过 1.0%, 这个过程就叫净化。

如果高温下溶液的物理化学性质不稳定, 经常用过滤的办法进行灭菌。在许多情况下, 无菌过滤是一项理想的技术。制药工业通常采用液体和气体的无菌过滤技术。溶液产品或者用于悬浮液的液体先要进行无菌过滤, 然后再进行无菌分装。进行无菌结晶前也要对结晶液进行无菌过滤以防微生物包裹在晶体中。

制药工业的各种要求很多, 仅用单一过滤器不能满足。药品生产者必须在过滤介质、设备能力、滤浆特性以及对最终产品质量要求之间寻求平衡。通常选择间歇加压式过滤器, 其原理既有表层过滤, 也有深层过滤。

表层过滤是过滤介质中的孔或洞将固体截留在表面。深层过滤允许滤液通过弯弯曲曲的孔隙或孔道进入过滤介质至一定深度, 在这一深度上, 固体颗粒的直径大于孔道直径。过滤介质内部形成一个密度梯度结构, 固体被截留在其中, 截留固体的力量既可能来自尺寸上的限制, 也可能来自过滤介质的吸附力。

15.2 Crystallization and pharmaceutical technology

A crystalline phase is created as a consequence of molecular **aggregation** processes in solution. These **prenucleation clusters** may achieve a certain size for a sufficient time to enable growth into **macroscopic** crystals. The rate and mechanisms by which **crystal**s form in liquid solutions are determined by numerous factors, including:

• **Solubility** or solubility product[1] (solubility product is important in solutions of **nonstoichiometric** composition[2]);

• **Supersaturation**: concentration of crystallizing **solute** or ions that **participate** in crystallization;

• **Diffusivity** or viscosity;

• Temperature;

• pH;

• Solvent;

• Soluble additives and **impurities**;

• **Reactivity** of surfaces toward nucleation;

• **Volume** of solution;

• Rate at which supersaturation is created: cooling rate, freezing rate, rate of pH change.

Understanding **crystallization** processes is important for the rational **formulation**, process development, and stability of pharmaceutical products. Whereas **thermodynamics** describes the **equilibrium** behavior of a system, pharmaceutical products most often encounter far-from-equilibrium conditions during processing, storage, or delivery. These conditions lead to the creation of **metastable** liquid or solid states[3]. Metastable liquid states may include freeze concentrated solutions, solutions of weak acids or bases exposed to a pH change, solutions prepared by dissolution of salts of weak acids or bases, and solutions prepared by dissolution of a high energy form. Metastable solid states include **amorphous** solids, **polymorphs**, and **solvates**[4]. Because crystallization provides a means to reduce the free energy of the system to the most stable state, crystallization mechanisms and **kinetics** determine the extent to which metastable states are reached and maintained.

Whereas knowledge of equilibrium phase diagrams[5] is useful in **identify**ing the concentration (or activity) and temperature **region**s of thermodynamic stability of solid phases, information on the crystallization kinetics is essential in determining solid phase

Remarks Column

aggregation [ægri'geiʃən] n. 聚合，集合

prenucleation [prinjuːk'leiʃən] n. [结晶] 成核前

cluster ['klʌstə] n. 聚集体；v. 丛生，成群

macroscopic [ˌmækrəu'skɔpik] adj. 肉眼可见的

crystals ['kristl] n. 晶体；adj. 结晶状的

solubility [ˌsɔljuˈbiliti] n. 溶解度

nonstoichiometric ['nɔnstɔikiə'metrik] adj. 非化学计量的

supersaturation ['sjuːpəˌsætʃə'reiʃən] n. [化] 过饱和

solute ['sɔljuːt] n. 溶质

participate [pɑː'tisipeit] v. 参与，参加

diffusivity [difju'siviti] n. 扩散常数

impurity [im'pjuəriti] n. 杂质

reactivity [ˌri(ː)æk'tiviti] n. 活性，反应能力

volume ['vɔljuːm (us) -jəm] n. 体积，量，卷

crystallization ['kristelai'zeiʃən] n. 结晶，结晶过程

formulation [ˌfɔːmu'leiʃən] n. 构想，设计

thermodynamics ['θəːməudai'næmiks] n. [物] 热力学

equilibrium [ˌiːkwi'libriəm] n. 平衡

metastable [ˌmetə'steibl] adj. 介稳的，亚稳的

outcomes. **Nucleation** and growth rates control the **isolation** of desired solid state **modifications**[6] as well as the particle size **distribution** (number of particles, mean diameter, and standard **deviation**[7]) and particle shape or **morphology**. The lack of information on crystallization processes leads to unwanted or previously unknown nucleation events that threaten the development of a pharmaceutical product.

amorphous [ə:mɔ:fəs] *adj.* 无定形的，无组织的

polymorph ['pɔlimɔ:f] *n.* 多形体，同质异像体

solvate ['sɔlveit] *n.* [化] 溶剂化合物

kinetics [kai'netiks] *n.* 动力学

identify [ai'dentifai] *v.* 识别，确定

region ['ri:dʒən] *n.* 区域，地方

nucleation [,nju:kli'eiʃən] *n.* [化] 成核，晶核形成

isolation [,aisəu'leiʃən] *n.* 离析，隔绝，孤立

modifications [,mɔdifi'keiʃən] *n.* 状态改变，更改，修改

distribution [,distri'bju:ʃən] *n.* 分布，分配，分发

deviation [,di:vi'eiʃən] *n.* 背离，偏差

morphology [mɔ:'fɔlədʒi] *n.* 形态学，结构

Notes

[1] solubility product，溶度积，化学术语，溶解反应平衡常数。

[2] solutions of nonstoichiometric composition，非化学计量组成溶液，比如，NaCl 分子中钠离子和氯离子的化学计量比为 1：1，如果溶液中钠离子和氯离子浓度比不等于 1：1，则为非化学计量溶液。

[3] metastable liquid or solid states，处于介稳态的液体或固体。介稳态：结晶学术语，是处于热力学稳定不稳定之间的一种状态，如果没有干扰，这种状态将一直持续下去。在某些场合也翻译为亚稳态。

[4] solvates，溶剂化合物，即由溶剂和溶质形成的化合物。

[5] equilibrium phase diagrams，平衡相图，一种热力学图表。

[6] state modifications，状态转变。

[7] standard deviation，统计学术语，标准方差。

参考译文

制药技术与结晶

溶液中分子的聚合过程导致了晶相的生成。这些核前聚集物可长成一定的尺寸，经过足够的

时间后生成肉眼可见的晶体。晶体在溶液中形成的速度和机理受多种因素制约，包括：

- 溶解度和溶度积（溶度积在非化学计量组成溶液中非常重要）；
- 过饱和状态　参与结晶的溶质或粒子浓度；
- 扩散系数和黏度；
- 温度；
- pH；
- 溶剂；
- 溶解的添加物或杂质；
- 生成晶核的表面活性；
- 溶液体积；
- 达成过饱和的速度　冷却速度，冰冻速度，pH 变化速度。

　　理解结晶过程对合理的制药产品设计、工艺开发以及制药产品的稳定性都很重要。如果说热力学研究的是一个系统的平衡问题的话，则制药产品在加工、储存或者运输过程中经常处于远离平衡的条件。这些条件导致介稳态液体或固体的出现。处于介稳态的液体有：降低了温度的浓缩溶液，改变了 pH 的弱酸或弱碱溶液，溶解弱酸或弱碱盐形成的溶液，以及溶解高能态物质所形成的溶液。固体的介稳态包括无定形固体、同质异形体和溶质与溶剂形成的化合物。因为结晶是使系统的自由能降低到最稳定状态的一个途径，结晶机理和动力学决定了到达介稳态的程度和介稳态的持续时间。

　　正像使用平衡相图可以确定固相浓度（活度）和温度的热力学稳定区域，结晶动力学知识在控制固相析出时必不可少。晶核形成和生长速率控制着哪个固体在相变中析出，也控制着晶体的大小分布（颗粒的数量，平均直径和标准方差）以及晶体形状或者晶体结构。对结晶过程缺乏了解意味着无法控制或无法预知形成了什么样的晶核，这对医药产品的开发非常不利。

15.3　Drying

There is hardly a pharmaceutical plant engaged in the **manufacture** of tablets or capsules that does not contain dryers. **Unfortunately**, the operation of drying is so taken for granted that efforts for achieving increased efficiency in the production of tablets do not include a study of drying .This chapter[1] introduces the industrial **pharmacist** to the theory and **fundamental** concepts of drying.

1. Definition

For the propose of this discussion, drying is defined as the removal of a liquid from a material by the application of heat, and is **accomplish**ed by the transfer of a liquid from a surface into an **unsaturated** vapor phase .This definition applies to the removal of a small amount of water from moisture-bearing table salt[2] as well as to the recovery of salt from the sea by evaporation .Drying and evaporation are **distinguishable** merely by the relative quantities of liquid removed from the solid.

There are , however, many nonthermal methods of drying ,for

Remarks Column
manufacture [ˌmænjuˈfæktʃə] vt. 制造，加工；n. 制造，制造业，产品
unfortunately [ʌnˈfɔːtʃənitli] adv. 不幸地
pharmacist [ˈfɑːməsist] n. 配药者，药剂师
fundamental [fʌndəˈmentl] adj. 基础的，基本的；n. 基本原则，基本原理
accomplish [əˈkɔmpliʃ] vt. 完成，达到，实现
unsaturated [ˈʌnˈsætʃəreitid] adj. 不饱和的
distinguishable [disˈtiŋwiʃəbl] adj. 可区别的，可辨识的

example ,the expression[3] of a solid to remove liquid(the squeezing of a wetted **sponge**), the **extraction** of liquid from a solid by use of a solvent or by the use of **desiccant**s(such as **anhydrous** calcium chloride), the absorption of **moisture** from gases by passage through a sulfuric acid column, and the desiccation of moisture from a solid by placing it in a sealed container with a moisture-removing material(silica gel in a bottle).

2. Purpose

Drying is most commonly used in pharmaceutical manufacturing as a unit process in the preparation of **granule**s, which can be dispensed in bulk or converted into tablets or capsules. Another application is found in the processing of materials, e.g., the preparation of dried aluminum hydroxide, the spray drying of **lactose**, and the preparation of powdered extracts. Drying also can be used to reduce bulk and weight, thereby lowering the cost of transportation and storage. Other uses include aiding in the **preservation** of animal and vegetable drugs by minimizing mold and bacterial growth in moisture-laden material and facilitating **comminution** by making the dried substance far more **friable** than the original, water-containing drug.

Dried products often are more stable than moist ones, as is the case in such diverse substances as **effervescent** salts[4], aspirin, **hygroscopic** powders, **ascorbic** acid[5], and penicillin. The drying reduces the chemical reactivity of the remaining water, which is expressed as a reduction in the water activity of the product. Various processes for the removal of moisture are used in the production of these materials. After the moisture is removed, the product is maintained at low water levels by the use of desiccants and/or low moisture **transmission** packaging materials. The proper application of drying techniques and moisture-protective packaging requires knowledge of the theory of drying, with particular reference to the concept of equilibrium moisture content.

sponge [spʌndʒ] n. 海绵,海绵状物,(外科用的)棉球,纱布

extraction [iks'trækʃən] n. 抽出,取出, [化]提取(法)萃取法,抽出物

desiccant ['desikənt] n. 干燥剂

anhydrous [æn'haidrəs] adj. 无水的

moisture ['mɔistʃə] n. 潮湿,湿气

granule ['grænjuːl] n. 小粒,颗粒

lactose ['læktəus] n. 乳糖

preservation [ˌprezə'veiʃən] n. 保存

hygroscopic [ˌhaigrə'skɔpik] adj. 吸湿的

friable['fraiəbl]adj. 易碎的, 脆的

effervescent[ˌefə'vesnt] adj.冒泡的, 兴奋的

ascorbic[əs'kɔːbik] adj. 维生素C的

transmission [træns'miʃən] n. 播送, 发射,传送, 传输, 转播

Notes

[1] 本文摘自教课书某章开头。

[2] table salt，食盐。

[3] expression, 在这里的意思是： the act of forcing something out by squeezing or pressing; "the expression of milk from her breast"，从某种物质挤出某种东西，类似 squeezing。

[4] effervescent salts： preparations made by adding sodium bicarbonate and tartaric and citric acids to the active salt; when thrown into water the acids break up the sodium bicarbonate, setting free the carbonic acid gas. 即泡腾产品，由小苏打、酒石酸和柠檬酸及药物活性物质制造，加到水里后

可酸碱反应放出二氧化碳气体。

[5] ascorbic acid，抗坏血酸即维生素 C。

参考译文

干　燥

几乎所有生产片剂或胶囊剂的制药厂都有干燥装置。但不幸的是，人们想当然地认为干燥操作没有什么好改善的，以至于在提高片剂生产效率的工作中竟然不考虑干燥。本节将向制药工作者介绍干燥理论和基本概念。

1. 定义

以下为了讨论方便，需要对干燥进行定义：干燥是通过加热的办法将液体从物料中移出的过程，它的最后一步是液体从(物料)表面向不饱和气相的传递。按照这个定义，从潮湿的食盐脱去少量水分以及用蒸发的办法从海水中回收盐的过程都属于干燥。干燥和蒸发的区别仅仅在于从固体中脱去液体量的不同。

但是，也有很多不通过加热的干燥方法，例如，通过压力将液体从固体中挤出（挤压湿海绵），使用某种溶剂或干燥剂（如无水氯化钙）将液体从固体中吸出，使潮湿的气体通过硫酸柱将水分脱下，将固体和干燥剂（如瓶装硅胶）放入密封的容器内使固体内的潮气转移出来。

2. 目的

作为一个单元操作，干燥广泛应用于制药工业生产的制粒过程中，所制得的颗粒既可以进行散装包装，也可以压成片剂或分装成胶囊。干燥还可以应用于物料的加工过程，如无水氢氧化铝的制备、乳糖的喷雾干燥以及将萃取物制成粉粒的过程。干燥也可用来减少体积和重量，从而降低运输和储存成本。其他的应用还有：干燥将湿物料中霉菌和细菌的生长降低到最低程度从而有助于动物和植物药的保存，使湿药物变干变脆从而有利于这些物料的粉碎。

干燥产品通常比潮湿产品更稳定，这样的物质很多，如泡腾产品、阿司匹林、吸湿性粉末、抗坏血酸（维生素 C）和青霉素。干燥降低了残留水分的化学反应能力，或者说减少了产品中水的活性。以上产品的生产过程中应用了各种除去水分的办法。除湿后，使用干燥剂或防潮包装材料将产品保存起来以维持低湿含量。正确地选择干燥技术和防潮包装要求有一定的干燥理论知识，特别是关于平衡水分的概念。

15.4　Mixing

The process of mixing is one of the most commonly employed operations in everyday life. Owing in part to the almost limitless variety of materials that can be mixed, much remains to be learned regarding the mechanisms by which mixing occurs.

For our purpose, mixing is defined as a process that tends to result in a randomization of dissimilar particles within a system. This[1] is to be distinguished from an ordered system in which the particles are arranged according to some iterative rule and thus follow a repetitive pattern. It is possible to consider the mixing of particles differing only by some vector quantity, such as spatial

Remarks Column

mixing ['mɪksɪŋ] *n.* 混合
randomization [ˌrændəmaɪˈzeɪʃən] *n.* 随机化，随机选择
iterative ['ɪtərətɪv] *adj.* 重复的，反复的；*n.* 反复体
vector ['vektə] *n.* [数]向量，矢量
spatial ['speɪʃəl] *adj.* 空间的

orientation or translational[2] velocity. In this chapter, however, we will deal solely with particles distinguishable by these.

1. Fluids Mixing

Fluids may generally be classified as Newtonian or non-Newtonian, depending on the relationship between their shear rates[3] and the applied stress. Forces of shear are generated by interactions between moving fluids and surfaces over which they flow during mixing. The rate of shear may be defined as the derivative of velocity with respect to distance measured normal to the direction of flow (dv/dx). The viscosity (dynamic) is the ratio of shear stress to the shear rate. For Newtonian fluids, the rate of shear is proportional to the applied stress, and such fluids have a dynamic viscosity that is independent of flow rate. In contrast, non-Newtonian fluids exhibit apparent dynamic viscosities that are a function of the shear stress.

The flow characteristics and mixing behavior of fluids are governed by three primary laws or principles: conservation of mass, conservation of energy, and the classic laws of motion. The equations that result from the application of these simple laws of conservation and motion to systems used for mixing are often complex and are beyond the scope of this discussion. An understanding of the fundamental principles of fluid dynamics, however, will help the reader to visualize [4] the overall[5] process of fluids mixing.

Mixing mechanisms for fluids fall essentially into four categories: bulk transport, turbulent flow, laminar flow, and molecular diffusion. Usually, more than one of these processes is operative in practical mixing situations.

2. Solids Mixing

The theory of solids mixing has not advanced much beyond the most elementary of concepts and, consequently, is far behind that which has been developed for fluids. This lag can be attributed primarily to an incomplete understanding of the ways in which particulate variables influence such systems and to the complexity of the problem itself.

When viewed superficially, such multi-particulate solids as pharmaceutical bulk powders or tablet granulations are seen to behave somewhat like fluids. That is, to the casual observer, they appear to exhibit fluid-like flow when they are poured from one container to another and seem to occupy a more or less constant bulk volume. Dissimilar powders can be intimately mixed at the particulate level much like miscible liquids, at least in principle.

orientation [ˌɔ(ː)rienˈteiʃən] n. 方向，方位，定位

velocity [viˈlɔsiti] n. 速度，速率
shear [ʃiə] v. 剪，剪切
applied [əˈplaid] adj. 应用的，实用的
stress [stres] n. 重压，逼迫，压力；vt. 强调
derivative [diˈrivətiv] adj. 引出的；n.导数，微分
respect [risˈpekt] n. 尊敬，关系；vt. 尊敬，不妨碍
dynamic [daiˈnæmik] adj. 动力的，动力学的，动态的
conservation[ˌkɔnsə(ː)ˈveiʃən] n. 保存，守恒
visualize [ˈvizjuəlaiz, ˈviʒ-] vt. 理解，形象化；vi. 显现
turbulent [ˈtəːbjulənt] adj. 狂暴的，吵闹的
turbulent flow 湍流
laminar [ˈlæminə(r)] adj.由薄片或层状体组成的，薄片状的
laminar flow 层流
superficially adv. 浅薄地，表面地
pharmaceutical [ˌfɑːməˈsjuːtikəl] n .药物；adj.制药(学)上的
granulation [ˌɡrænjuˈleiʃən] n. 使成粒状，颗粒
Intimately[ˈintimitli] adv. 密切地

miscible [ˈmisibl] adj. 易混合的；
miscible liquids 互溶液体

Contrary to these similarities with fluids, however, the mixing of solids presents problems that are quite different from those associated with miscible liquids. The latter, once mixed, do not readily separate and can be poured, pumped, and otherwise subjected to normal handling without concern for un-mixing. In addition, they can be perfectly mixed in any standard equipment, with the primary concerns being power efficiency and time required. In contrast, well-mixed powders are often observed to undergo substantial segregation during routine handling following the mixing operation. Such segregation of particulate solids can occur during mixing as well and is perhaps the central problem associated with the mixing and handling of these materials.

readily ['redili] *adv.* 乐意地, 欣然, 容易地

segregation [segrɪ'geɪʃ(ə)n] *n.* 分离, 离析

routine [ruː'tiːn] *n.* 例行公事, 程序

Notes

[1] 编者认为 this 指 mixing。

[2] translational *adj.* 平移的。

[3] shear rate 剪切率, 流体力学术语。

[4] visualize 这里同 understand, 理解, 掌握。

[5] overall *adj.* 大体的。

参考译文

混　合

混合是我们日常生活中最经常使用的操作之一。部分因为涉及几乎所有无穷无尽的物料, 混合过程的机理还存在很多不清楚的地方。

在本书中, 我们把混合定义为: 对一个系统内各不相同的粒子进行随机化分布的过程。这与将粒子按照某个规则进行安排形成以一定规律重复排列的有序系统截然不同。我们有可能将粒子混合的不同理解为某些矢量的不同, 比如空间指向矢量和位移速度矢量。因此, 在本节中, 我们的研究仅限于能被上述一些矢量表示的粒子。

1. 流体混合

流体依据其剪切率和所施加的剪切应力之间的关系通常分成牛顿流体和非牛顿流体。剪切力产生于流动的流体和其作用面之间的相互作用。剪切率是速度变化对垂直于流动方向上距离的导数 (d*v*/d*x*)。动力黏度是剪切应力对剪切率的比值。对于牛顿流体, 剪切率正比于所施加的剪切应力, 这种流体的动力黏度与流动速度无关。相反, 非牛顿流体只有表观动力黏度, 其大小是剪切应力的函数。

流体的流动特性和混合行为遵循三个主要定律或原理: 质量守恒定律、能量守恒定律和经典的运动定律。将这些简单的守恒定律和运动定律应用于混合系统得到的公式通常非常复杂, 超出本章所讨论的范围。但是, 理解流体动力学的基本原理, 有助于读者大体掌握流体的混合过程。

流体混合机理基本有四种: 整块移动、湍流、层流和分子扩散。通常, 实际混合情况有一种

以上的混合机理在起作用。

2. 固体混合

固体混合理论除了一些最基本的概念外，并没有多大进展，因此远远落后于流体混合理论。落后的主要原因是：①还不能完全理解有关微粒的各种变量如何影响混合系统；②固体混合本身的复杂性。

从表面上看，由众多粒子组成的固体混合和流体有些相似，例如，制药中的散装粉料或压片用的颗粒。也就是说，乍一看，当这些物料从一个容器倒向另一个时，看起来和流体一样能自由流动，也会占据或多或少的恒定容积。不同的粉末可以在粒子水平上充分混合，至少在大体上和液体的混合差别不大。但是，与这些类似性相反，固体物料在混合时所遇到的问题与液体物料大大不同。液体一旦混合后很难再分开，混合后的物料可以倾倒、用泵打，或者进行其他常规性的处理而不用担心混合物再次分开。此外，在任何标准设备里液体都能充分混合，除了能耗的高低和所需时间的长短外，其他不用太多考虑。与此相反，充分混合好的固体粉末，在随后的常规处理中经常产生非常明显的离析。这些固体粒子的离析也会发生在混合过程中，这也许是混合和处理这些固体物料最核心的问题所在。

Reading material

The use of Milling

Extraction or leaching from animal glands (liver and pancreas), and from crude vegetable drugs, is facilitated by comminution. The time required for extraction is shortened by the increased area of contact between the solvent and the solid and the reduced distance the solvent has to penetrate into the material. The control of particle size in the extraction process provides for more complete extraction and a rapid filtration rate when the solution is filtered from the marc. Similarly, the time required for dissolution of solid chemicals in the preparation of solutions is shortened by the use of smaller particles.

The drying of wet masses may be facilitated by milling, which increases the surface area and reduces the distance the moisture must travel within the particle to reach the outer surface. Solvolytic decomposition of solids initially occurs at surface irregularities and is increased by the presence of solvates or moisture. Micronization and subsequent drying increase the stability because the occluded solvent is removed. In the manufacture of compressed tablets, the granulation of the wet mass results in more rapid and uniform drying. The dried tablet granulation is then milled to a particle size and distribution that will flow freely and produce tablets of uniform weight. The flow-ability of powders and granules in high-speed filling equipment and in tablet presses affects product uniformity. Relationships between flow rate and particle size have been reported. The role of size reduction in tablet manufacturing has been discussed.

The mixing or blending of several solid ingredients of a pharmaceutical is easier and more uniform if the ingredients are approximately the same size. This provides a greater uniformity of dose. Solid pharmaceuticals that are artificially colored are often milled to distribute the coloring agent to ensure that the mixture is not mottled and is uniform from batch to batch. Even the size of a pigment affects its color.

Lubricants used in compressed tablets and capsules function by virtue of their ability to coat the surface of the granulation or powder. A fine particle size is essential if the lubricant is to function properly. The milling of ointments, creams, and pastes provides a smooth texture and better appearance in addition to improved physical stability.

New Words

milling ['miliŋ] *n.* 磨, 制粉, [机]轧齿边

marc [mɑːk] *n.* (水果, 种子等经压榨后的)榨渣

micronization [,maɪkrəʊnaɪzeɪʃ ə·n] *n.* 微粉化

tablet ['tæblit] *n.* 药片, 片剂

ingredient [inˈgriːdiənt] *n.* 成分, 因素

mottle ['mɔtl] *vt.* 使成杂色, 使有斑点; *n.* 杂色, 斑点

pigment ['pigmənt] *n.* [生]色素, 颜料

capsule ['kæpsjuːl] *n.* 胶囊

Chapter 16　Industrial pharmacy

16.1　Tablets

1.　Introduction

Tablets are solid dosage forms containing medical substances with suitable diluents. They may be classed according to the method of manufacture, as compressed tablets or molded tablets.

The vast majority of all tablets manufactured are made by compression, and compressed tablets are the most wildly used dosage form now. Compressed tablets are prepared by the application of high pressures, utilizing steel punches and dies, to powders or granulations. Tablets can be produced in a wide variety of size, shapes, and surface markings, depending upon the design of the punches and dies. Capsule-shaped tablets are commonly referred to as caplets. Boluses are large tablets intended for veterinary use, usually for large animals.

Molded tablets are prepared by forcing dampened powders under low pressure into die cavities. Solidification depends upon crystal bridges built up during the subsequent drying process, and not upon the compaction force.

Buccal tablets are intended to be inserted in the buccal pouch, and sublingual tablets are intended to be inserted beneath the tongue, where the active ingredient is absorbed directly through the oral mucosa. Few drugs are readily absorbed in this way, but for those that are (such as nitroglycerin and certain steroid hormones), a number of advantages may result.

Soluble, effervescent tablets are prepared by compression and contain, in addition to active ingredients, mixtures of acids(citric acid, tartaric acid) and sodium bicarbonate, which release carbon dioxide when dissolved in water. They are intended to be dissolved or dispersed in water before administration. Effervescent tablets should be stored in tightly closed containers or moisture-proof packs and labeled to indicate that they are not to be swallowed directly.

2.　Formulation of compressed tablets

Most compressed tablets consist of the active ingredient and a diluent, binder, disintegrating agent, and lubricant. Pigments,

Remarks Column

New words

tablets['tæblits] *n.* 片剂

compress [kəm'pres] *vt.* 压紧, 压缩

compression [kəm'preʃən] *n.* 挤压, 压缩

granulation [ˌgrænjuˈleiʃən] *n.* 使成粒状,成粒

caplet ['kæplit] *n.* 囊片(指为防不良物质掺入而设计的一种椭圆胶囊形糖衣药片)

bolus ['bəuləs] *n.* 大丸药

veterinary ['vetərinəri] *adj.* (为医治)动物(尤指家禽家畜)疾病的;兽医的

dampen ['dæmpən] *vt.* 加湿

solidification [ˌsolidifiˈkeiʃən] *n.* 凝固

compaction [kəmˈpækʃən] *n.* 压紧, 压实

dissolve [diˈzolv] *vt.* (使)溶解

adminstration [ədˌminisˈtreiʃən] *n.* 管理, 服药

moisture-proof adj. 防潮的

formulation [ˌfoːmjuˈleiʃən] *n.* 配方

diluent ['diljuənt] *n.* 稀释剂

binder ['baində] *n.* 黏合剂

lubricant ['ljuːbrikənt] *n.* 润滑剂

pigment ['pigmənt] *n.* 颜料,天然色素

flavor ['fleivə] *n.* 芳香剂

lactose ['læktəus] *n.* 乳糖

starch [staːtʃ] *n.* 淀粉

acacia [əˈkeiʃə] *n.* 阿拉伯树胶

flavors and sweetening agents may also be present. Diluents are added where the quantity of active ingredient is small or difficult to compress. Common tablet fillers include lactose, starch, dibasic calcium phosphate, and microcrystalline cellulose.

Binders give adhesiveness to the powder during the preliminary granulation. While binders may be added dry, they are more effective. Common binders include acacia, gelatin, sucrose, povidone, methylcellulose, carboxymethylcellulose, and hydrolyzed starch pastes.

A disintegrating agent serves to assist in the fragmentation of the tablet after administration. The most wildly used tablet disintegrating agent is starch. Effervescent mixture are used in soluble tablet systems as disintegrating agents. The concentration of the disintegrating agent, method of addition, and degree of compaction play a role in effectiveness.

Lubricants reduce friction during the compression. In addition, they aid in preventing adherence of tablet material to the dies and punches. Metallic stearates, stearic acid, hydrogenated vegetable oils, and talc are used as lubricants. Most lubricants are hydrophobic, and tend to reduce the rates of tablet disintegraion and dissolution. Consequently, excessive concentrations of lubricant shoule be avoided.

Glidants are agents that improve powder fluidity, and they are commonly employed in direct compression where no granulation step is involved. The most effective glidants are the colloidal pyrogenic silicas.

Colorants are often added to tablet formulations for esthetic value. Most colorants are photosensitive and they fade when exposed to light.

gelatin ['dʒelətin] n. 凝胶
sucrose ['sjuːkrəus] n. 蔗糖
povidone [pɔvai'dəun] n. 聚维酮
methylcellulose [ˌmeθil'seljuləs] n. 甲基纤维素
carboxymethylcellulose [kɑːbəuksiˌmeθil'seljuləs] n. 羧甲基纤维素
talc [tælk] n. 滑石粉
hydrophobic [ˌhaidrəu'fəubik] adj. 疏水的
glidant ['glidənt] n. 助流剂
fluidity [flu(ː)'iditi] n. 流动性
colorant ['kʌlərənt] n. 着色剂
photosensitive [ˌfəutəu'sensitiv] adj. 感光性的

Expressions and Technical Terms

solid dosage form 固体剂型
compressed tablets 压制片
molded tablets 模制片
punches and dies 冲床和模具
be referred to as 被称为
die cavity 模槽
buccal tablets 口含片
sublingual tablets 舌下片
oral mucosa 口腔黏膜
soluble tablets 溶液片
effervescent tablets 泡腾片
sodium bicarbonate 碳酸氢钠
carbon dioxide 二氧化碳
disintegrating agent 崩解剂
sweetening agent 甜味剂
dibasic calcium phosphate 磷酸氢钙
microcrystalline cellulose 微晶纤维素
hydrolyzed starch pastes 水解淀粉糊
metallic stearates 硬脂酸盐
stearic acid 硬脂酸
hydrogenated vegetable oils 氢化植物油

16.2　Capsules

Capsules are solid dosages forms in which the drug is enclosed within either a hard or soft shell. The shells are susally formed from gelatin; however, they also may be made from starch or other suitable substances. The two main types of capsules are hard-shell capsules, which are normally used for dry, powdered ingredients, and soft-shell capsules, primarily used for oils and for active ingredients that are dissolved or suspended in oil.

In extemporaneous prescription practice, hard-shell capsules may be hand-filled; this permits the prescriber a latitude of choice in selecting either a single drug or a combination of drugs at the exact dosage level considered for the individual patient. This flexibility gives hard-shell capsules an advantage over compressed tablets.

Hard gelatin capsules are made by a process that involves dipping shaped pins into gelatin solutions, after which the gelatin films are dried, trimmed, and removed from the pins, and the body and cap pieces are joined. Starch capsules are made by injection molding a mixture of starch and water, after which the capsules are dried. The empty capsules should be stored in tight containers until they are filled. Since gelatin is of animal origin and starch is of vegetable origin, capsules made with these materials should be protected from potential sources of microbial contamination.

In hard gelatin capsule filling operations, the body and cap of the shell are separated prior to dosing. In hard starch shell filling operations, the bodies and caps are supplied separately and are fed into separate hoppers of the filling machine. Machines employing various dosing principles may be employed to fill powders into hard-shell capsules; however, most fully automatic machines form powder plugs by compression and eject them into empty capsule bodies. Powder formulations often require adding fillers, lubricants, and glidants to the active ingredients to facilitate encapsulation. The formulation, as well as the method of filling, particularly the degree of compaction, may influence the rate of drug release. The addition of wetting agents to the powder mass is common where the active agent is hydrophobic. Disintegrants also may be included in powder formulations to facilitate deaggregation and dispersal of capsule plugs in the gut.

Soft-shell capsules made from gelatin or other suitable material require large-scale production methods. The soft gelatin

Remarks Column

New words

capsules ['kæpsjuːlz] *n.* 胶囊

extemporaneous [ik,stempə'reiniəs] *adj.* 临时的

prescription [pris'kripʃən] *n.* 处方, 药方

flexibility [,fleksə'biliti] *n.* 灵活性

trim [trim] *vt.* 修剪，切割

microbial [mai'krəubiəl] *adj.* 微生物的，由细菌引起的

contamination [kən,tæmi'neiʃən] *n.* 污染

dosing ['dəusiŋ] *n.* 配料

hopper ['hɔpə] *n.* 加料斗

facilitate [fə'siliteit] *vt.* 使容易，促进

encapsulation [in,kæpsju'leiʃən] *n.* 灌封，包裹　the condition of being enclosed (as in a capsule)

disintegrant [dis'intigrənt] *n.* 崩解剂

deaggregation [di,ægri'geiʃən] *n.* 分解

gut [gʌt] *n.* 肠

plasticize ['plæstisaiz] *v.* 塑化

plasticizer ['plæstisaizə] *n.* 增塑剂

polyol ['pɔliɔl] *n.* 多元醇，多羟基化合物

sorbitol ['sɔːbitəl] *n.* 山梨(糖)醇

glycerin ['glisərin] *n.* 甘油,丙三醇

preservative [pri'zəːvətiv] *n.* 防腐剂

vehicle ['viːikl] *n.* 赋型剂

oleaginous [,əuli'ædʒinəs] *adj.* 油质的

shell is somewhat thicker than that of hard-shell capsules and may be plasticized by the addition of a polyol such as sorbitol or glycerin.The ratio of dry plasticizer to dry gelatin determines the "hardness" of the shell and may be varied to accommodate environmental conditions as well as the nature of the contents. Like hard shells, the shell composition may include approved dyes and pigments, opaquing agents such as titanium dioxide, and preservatives. Flavors may be added and up to 5% sucrose may be included for its sweetness and to produce a chewable shell. Soft gelatin shells normally contain 6% to 13% water. Soft-shell capsules are filled with liquid contents and active ingredients are dissolved or suspended in a liquid vehicle. An oleaginous vehicle such as vegetable oil was commonly used; however, nonaqueous, water-miscible liquid vehicles such as the lower-molecular-weight polyethylene glycols are more common today due to bioavailability problems.

Available in a wide variety of sizes and shapes, soft-shell capsules are both formed, filled, and sealed in the same machine; and this is a rotary die process, although a plate process or reciprocating die process sometimes also may be employed. Soft-shell capsules also may be manufactured in a bubble process that forms seamless spherical capsules. With suitable equipment, powders and other dry solids also may be filled into soft-shell capsules.

16.3 Injections

1. Introduction

Parenteral articles are preparations intended for injection through the skin or other external boundary tissue, rather than through the alimentary canal, so that the active substances they contain are administered, using gravity or force, directly into a blood vessel, organ, tissue, or lesion. Parenteral articles are prepared scrupulously by methods designed to ensure that they meet Pharmacopeial requirements for sterility, pyrogens, particulate matter, other contaminants, and where appropriate, contain inhibitors of the growth of microorganisms. An injection is a preparation intended for parenteral administration or for constituting or diluting a parenteral article prior to administration.

2. Classification

The following nomencalture pertains to five general types of preparations, all of which are suitable for, and intended for,

nonaqueous [ˈnɔnˈeikwiəs] adj. 非水的

bioavailability [ˌbaiəuəˌveiləˈbiliti] n. (药物或营养素的)生物药效率

seal[si:l] v. 密封

Expressions and Technical Terms

hard-shell capsules 硬胶囊剂

soft-shell capsules 软胶囊剂

active ingredients 活性成分

injection molding 喷射模塑法

body and cap 囊体和囊帽

prior to 在…之前

filling machine 灌装机

wetting agents 润湿剂

large-scale production 大规模生产

opaquing agents 避光剂

titanium dioxide 二氧化钛

polyethylene glycols 聚乙二醇

rotary die process 旋转式模压法

plate process 钢板式模压法

reciprocating die process 往复式模压法

Remarks Column

New words

injections [inˈdʒekʃənz] n. 注射剂

lesion [ˈli:ʒən] n. 损伤，伤口

sterility [steˈriliti] n. 无菌

pyrogen [ˈpaiərəudʒin] n. 热原(质)

microorganism [ˌmaikrəuˈɔ:gənizəm] n. 微生物

dilute [daiˈlju:t] vt. 稀释

isotonic [ˌaisəuˈtɔnik] adj. 等渗的

mercury [ˈmə:kjuri] n.汞，水银

parenteral administration. They may contain buffers, preservatives , or other added substances.

① [DRUG] Injection—Liquid preparation that are drug substances or solutions thereof.

② [DRUG] for Injection—Dry solids that, upon the addition of suitable vehicles, yield solutions conforming in all respects to the requirements for injection.

③ [DRUG]Injectable Emulsion—Liquid preparations of drug substances dissolved or dispersed in a suitable emulsion medium.

④ [DRUG]Injectable Suspension—Liquid preparations of solids suspended in a suitable liquid medium.

⑤ [DRUG]for Injectable Suspension—Dry solids that, upon the addition of suitable vehicles, yield preparations conforming in all respects to the requirements for Injectable Suspensions.

3. Ingredients—Vehicles and added substances

Aqueous Vehicles—The vehicles for aqueous injections meet the requirements of the Pyrogen Test or the Bacterial Endotoxins Test, whichever is specified. Water for injection generally is used as the vehicle, unless otherwise specified in the individual monograph. Sodium chloride may be added in amounts sufficient to render the resulting solution isotonic; and Sodium Chloride Injection, or Ringer's Injection, may be used in whole or in part instead of water for injection.

Other vehicles—Fixed oils used as vehicles for nonaqueous injections are of vegetable origin, are odorless or nearly so , and have no odor suggesting randidity. They meet the requirements of the test for Solid paraffin under Mineral Oil, the cooling bath being maintained at 10, have Sponification Value between 185 and 200, have an Iodine Value between 79 and 141, and meet the requirements of the following tests.

Added substances—Suitable substances may be added to preparations intended for injection to increase stability and usefulness, provided they are harmless in the amounts administered and do not interfere with the therapeutic efficacy or with the responses to the specified assays and tests. No coloring agent may be added, solely for the purpose of coloring the finished preparation, to a solution intended for parenteral administration.

Observe special care in the choice and use of added substances in preparations for injection that are administered in a volume exceeding 5ml. The following maximum limits prevail unless otherwise directed: for agents containing mercury and the

cationic [ˌkætaiˈɔnik] adj. 阳离子的

chlorobutanol [ˌklɔrəˈbjutənəul] n. 氯丁醇(消毒防腐药)

cresol [ˈkriːsɔl] n. 甲酚

phenol [ˈfiːnəl] n. 苯酚,石碳酸

equivalent [iˈkwivələnt] adj. 相等的, 相当的

sulfite [ˈsʌlfait] n. 亚硫酸盐

bisulfite [ˌbaiˈsʌlfait] n. 酸性亚硫酸盐

metabisulfite [ˈmetəbaiˈsʌlfait] n. 偏亚硫酸氢盐

radionuclide [ˌreidiəuˈnjuːklaid] n. 放射性核, 放射性核素

antimicrobial [ˌæntimaiˈkrəubiəl] n. 抗菌剂,杀菌剂

Expressions and Technical Terms
parenteral articles 注射用药品
external boundary tissue 外周组织
the alimentary canal 消化道
blood vessel 血管
particulate matter 不溶性微粒
injectable emulsion 注射乳剂
injectable suspension 注射混悬剂
added substances 添加剂
pyrogen test 热原检查
bacterial endotoxins test 细菌内毒素检查
water for injection 注射用水
sodium chloride 氯化钠
sodium chloride injection 氯化钠注射液
Ringer's injection 林格氏注射剂
sponification value 皂化值
iodine value 碘值
interfere with 干扰
therapeutic efficacy 疗效
specified assay 含量测定
coloring agent 着色剂

cationic surface-active compounds, 0.01%; for chlorobutanol, cresol, phenol, and similar types of substances, 0.5%; and for sulfur dioxide, or an equivalent amount of the sulfite, bisulfite, or metabisulfite of potassium or sodium, 0.2%.

A suitable substance or mixture of substances to prevent the growth of microorganisms must be added to preparations intended for injection that are packaged in multiple-dose containers, regardless of the method of sterilization employed, unless one of the following conditions prevails: (1) there are different directions in the individual monograph; (2) the substance contains a radionuclide with a physical half-life of less than 24 hours; (3) The active ingredients are themselves antimicrobial. Such substances are used in concentrations that will prevent the growth of or kill microorganisms in the preparations for injection.

surface-active compounds 表面活性剂
multiple-dose container 多剂量容器
physical half-life 物理半衰期

16.4 Packaging

The container used for packaging is that which holds the article and is in direct contact with the article. Prior to being filled, the container should be clean. Special cleaning procedures may be necessary to ensure that each container is clean and that extraneous matter is not introduced into or onto the article. The container does not interact physically or chemically with the article placed in it so as to alter the strength, quality, or purity of the article beyond the official requirements. The pharmacopeial requirements for the use of specified containers apply also to articles as packaged by the pharmacist or other dispenser, unless otherwise indicated in the individual monograph.

Light-Resistant Container — A light-resistant container protects the contents from the effects of light by the specific properties of the material of which it is composed, including any coating applied to it. A colorless or a translucent container may be made light-resistant by means of an opaque covering, in which case the label of the container bears a statement that the opaque covering is needed until the contents are to be used or administered. Where it is directed to "protect from light" in an individual monograph, preservation in a light-resistant container is intended.

Well-Closed Container—A well-closed container protects the contents from extraneous solids and from loss of the article under the ordinary or customary conditions of handling, shipment,

Remarks Column
New words
extraneous [ik'streiniəs] adj. 外部的, 外来的

pharmacist ['fɑːməsist] n. 药剂师
dispenser [dis'pensə] n. 配药师, 药剂师

translucent [trænz'luːsnt] adj. 半透明的

light-resistant adj. 耐光的

efflorescence [ˌeflɔː'resəns] n. 风化

deliquescence [ˌdeli'kwesns] n. 潮解

closure ['kləuʒə] n. 封塞

impervious [im'pəːviəs] adj. 不可渗透的, 透不过的

storage and distribution.

Tight Container—A tight container protects the contents from contamination by extraneous liquids, solids or vapors; from loss of the article; and from efflorescence, deliquescence, or evaporation under the ordinary or customary conditions of handling, shipment, storage and distribution; and is capable of tight closure. Where a tight container is specified, it may be replaced by a hermetic container for a single dose of an article.

Hermetric Container—A hermetic container is impervious to air or any other gas under the ordinary or customary conditions of handling, shipment, storage and distribution.

Single-Unit Container—A single-unit container is one that is designed to hold a quantity of drug product intended for administration as a single dose or a single finished device intended for use promptly after the container is opened. Preferably, the immediate container and the outer container or protective packaging shall be so designed as to show evidence of any tampering with the contents. Each single-unit container shall be labeled to indicate the identity, quantity and strength, name of the manufacturer, lot number, and expiration date of the article.

Single-Dose Container — A single-dose container is a single-unit container for articles intended for parenteral administration only. Examples of single-dose containers include prefilled syringes, fusion-sealed containers and closure-sealed containers.

Unit-Dose Container—A unit-dose container is a single-unit container for articles intended for administration by other than the parenteral route as a single dose.

Multiple-Unit Container — A multiple-unit container is a container that permits withdrawal of successive portions of the contents without changing the strength, quantity, or purity of the remaining portion.

Mutiple-Dose Container — A multiple-dose container is a multiple-unit container for articles intended for parental administration only. Closures for multiple-dose containers permit the withdrawal of the contents without removal or destruction of the closure. The closure permits penetration by a needle and, upon withdrawal of the needle, closes at once, protecting the container against contamination. Validation of the multiple-dose container integrity must include verfication that such a package prevents microbial contamination or loss of product contents under anticipated conditions of multiple entry and use.

penetration [peni'treiʃən] n. 穿透，穿入

validation [væli'deiʃən] n. 确认，验证

integrity [in'tegriti] n. 完整，完全

Expressions and Technical Terms
opaque covering 不透明的遮盖物（a partially *opaque covering* 半透明的遮盖物）
tamper with 影响，损害
lot number 批号
expiration date 到期日期
prefilled syringes 预充注射器
fusion-sealed containers 熔封容器
closure-sealed containers 塞封容器
light-resistant container 避光容器
well-closed container 密封容器
tight container 紧密容器
hermetric container 气密容器
single-unit container 单元容器
single-dose container 单剂量注射剂容器
unit-dose container 单剂量容器（用于除注射剂以外的其他剂型）
multiple-unit container 多单元容器
mutiple-dose container 多剂量容器

Notes

[1] special background 工业药剂学（industrial pharmacy）是一门研究药物制成稳定制剂的规律和生产设计的一门应用技术学科。该学科的目标是使药物通过剂型的大量生产，向病员提供疗效理想、副作用和毒性小、无危害性、成本低廉和服用方便的药剂。任何一种药物都不可能以原药粉的形式给病人使用，必须制成最佳的给药形式，如片剂、胶囊剂、注射剂、栓剂、软膏剂、气雾剂、膜剂等。

[2] Compressed tablets are prepared by the application of high pressures, utilizing steel punches and dies, to powders or granulations. 压制片是通过利用高压并使用铁制的冲床和模具将原料制成粉末或颗粒的方式来制备的。现在分词 utilizing 表示伴随状语。

[3] Soluble, effervescent tablets are prepared by compression and contain, in addition to active ingredients, mixtures of acids(citric acid, tartaric acid) and sodium bicarbonate, which release carbon dioxide when dissolved in water. 溶液片、泡腾片是通过压制方式制备的。除了活性成分外，溶液片和泡腾片中还含有混合酸（如柠檬酸、酒石酸）和碳酸氢钠的混合物，当其溶解在水中时，会释放出 CO_2。其中，which 引导的非限制性定语从句修饰 mixtures of acids and sodium bicarbonate。

[4] Glidants are agents that improve powder fluidity, and they are commonly employed in direct compression where no granulation step is involved. 助流剂可以提高粉末的流动性，它们经常被用于直接压制中，直接压制不用进行粒化。and 作为连词连接前后两个句子，前面一外句子中，that 引导了定语从句修饰 agents；后面一个句子，where 引导的定语从句修饰 direct compression。

[5] Most colorants are photosensitive and they fade when exposed to light. 大多数着色剂具有感光性，当被暴露在光线下，颜色会褪去。When 引导的时间状语从句省略了主语 they are。

[6] The two main types of capsules are hard-shell capsules, which are normally used for dry, powdered ingredients, and soft-shell capsules, primarily used for oils and for active ingredients that are dissolved or suspended in oil. 其中，The two main types of capsules are hard-shell capsules and soft-shell capsules 为主句，which 引导的定语从句，修饰 hard-shell capsules；过去分词 used for 修饰的是 soft-shell capsules，接着，that 引导的定语从句又修饰 active ingredients。

[7] Since gelatin is of animal origin and starch is of vegetable origin, capsules made with these materials should be protected from potential sources of microbial contamination. 由于凝胶来源于动物，淀粉来源于植物，用这些材料制得的胶囊必须防止潜在的微生物污染。since 作为连词表示原因，protect…from 表示保护…防止。

[8] Machines employing various dosing principles may be employed to fill powders into hard-shell capsules.这里现在分词 employing 作定语，修饰 machines。

[9] Parenteral articles are preparations intended for injection through the skin or other external boundary tissue, rather than through the alimentary canal, so that the active substances they contain are administered, using gravity or force, directly into a blood vessel, organ, tissue, or lesion. 注射用药品是通过皮肤或其他外周组织进行注射的制剂，而不是通过消化道给药，注射剂中的有效成分可通过重力或外力直接进入血管、组织或伤口。这是 so that 引导的结果状语从句，过去分词 intended 作 preparation 的定语，through, rather than through 引导方式状语，表示通过这种方式，而不是通过另外一种方式；从句中现在分词 using 表示伴随状语。

[10] Parenteral articles are prepared scrupulously by methods designed to ensure that they meet pharmacopeial requirements for sterility, pyrogens, particulate matter, other contaminants. 制备注射剂

的方法应能保证其符合无菌、无热原、无不溶性微粒和其他污染物的药典要求。过去分词 designed to 作 methods 的定语，ensure that 后面加宾语从句。

[11] Suitable substances may be added to preparations intended for injection to increase stability and usefulness, provided they are harmless in the amounts administered and do not interfere with the therapeutic efficacy or with the responses to the specified assays and tests. 为提高稳定性和方便使用，注射用制剂中可加入适当的物质，这些物质应在该药量下无害，不影响疗效，不干扰规定的含量测定和检查。其中，provided 不是过去分词，而是连词，表示"假如，只要"。

[12] The container does not interact physically or chemically with the article placed in it so as to alter the strength, quality, or purity of the article beyond the official requirements. 容器不应与放置在其中的药品发生物理和化学相互作用以致引起药品含量、质量和纯度超出药典规定。过去分词 placed 作 article 的定语，so as to 引导目的状语。

[13] The pharmacopeial requirements for the use of specified containers apply also to articles as packaged by the pharmacist or other dispenser, unless otherwise indicated in the individual monograph. 药典规定使用指定的容器也适用于药剂师或其他配药员包装的药品，除各品种正文另有规定外。unless otherwise indicated 表示"除非另作规定"。

[14] A light-resistant container protects the contents from the effects of light by the specific properties of the material of which it is composed, including any coating applied to it. 由于容器所用材料的特殊性质以及容器的外部涂层，避光容器可以保护内容物不受光线影响。过去分词 applied 修饰 coating，which 引导的定语从句修饰 material。

Exercises

1. Put the following into Chinese

A tablet is a mixture of active substances and excipients, usually in powder form, pressed or compacted into a solid. The excipients include binders, glidants and lubricants to ensure efficient tabletting; disintegrants to ensure that the tablet breaks up in the digestive tract; sweeteners or flavours to mask the taste of bad-tasting active ingredients; and pigments to make uncoated tablets visually attractive. A coating may be applied to hide the taste of the tablet's components, to make the tablet smoother and easier to swallow, and to make it more resistant to the environment, extending its shelf life.

2. Put English sentences into Chinese

(1) The type of glass preferable for each parenteral preparation is usually stated in the individual monograph.

(2) A container for a sterile solid permits the addition of a suitable solvent and withdrawal of portions of the resulting solution or suspension in such manner that the sterility of the product is maintained.

(3) In addition, the solutes and the vehicle must maintain their specified total and relative quantities or concentrations when exposed to anticipated extreme conditions of manufacturing and processing, and storage, shipment, and distribution.

3. Cloze

Wet granulation is a process of ___(1)___ a liquid binder or adhesive to the powder mixture. The amount of liquid must be properly managed, and over wetting will cause the granules to be too hard and

（2）　wetting will cause them to be too soft and friable. Aqueous solutions have the advantage of being 　（3）　 to deal with than solvents.

Procedure of Wet Granulation

Step 1: Weighing and Blending—the active ingredient, filler, disintegrating agents, are weighed and mixed.

Step 2: The wet granulate is prepared by adding the liquid binder. Examples of binders include aqueous preparations of cornstarch, natural gums such as acacia, cellulose derivatives such as methyl cellulose, CMC, gelatin, and povidone. Ingredients are placed within a granulator which helps ensure correct density of the composition.

Step 3: Screening the damp mass into pellets or granules

Step 4: Drying the granulation

Step 5: Dry screening: After the granules are dried, pass through a screen of smaller size than the one used for the wet mass to select granules of uniform size.

Step 6: Lubrication- A dry lubricant, antiadherent and glidant are added to the granules either by dusting over the spread-out granules 　（4）　 by blending with the granules. It reduces friction between the tablet and the walls of the die cavity. Antiadherent reduces sticking of the tablet to the die and punch.

Step7: Add disintegrants-Disintegrants expand and dissolve when it is 　（5）　 contact with water, causing the tablet to break apart in the digestive tract and releasing the active ingredients for absorption. Examples of disintegrants include: crosslinked polyvinyl pyrrolidone, sodium starch glycolate, crosslinked sodium carboxymethyl cellulose.

Step 8: Tablet pressing—In the tablet-pressing process, it is important that all ingredients be dry, powdered or granular, uniform in particle size, and 　（6）　 flowing. In this step, tablets presses are used, which range from small, inexpensive bench-top models that make one tablet at a time, 　（7）　 more than a few thousand an hour, and with only around a half-ton pressure, 　（8）　 large, computerized, industrial models that can make hundreds of to millions of tablets an hour with much greater pressure.

Step 9: Tablet 　（9）　. This is the last stage in tablet formulation and it is done to protect the tablet 　（10）　 temperature and humidity constraints. It is also done to mask the taste, give it special characteristics, and prevent inadvertent contact with the drug substance. The most common forms of tablet coating are sugar coating and film coating.

（1）A. used 　　B. using 　　C. use 　　D. uses 　　（　　）
（2）A. beneath 　　B. from 　　C. under 　　D. down 　　（　　）
（3）A. safer 　　B. safe 　　C. dangerous 　　D. safest 　　（　　）
（4）A. 不填 　　B. or 　　C. and 　　D. than 　　（　　）
（5）A. on 　　B. to 　　C. in 　　D. by 　　（　　）
（6）A. clear 　　B. clearly 　　C. freely 　　D. free 　　（　　）
（7）A. not 　　B. no 　　C. on 　　D. for 　　（　　）
（8）A. to 　　B. for 　　C. on 　　D. by 　　（　　）
（9）A. coated 　　B. coat 　　C. coating 　　D. stain 　　（　　）
（10）A. from 　　B. by 　　C. on 　　D. in 　　（　　）

4. Put the following into English

口含片 　　　　崩解剂 　　　　泡腾片 　　二氧化碳 　　　　硬胶囊剂

| 喷射模塑法 | 灌装机 | 润湿剂 | 避光剂 | 外周组织 |
| 注射乳剂 | 氯化钠注射液 | 熔封容器 | 半透明的遮盖物 | 预充注射器 |

参考译文

16.1　片剂

1.　简介

片剂是一种固体剂型，含有药物成分，并加入了适当的稀释剂。根据加工方法，片剂被分成两类：压制片或模制片。

大部分片剂是通过压制的方式来制备的，压制片是当今使用最广泛的剂型。压制片是通过利用高压并使用铁制的冲床和模具将原料制成粉末或颗粒的方式来制备的。根据冲床和模具的设计形状，可以制备成各种大小、形状和表面斑纹不同的片剂。胶囊形状的片剂通常指囊片。丸剂是大的片剂用作兽药，通常用于大型动物。

模制片的制备是在低压下将潮湿粉末挤入模槽。在接下来的干燥过程中，湿粉固化取决于晶体桥的逐渐形成，而不是取决于挤压力。

口含片要求放入颊囊，舌下片要求放入舌下，活性成分通过口腔黏膜被直接吸收。大多数药物都很难以这种方式被吸收，但是对于那些如硝酸甘油和某些类固醇激素，能以这种方式被吸收。

溶液片、泡腾片是通过压制方式制备的。除了活性成分外，溶液片和泡腾片中还含有混合酸（如柠檬酸、酒石酸）和碳酸氢钠的混合物，当其溶解在水中时，会释放出 CO_2。在服用溶液片、泡腾片以前，要求先将它们溶解于或分散于水中。泡腾片必须贮藏在紧闭容器或防潮包装中，并且要在标签上注明不能直接被吞服。

2.　压制片的配方

大多数压制片由活性成分、稀释剂、黏合剂、崩解剂和润滑剂组成。其中也含有色素、芳香剂和甜味剂成分。当活性成分的量较少或难以压缩时，就必须加入稀释剂。常用的片剂填充剂有乳糖、淀粉、磷酸氢钙和微晶纤维素。

在初级粒化过程中，黏合剂使粉末具有黏性。当黏合剂在干燥的情况下被加入，黏合效果更好。常用的黏合剂有阿拉伯树胶、凝胶、蔗糖、聚维酮、甲基纤维素、羧甲基纤维素和水解淀粉糊。

崩解剂的作用是在片剂服用后有助于将其裂碎成细小颗粒。使用最广泛的片剂崩解剂是淀粉。泡腾混合物作为崩解剂被用于可溶性的片剂体系中。崩解剂的浓度，添加方法和压实度对崩解效果影响很大。

在压制过程中，润滑剂可以降低摩擦。除此之外，润滑剂有助于防止片剂成分黏结在模子和冲床上。硬脂酸盐、硬脂酸、氢化植物油和滑石粉都被用作润滑剂。大多数润滑剂是疏水性的，并且可以降低片剂的崩解速度和溶解速度。因此，应避免润滑剂的浓度过量。

助流剂可以提高粉末的流动性，它们经常被用于直接压制中，直接压制不用进行粒化。最有效的助流剂为热解硅酸盐胶体。

为了产品的美观，着色剂经常被添加到片剂中。大多数着色剂具有感光性，当被暴露在光线下，颜色会褪去。

16.2　胶囊剂

胶囊是一种固体剂型，其将药物填装于硬质或软质的胶囊壳中。胶囊壳通常是由凝胶制成的；然而，胶囊壳同样也能由淀粉或其他适当的物质制成。胶囊的两种主要类型为硬胶囊剂和软胶囊剂，硬胶囊剂通常适用于干燥的粉末状成分，而软胶囊剂主要适于油状物及能够溶解或悬浮于油状物中的活性成分。

临时开处方时，硬胶囊剂可以通过手工方式来灌制；这就允许开方者有多种选择，根据病人的情况，或者选择准确剂量的单种药物，或者选择准确剂量的多种药物的混合物。这种灵活性就使硬胶囊剂比压制片剂更有优势。

硬质凝胶胶囊的制备程序如下：首先将蘸胶针加入凝胶溶液中（即蘸胶），然后将凝胶薄膜进行干燥，切割，拔壳，并将囊体和囊帽拼接起来。淀粉胶囊通过将淀粉与水的混合物进行注模而制得，然后将胶囊干燥。空胶囊在被填装之前必须贮藏在紧闭的容器中。由于凝胶来源于动物，淀粉来源于植物，用这些材料制得的胶囊必须防止潜在的微生物污染。

在硬质凝胶胶囊的灌装操作中，在配料之前，先将胶囊壳的囊体和囊帽分开。在硬质淀粉胶囊灌装操作中，囊体和囊帽应分开制备，然后分别放入灌装机的不同的进料斗中。采用不同定量规则的灌装机可以将粉末填入硬质胶囊壳中；然而，全自动的灌装机将粉末压制成栓型，并将它们喷射入空的胶囊壳体中。粉末的配方经常需要在活性成分中添加填充剂、润滑剂和助流剂来促进胶囊化。配方以及灌装方法，尤其是压实度可能会影响药物的释放速度。若活性剂是疏水的，在粉末中加入润湿剂是很常见的。粉末配方中也可以含有崩解剂，可以促进胶囊在肠道内的分解和扩散。

由凝胶或其他合适材料制得的软胶囊需要大规模的生产方式。软质凝胶胶囊壳比硬胶囊壳稍微厚一些，并能够通过加入多元醇如山梨醇或甘油来塑化。干的增塑剂与干凝胶的比例决定了胶囊壳的"硬度"，并且可以为适应环境条件和内容物性质而不同。像硬质胶囊壳，壳的组成可以包括许可的染料和色素，避光剂如二氧化钛，以及防腐剂。软胶囊壳中可以加入芳香剂，可添加多于5%的蔗糖作为甜味剂，并赋予胶囊壳可嚼性。软质凝胶胶囊壳通常含有6%~13%的水分。软胶囊壳内填充了液体物质，活性成分溶解或悬浮于液体赋型剂中。常用的油质赋型剂如植物油；然而，由于生物药效率问题，非水性的、混水的液体赋型剂如较低分子量的聚乙二醇现在更加常用。

软胶囊壳的成型、填充和密封过程都是在同一机器上加工完成的，通过这种方式，可以制成各种大小、形状不同的软胶囊。这是旋转式模压法，而有时也可以使用钢板式模压法或往复式模压法。软胶囊也可以用鼓泡式模压法来生产，通过这种方法可以制得无缝球形胶囊。通过适当的设备，粉末和其他干燥固体也可以填充入软胶囊。

16.3　注射剂

1. 简介

注射用药品是通过皮肤或其他外周组织进行注射的制剂，而不是通过消化道给药，注射剂中的有效成分可通过重力或外力直接进入血管、组织或伤口。制备注射剂的方法应能保证其符合无菌、无热原、无不溶性微粒和其他污染物的药典要求。必要时，注射剂中含有微生物生长抑制剂。注射剂是一种注射给药的制剂，或是在给药前配制或稀释成注射用药品的制剂。

2. 分类

下列术语适用于 5 种注射给药的一般剂型。这些制剂可能含有缓冲剂、防腐剂或其他添加剂。

① [药物]注射液——药物或其溶液的液体制剂。

② 注射用[药物]——干固体,加适宜溶剂制成的溶液符合注射剂项下全部规定。

③ [药物]注射乳剂——药物溶解或分散于乳胶介质中的液体制剂。

④ [药物]注射混悬剂——固体混悬在适宜液体介质中的液体制剂。

⑤ 注射混悬剂用[药物]——干固体,加适宜介质而成的制剂符合注射混悬剂项下全部规定。

3. 成分——溶剂和添加剂

水溶性溶剂——水溶性注射剂用的这类溶剂,应按规定符合热原检查和细菌内毒素检查,除各品种正文另有规定外。一般用注射用水作为溶剂,除各品种正文另有规定外。可加一定量氯化钠调节等渗;或部分或全部用氯化钠注射液或林格氏注射剂代替注射用水。

其他溶剂——用于非水注射剂溶剂的脂肪油,是植物来源,无臭或几乎无臭,不得有腐臭。应符合矿物油项下固体石蜡检查项的要求。冷却温度维持在 10℃,皂化值为 185~200,碘值为 79~141,并符合下列检查要求。

添加剂——为提高稳定性和方便使用,注射用制剂中可加入适当的物质,这些物质应在该药量下无害,不影响疗效,不干扰规定的含量测定和检查。肠道外给药的溶液中不得添加仅为对最终制剂着色的着色剂。

对用药量超过 5ml 的注射制剂,应特别注意添加剂的选择和使用。除另有规定外,按下列最高限度:含汞和阳离子表面活性剂的添加剂为 0.01%;氯丁醇、甲酚、苯酚及类似物为 0.5%、二氧化硫,或相当量的亚硫酸盐、亚硫酸氢盐和偏亚硫酸氢盐(钾或钠盐)为 0.2%。

多剂量容器包装的注射用制剂必须添加防止微生物生长的适宜物质,不论其灭菌方法,但不包括下列情况之一:①各品种正文另有规定;②添加物含有物理半衰期少于 24h 的放射性核素;③有效成分本身为抗菌药。这类添加剂的使用浓度应能防止注射用制剂中微生物的生长或杀灭注射用制剂中的微生物。

16.4 包装

用于包装的容器能够将物品包裹住并且与药品直接接触。在被填装之前,容器必须清洗干净。为了保证每个容器是干净的,药品内部与表面没有杂质,特殊的清洁程序是必要的。容器不应与放置在其中的药品发生物理和化学相互作用以致引起药品含量、质量和纯度超出药典规定。药典规定使用指定的容器也适用于药剂师或其他配药员包装的药品,除各品种正文另有规定外。

避光容器——由于容器所用材料的特殊性质以及容器的外部涂层,避光容器可以保护内容物不受光线影响。无色的或半透明的容器可以通过在外粘上一层不透明的遮盖物使其具有耐光性。在这种情况下,容器的标签上应该声明,直到药物被使用或服用后,方可揭去这层不透明的遮盖物。如果正文中指出要避光的,那么就必须将药品保存在避光容器中。

密封容器——密封容器能够保护内容物不受在正常操作、运输、销售和使用中引起的杂质的污染和药品的损失。

紧密容器——紧密容器能够保护内容物不受在正常操作、运输、销售和使用中引起的外界液体、固体或气体的污染,以及药品的损失、风化、潮解和挥发,并且能够旋紧封塞。如果指定需要紧密容器,那么也可以用气密容器来代替盛放单剂量的药品。

气密容器——密封容器是在正常操作、运输、销售和使用中不透空气和其他任何气体的容器。

单元容器——单元容器是设计用来贮存一定量作为单剂量服用的药物产品，或容器打开后可以立即使用的单个成品。直接包装和外面包装或保护性包装最好设计成能够显示出损害包装物的标记。每个单元容器必须有标示标明药品的特性、质量和含量、品名、批号和保质期。

单剂量注射剂容器——单剂量容器是专门用于注射用制剂的一种单元容器。单剂量容器包括预充注射器、熔封容器和塞封容器。

单剂量容器（用于除注射剂以外的其他剂型）——单剂量容器是一种单元容器，用于单剂量除了注射途径以外的其他服用途径。

多单元容器——多单元容器在连续抽取内容物时不用改变剩余药品的含量、质量和纯度。

多剂量容器——多剂量容器是专门用于注射用制剂的一种多单元容器。多剂量容器的封塞抽取内容物时不应取下或破坏。封塞应便于针头穿刺，针头抽出后，立即关闭，防止容器被污染。多剂量容器的完好性验证应包括在多次使用的预期条件下确认该包装能防止微生物污染或内容物的流失。

Reading material

Direction of Prednisone

DRUG NAME: Prednisone

DESCRIPTION:

Deltasone tablets contain prednisone which is a glucocorticoid. Glucocorticoids are adrenocortical steroids, both naturally occurring and synthetic, which are readily absorbed from the gastrointestinal tract. Prednisone is a white, odorless, crystalline powder. It is very slightly soluble in water; slightly soluble in alcohol, in chloroform, in dioxane, and in methanol.

The chemical name for prednisone is pregna-1,4-diene-3,11,20-trione-17,21- dihydroxy- and its molecular weight is 358.43.

PHARMACOLOGICAL   ACTIONS:

Naturally occurring glucocorticoids, which also have salt-retaining properties, are used as replacement therapy in adrenocortical deficiency states. Their synthetic analogs are primarily used for their potent anti-inflammatory effects in disorders of many organ systems.

Glucocorticoids cause profound and varied metabolic effects. In addition, they modify the body's immune responses to diverse stimuli.

INDICATIONS:

Acute severe bacterial infection;

Severe anaphylactic disease;

Lupus erythematosus;

Rheumatosis;

Rheumatoid Arthritis;

Nephrotic syndrome;

Severe Bronchial asthma;

Thrombocytopenic purpura;

Neutropenia;

Acute lymphoblastic leukemia;

Adrenocortical insufficiency;

Exfoliative dermatitis;

Pemphigus;

Dermatoneuritis;

Eczema

CONTRAINDICATIONS:

Systemic fungal infections and known hypersensitivity to components.

DOSAGE and ADMINISTRATION:

The initial dosage of prednisone tablets may vary from 5-60 mg of prednisone per day depending on the specific disease entity being treated. The initial dosage should be maintained or adjusted until a satisfactory response is noted. **It should be emphasized that dosage requirements are variable and must be individualized on the basis of the disease under treatment and the responseof the patient.**

ADVERSE REACTION:

Long-term use of prednisone will cause adrenogenital syndrome, neuropsychiatric symptoms, digestive ulcer, osteoporosis, growth inhibition and heavier infection.

PRECAUTIONS:

The interaction should be considered when taking drugs of lowering blood sugar, anti-hieronosus, thiazide emictory, salicylate, anticoagulant, cardiotonic and so on , and the dosage of Prednisone should be adjusted.

SPECIFICATION and PACKAGE:

Tablets:5mg/pill;

plastic bottle and 100 pills/bottle.

STORAGE:

Store at room temperature 20-25°C.

强的松片说明书

【药品名称】

强的松

【说明】

强的松片剂含有强的松成分，强的松是一种肾上腺皮质激素。肾上腺皮质激素是一种肾上腺皮质类固醇，有天然的和合成的两种，它很容易被胃肠道吸收。强的松是一种白色无味的结晶状粉末，在水中难溶，微溶于乙醇、氯仿、二氧乙烷和甲醇。

化学名：1, 4-二烯-3, 11, 20-三酮-17, 21-二羟基孕甾

分子量：358.43

【药理作用】

天然的肾上腺皮质激素，同时也具有钠潴留特性，可以用作肾上腺皮质缺陷症状的代替治疗药物。合成类似物由于具有潜在的抗炎功效，主要用于治疗许多脏器系统的异常病症。

肾上腺皮质激素可以对代谢产生较大且不同的影响。同时，它们可以改变机体对不同外界刺激的免疫反应。

【适应证】

主要用于各种急性严重细菌感染、严重过敏性疾病、红斑狼疮、风湿病、类风湿性关节炎、肾病综合征、严重支气管哮喘、血小板减少性紫癜、粒细胞减少症、急性淋巴性白血病、各种肾上腺皮质功能不全

症、剥脱性皮炎、天疱疮、神经性皮炎、湿疹等。

【禁忌证】

全身真菌感染者禁用，对本品及肾上腺皮质激素类药物有过敏史患者禁用。

【用量用法】

强的松片剂，根据所治疗的特定疾病，开始每日 5~60mg，病情稳定后，可维持或调整最初剂量。**必须强调**，强的松服用剂量应该以治疗的病症和病人的反应为基础，并且因人而异。

【不良反应】

长期服用引起柯兴综合征，诱发神经精神症状以及消化系统溃疡、骨质疏松、生长发育受抑制和加重感染。

【注意事项】

与降糖药、抗癫痫药、噻嗪类利尿药、水杨酸盐、抗凝血药、强心苷等合用须考虑相互作用，应适当调整剂量。

【规格与包装】

片剂：5mg/片；塑料瓶装，每瓶 100 片。

【贮藏】

室温保存（20~25℃）。

Chapter 17　Medicine analysis

Today, modern **pharmaceutical** analysis entails much more than the analysis of active pharmaceutical **ingredients** or the formulated product. There are many reasons for this change, not the least of which is our ability to better understand **physicochemical** properties of pharmaceutical compounds through the use of advanced **instrumental** methods. Furthermore, there is a need for quality assurance of pharmaceutical products throughout their shelf life. This requires that we study interactions of the drug substance with the **excipients** in the presence of residual solvents, as well as other potential **degradation reactions** that may occur in the formulated product over a period of time under various **stress conditions** (these include conditions they may be subjected to during storage or shipment in the final package configuration).

The pharmaceutical industry is under increased scrutiny from the government and public interest groups to contain costs and yet consistently deliver to market safe, efficacious products that fulfill unmet medical needs. As part of the crusade to **hold the line** on **prescription drug** prices, the industry has **streamlined** its operations with respect to drug discovery, development, and manufacturing. The drive to bring innovative products to market faster without negatively impacting quality or safety has caused every company to challenge all existing processes and to look for ways to increase capacity, shorten time lines, and "do more with less".

Analytical chemistry has played a major role in the changes facing the pharmaceutical industry today. Traditionally viewed as a service organization, the analytical department has become a significant partner in the drug development process. Indeed, the demand for analytical data has become a critical path activity for the selection of **candidate** molecules for full development. Working under sample-limited conditions and in full

Remarks Column
pharmaceutical[ˌfɑːməˈsjuːtikəl]*n.* 药物；*adj.* 制药(学)上的
ingredient[inˈgriːdiənt]*n.* 成分，因素
physicochemical[ˌfizikəuˈkemikəl]*adj.* 物理化学的
instrumental[ˌinstruˈmentl]*adj.* 仪器的，器械的，乐器的
excipient[ikˈsipiənt]*n.* 赋型剂
streamlined[ˈstriːmlaind]*adj.* 最新型的，改进的
candidate[ˈkændidit]*n.* 候选人，投考者

compliance of current good manufacturing practices (cGMP), pharmaceutical analysts are called on to generate accurate and **precise** data-almost on demand. The science and technology utilized today, **coupled with** the new regulations that are now binding, have made pharmaceutical analysis much more complicated compared to what it was as little as ten years ago.

The pharmaceutical analyst plays a major role in assuring identity, safety, efficacy, **purity**, and quality of a drug product. Safety and efficacy studies require that drug substance and drug product meet the established identity and purity as **bioavailability/dissolution** requirements. The need for pharmaceutical analysis is driven largely by regulatory requirements. This stems from the fact that regulatory considerations **loom large** when a commercial product does not meet its purported quality. The International Conference on Harmonization (ICH) that has attempted to **harmonize** the requirements by regulatory authorities in the United States, Europe, and Japan.

precise[pri'sais]*adj*.精确的，准确的；*n*.精确

purity['pjuəriti]*n*.纯净，纯洁，纯度

bioavailability[,baiəuə,veilə'biliti]*n*.（药物或营养素的）生物药效率，生物利用度
dissolution[disə'lju:ʃən]*n*.分解，解散

harmonize['hɑːmənaiz]*v*.协调

Expressions and Technical Terms

degradation reactions　分解反应
stress conditions　应力状态
hold the line　保持不变
prescription drug　处方药
Analytical chemistry　分析化学
coupled with　加上，外加
loom large　显得突出

Notes

[1] special background　药物分析（习惯上称为药品检验）是运用化学的、物理学的、生物学的以及微生物学的方法和技术来研究化学结构已经明确的合成药物或天然药物及其制剂质量的一门学科。它包括药物成品的化学检验，药物生产过程的质量控制，药物贮存过程的质量考察，临床药物分析，体内药物分析等。

药物分析是分析化学中的一个重要分支，它随着药物化学的发展逐渐成为分析化学中相对独立的一门学科，在药物的质量控制、新药研究、药物代谢、手性药物分析等方面均有广泛应用。随着生命科学、环境科学、新材料科学的发展，生物学、信息科学、计算机技术的引入，分析化学迅猛发展并已经进入分析科学这一崭新的领域，药物分析也正发挥着越来越重要的作用，在科研、生产和生活中无处不在，尤其在新药研发以及药品生产等方面扮演着重要的角色。

[2] This requires that we study interactions of the drug substance with the excipients in the presence of residual solvents, as well as other potential degradation reactions that may occur in the formulated product over a period of time under various stress conditions. 我们需要研究在残留溶剂中药物物质与赋型剂的相互作用，同样也需要研究药品在各种应力条件下（包括药品在储存或装

船时的特殊包装结构）一段时间后，所可能发生的其他潜在的降解反应。这里"excipients"是"赋型剂"的意思，指构成药物或抗原的辅料的无活性物质（如阿拉伯胶、糖浆、羊毛脂或淀粉）；尤指在药物混合物中有足够量液体的情况下，为使混合物有黏性，以便制备丸剂或片剂而加入的物质。

Exercises

1. Put the following into Chinese

Methods used in pharmaceutical analysis must be sufficiently accurate, specific, sensitive and precise to conform to the regulatory requirements as set out in the relevant guidelines of "The International Conference of Technical Requirements for the Registration of Pharmaceutical for Human Use" (ICH),which are applied by the licensing authorities and by some pharmacopoeias.

2. Put the following into English

处方药　成分　器械的　赋型剂　精确的　纯度

3. Writing

Write summary of this text (no more than 120 words).

参考译文

药 物 分 析

当今，现代药物分析不只是药物活性成分分析和产品分析。这种变化的原因是多方面的，至少包括我们能更好地通过使用先进的仪器的方法，来了解药品成分的理化特性。此外，需要有技术能保证药品在保质期内药物化学成分的质量。

我们需要研究在残留溶剂中药物物质与赋型剂的相互作用，同样也需要研究药品在各种应力条件下（包括药品在储存或装船时的特殊包装结构）一段时间后，所可能发生的其他潜在的降解反应。

政府和公众权益机构对制药行业的审查越来越严，包括药物的价格和药品的安全性，保证有效的产品以满足医疗的需要。作为改革一直保持不变的处方药价格的一部分，医药产业已经开始精简药物发现、开发和生产的过程。这种改革使新产品进入市场的速度加快，并且没有质量和安全方面的负面影响，这使得每一个公司都要改变现有的生产工艺，并寻找新的方法提高产能、缩短时间，做到"少花钱，多办事"。

分析化学在当今医药工业的变革中起着非常重要的作用。传统的观点认为分析化学只是一个服务机构，在当今的药物开发过程中分析部门已成为一个重要的合作伙伴。事实上，对分析数据的需求已经成为挑选候选分子进行充分开发的一个关键途径。在有限的样本和充分遵守目前的《生产质量管理规范》（cGMP）的条件下，要求医药分析者提供正确和精确的数据。现代科学技术的应用，再加上现在正在实施的新的条例，都使药物分析变得比10年前更加复杂。

药物分析师在保证药物的成分、安全性、有效性、纯度和质量方面起着非常重要的作用。安全性和有效性的研究需要原料药和制剂产品满足已制定的成分和纯度，如对生物利用度/溶出度的要求。对药物分析的需求在很大程度上是法律法规的要求。这种监管往往在商业产品不符合其声称的质量时显得尤为突出。一些国际会议已在尝试协调将美国、欧洲和日本的检测标准统一。

Natural Products/Traditional Herbal Medicine Analysis

For traditional herbal medicines (THM), also known as natural products or traditional Chinese medicines (TCM), analytical laboratories need to expand their understanding of their **pharmacology** to provide evidence-based validation of their **effectiveness** as medicines and to establish safety **parameters** for their production. The challenges in analyzing THM or TCM samples arise from the complexity of the matrix as well as variability from sample to sample.

Conventional Western pharmaceutical industry-standard techniques such as purification and qualitative and quantitative chromatography and mass spectrometry are being applied to determine active drug candidates and to characterize the efficacy of their candidate **remedies**.

Waters provides high-quality separations and detection capabilities to identify active compounds in highly complex samples that results from natural products and THMs. Our workflow-based approach to THM analysis, when combined with user-friendly software, enables you to perform fast sample analysis while obtaining maximum information.

Metabonomics-based analysis, using UPLC, exact mass MS, and MarkerLynx Software data processing for multivariate statistical analysis, can help quickly and accurately characterize these medicines and also their effect on human **metabolism**.

Preparative-scale fractionation and purification is used along with classic quantitative bioanalytical tools used in drug development.

New Words

pharmacology[ˌfɑːməˈkɒlədʒi]　*n.*药理学

effectiveness [iˈfektivnis]　*n.*效力

parameters [ˌpærəˈmetrik]　*adj.*参（变）数的，参（变）量的

remediless[ˈremidilis]　*adj.*不可救药的

metabolism[meˈtæbəlizəm]　*n.*新陈代谢，变形

Expressions and Technical Terms

traditional herbal medicines　传统草药

traditional Chinese medicines　传统中医

mass spectrometry　质谱学

user-friendly　用户界面友好的，用户容易掌握使用的

multivariate statistical analysis　多元统计分析

Chapter18　Modernization of traditional Chinese medicine

Modernization of TCM basic theory means combining it with modern science and modern medicine. Its aim is using scientific experiments to study TCM and to make a canonical, quantitative, and correct description for the concept and theory of TCM. **Multidisciplinary** cooperation becomes necessary to **elucidate** the physical foundation, action mechanism, and **prescription compatibility** of TCM **pharmacodynamic** action. At the same time, we should highly value the research and innovation of the basic theory of TCM, especially the research theory related to the development of the modernization of TCM, for example, the theory of syndromes, formulation, nature of a drug, etc., to determine their scientific meanings.

In the new era of "modernization" of TCM over the past decade, advanced chemical, **pharmacological** and biological technologies have **facilitated** an increasing number of researchers in the search for possible ways to explore the potential healthcare benefits of is "mysterious" **millennia-old** healing system. Research institutes and drug companies have been actively exploring Chinese material medica (CMM) as a source for new drug discovery and development. Furthermore, due to an increasing interest among people outside of China in Chinese materia medica as an **alternative therapeutic modality**, many scientific studies have been conducted on its various aspects, including **taxonomy, authentication,** isolation and elucidation of chemical constituents, **pharmacology, toxicology,** bioactivity screening, and others. Although different branches of science and their techniques have been involved, much of the approach and research methodology is basically modeled after those for modern conventional drugs and Western **phytomedicines** which are rooted in chemistry and molecular biology in a **reductionism** manner. Hence when conducting research on Chinese herbs, most investigators tend to treat them as if they were single-entity chemical drugs with little concern of the documented traditional explanations and ignoring the **seemingly** inaccessible ancient Chinese theories.

Remarks Column
modernization *n.* 现代化
canonical *adj.* 规范的 权威的 权威性的
multidisciplinary *adj.*包括各种学科的, 有关各种学问的
elucidate *vt.*阐明，说明
prescription compatibility 方剂配伍
pharmacodynamic *adj.*药效的
syndromes *adj.*综合病征的；症候群的
pharmacological 药理学
facilitate *vt.*使容易，使…不费力；帮助，促进
millennia-old *adj.*千年的
alternative therapeutic modality 替代治疗方式
taxonomy *n.*分类学
authentication *n.*证明，鉴定
toxicology *n.* 毒理学
phytomedicines *n.*植物药物
reductionism *n.*简化法
seemingly *adj.*表面上；好像

Since last century, enormous numbers of "single components" have been isolated and chemical structures and pharmacological activities have been studied and thousands of research papers have been published elsewhere. But the success stories unfortunately have been few and far between. One exception is of **artemisinin** isolated from ***Artemisia annua*** **L.** ("Qing Hao" in Chinese; Family: Compositae) that was used to treat fever according to ancient Chinese herbal **compendia**, it is the currently the most effective treatment for **malaria**. On the other hand, many researchers and drug industries in China intend to develop modernized TCM **proprietary** products based on the concept of **holistic** feature of TCM. But many are still **perplexed** on how to connect the high tech and analytical **precision** to tradition and practical application, because the fundamental **tenets** held dear by both modern medicine and TCM have not yet been equally addressed. CMM research results so far have not been deemed acceptable by both the TCM and the scientific communities. This is probably the major reason why CMM has not been universally accepted as a **legitimate** healthcare modality in the modern world. In order to bridge the communication gap, those involved in any research aspects of CMM, including modernization and development of quality control methods, should have a clear understanding of the fundamental differences between CMM and modern chemical drugs so that the results will be **relevant** to both fields.

artemisinin *n.*青蒿素
Artemisia annua L.黄花蒿
compositae *n.* 菊科
malaria *n.*疟疾

proprietary *adj.* 专利的，独家制造的
holistic *adj.*整体的，全盘的
perplexed *adj.*困[迷]惑的，茫然不知所措的
tenets *n.*宗旨

legitimate *adj.*合法的，合理的

relevant *adj.* 有重大意义[作用]的；实质性的

Notes

[1] special background 中药是在西方医学传入我国以后，人们对我国传统医药学的称呼，是与西医相对而言的。中药按加工工艺分为中成药、中药材。中药主要起源于中国，除了植物药以外，动物药如蛇胆、熊胆、五步蛇、鹿茸、鹿角等；介壳类如珍珠、海蛤壳；矿物类如龙骨、磁石等都是用来治病的中药。少数中药源于外国，如西洋参。目前，随着对中药资源的开发和研究，许多民间药物也归入中药的范畴。所以，中药是以中医理论为基础，用于防治疾病的植物、动物、矿物及其加工品，不论产于中国、外国均称中药。中药有着独特的理论体系和应用形式，充分反映了我国自然资源及历史、文化等方面的特点。

[2] Its aim is using scientific experiments to study TCM and to make a canonical, quantitative, and correct description for the concept and theory of TCM. 其目的是以科学试验来研究中医并且用规范化、量化，和准确的语言来描述中医的概念和理论。

[3] Research institutes and drug companies have been actively exploring Chinese material medica (CMM) as a source for new drug discovery and development. 中药材中的活性成分，也一直是各大研究机构和制药企业新药发现与研究的重要来源。

[4] Hence when conducting research on Chinese herbs, most investigators tend to treat them as if

they were single-entity chemical drugs with little concern of the documented traditional explanations and ignoring the seemingly inaccessible ancient Chinese theories. 因此，当对中草药进行研究时，大多数的研究者往往像研究单体化合物一样来研究中药，而忽视了中国传统文献中的记载和详尽的解释，也同时忽略了看似难懂的中国古代理论。

[5] One exception is of artemisinin isolated from Artemisia annua L. ("Qing Hao" in Chinese; Family: Compositae) that was used to treat fever according to ancient Chinese herbal compendia, it is the currently the most effective treatment for malaria. 从青蒿中提取青蒿素是一个例外（中文名：青蒿，科：菊科）。青蒿在古代用来治疗发热，现在却是治疗疟疾最有效的方法。

[6] But many are still perplexed on how to connect the high tech and analytical precision to tradition and practical application, because the fundamental tenets held dear by both modern medicine and TCM have not yet been equally addressed. （中国的许多研究人员和药厂尝试发展以传统中医为背景的现代中医药产品）但仍然困惑于如何将现代高科技和精确分析融入到传统中医药中，因为现代医学和中医的基本理论都尚未被完全阐明。

Exercises

1. Put English sentences into Chinese

(1) Given the worldwide hegemony of biomedicine throughout most of this century, the global emergence of TCM is a monumental event.

(2) The future of Chinese medicine in the west will also depend largely on what answers can be provided about safety and efficacy.

(3) Technologies related closely to the realization of TCM modernization are analytical chemistry and molecular biology.

2. Put the following into English

中药学　　定量的　　方剂配伍　　新药研发　　分类学
鉴定　　分离与提取　　生物活性物质筛选　　专利

3. Writing

Write summary of this text (no more than 200 words).

参考译文

中医现代化的基础理论联合了现代科学和现代医学。其目的是以科学试验来研究中医并且用规范化、量化，和准确的语言来描述中医的概念和理论。而且必须用多学科联合的方法来阐明物质的组成、作用机理和中医药效学的方剂配伍等。同时我们也要高度重视中医基础理论的研究和创新，尤其是中医现代化的发展，譬如，科学的定义诊断以及中药的组成和性质等。

在过去十年中医药现代化过程中，随着化学技术、药理学和生物技术的发展，大批的科学家深入探讨中医药这个神秘的千年医疗体系潜在的治疗优势。中药材中的活性成分，也一直是各大研究机构和制药企业新药发现与研究的重要来源。此外，由于越来越多的外国人把中药作为一种替代疗法来使用，因此，大量的研究也渗透入中药学研究的各个方面，其中包括：中药的分类、鉴别和认证，中药的提取和分离，以及药理、毒理，生物活性筛选等其他方面。尽管我们可以使用大量的现代科学技术方法，但是许多方法仍是模仿现代西药的研究方法，而这些方法都来源于化学和分子生物学。因此，当对中草药进行研究时，大多数的研究者往往像研究单体化合物一样来研究中药，而忽视了中国传统文献中的记载和详尽的解释，也同时忽略了看似难懂的中国古代理论。

20 世纪以来，大量的单组分提取的研究不再被重视，人们发表了大量关于化学构成和药理活性的文章。但不幸的是成功的例子很少。从青蒿中提取青蒿素是一个例外（中文名：青蒿，科：菊科）。青蒿在古代用来治疗发热，现在却是治疗疟疾最有效的方法。另一方面，中国的许多研究人员和药厂尝试发展以传统中医为背景的现代中医药产品，但仍然困惑于如何将现代高科技和精确分析融入到传统中医药中，因为现代医学和中医的基本理论都尚未被完全阐明。中药的研究结果至今未被中医和科学界完全认可，这也是现代社会未普遍接受中药为正规医疗模式的原因。为加大中西医结合的力度，中医的研究包括现代化和质量控制必须与现代西医在原则上区分开来，以便结果可以同时运用到这两个领域。

Reading material

Unique features of CMM versus Western medicine

As a unique holistic healthcare system, TCM aims to restore and maintain the dynamic balance of a person, thus achieving a harmony between the person and nature. TCM does not focus solely on the disease defined by specific **pathological** changes, but instead concentrates on the overall functional state of the patient. Thus, while Western medicine focuses on a person's disease, TCM focuses on the diseased person. This means in addition to disease treatment, TCM takes care of a person's total well being more seriously. In Western medicine, drugs are developed to counteract or neutralize pathological targets or to eliminate **pathogenic** factors, whereas in TCM, the therapy is aimed at specific responses (e.g., patterns), which reflect changes at the multi-system and **multiorgan** levels of the human body. The goal is to restore balance to the multi-functional body, which is not too different from the Western concept of **homeostasis**, though the latter currently does not seem to play a role in modern drug therapy. This TCM approach to health and disease also distinguishes it from most of the traditional forms of herbal medicine systems with primarily transferred from person to person by oral means. Examples are the shamanic medicine of Amazonia and Africa as well as other indigenous medicines practiced in tropical Asia. Unlike modern **allopathic** medicine, the development of CMM started directly with humans by trial and error. The results were eventually documented in writing and their efficacy and toxicity vetted over time, starting at least 3000 years ago. In contrast, a modern drug may have undergone an extensive development and approval process (from animal studies through human clinical trials) before it is finally being used on humans, but its true potential (for better or worse) will not be known until it is actually used by humans over time. Examples of the results of modern drug development, based on sound science as known at the time, which has not produced favorable results as expected, are many, with **thalidomide** being probably the most notorious. But there are also unexpected pleasant surprises from certain drugs that, after decades of prolonged use, have proven to be useful in other human conditions than those for which they were originally designed. A notable example is the **analgesic**, **acetyl salicylic acid** (Aspirin TM), which is now being also used in the prevention of **cardiovascular** disease (coronary heart disease and **cerebrovascular** disease, including heart attack and stroke). None of these results (good or bad) could have been predicted during the drug development process as practiced in the Western world. They can only be discovered by actual human use over time, such aswith CMM. Compared to the three-millennia-plus recorded history for some of the CMM, none of the modern drugs have a human use history of more than even a couple of 100 years.

New Words

pathological　*adj.* 病理的，病态的

pathogenic　*adj.* 致病的，病原的，发病的

multiorgan 多引线

homeostasis 动态静止，动态平衡 *n.* （社会群体的）自我平衡，原状稳定

allopathic　*adj.* 对抗疗法的

thalidomide　*n.* 镇静剂，安眠药之一种

analgesic　*adj.* 止痛的，不痛的

　　　　　　n. [医]止痛剂

cardiovascular　*adj.* 心脏血管的

cerebrovascular　*adj.* [医]脑血管的

Chapter 19 Frontiers of pharmaceutical engineering

19.1 Interferon

Interferons (IFNs) are natural <u>proteins</u> produced by the cells of the <u>immune system</u> of most **vertebrates** in response to challenges by foreign agents such as <u>viruses</u>, **parasites** and <u>tumor</u> cells. Interferons belong to the large class of **glycoproteins** known as **cytokines**. Interferons are produced by a wide variety of cells in response to the presence of double-stranded <u>RNA</u>, a key indicator of viral infection. Interferons assist the immune response by inhibiting viral replication within host cells, activating natural killer cells and **macrophages**, increasing <u>antigen presentation</u> to lymphocytes, and inducing the resistance of host cells to viral infection.

1. Types of interferon

There are three major classes of interferons that have been described for humans according to the type of receptor through which they signal:

<u>Interferon type I</u>: All type I IFNs bind to a specific cell surface receptor complex known as the <u>IFN-α</u> receptor (<u>IFNAR</u>) that consists of <u>IFNAR1</u> and <u>IFNAR2</u> chains. The type I interferons present in humans are IFN-α, <u>IFN-β</u> and <u>IFN-ω</u>.

<u>Interferon type II</u>: Binds to <u>IFNGR</u>. In humans this is <u>IFN-γ</u>.

<u>Interferon type III</u>: Signal through a receptor complex consisting of IL10R2 (also called CRF2-4) and <u>IFNLR1</u> (also called CRF2-12)

2. Pharmaceutical uses

Just as their natural function, interferons have antiviral, antiseptic and antioncogenic properties when administered as drugs.

Interferon **therapy** is used (in combination with

Remarks Column

interferon[ˌintə(ː)ˈfiərɔn]*n.* 干扰素

vertebrate[ˈvəːtibrit]*n.* 脊椎动物

parasitic[ˌpærəˈsitik]*adj.*寄生的

glycoprotein[ˌglaikəuˈprəutiːn]

n. 糖蛋白类，糖蛋白

cytokine[ˈsaitəuˌkain] *n.* 细胞因子

macrophage[ˈmækrəfeidʒ]*n.* 巨噬细胞

therapy[ˈθerəpi]*n.* 治疗

chemotherapy and radiation) as a treatment for many cancers.

More than half of **hepatitis** C patients treated with interferon respond with viral elimination (sustained virological response), better blood tests and better liver **histology** (detected on biopsy). There is some evidence that giving interferon immediately following infection can prevent chronic hepatitis C. However, people infected by HCV often do not display **symptoms** of HCV infection until months or years later making early treatment difficult.

Interferons (interferon beta-1a and interferon beta-1b) are also used in the treatment and control of multiple **sclerosis**, an autoimmune disorder.

Administered intranasally in very low doses, interferon is extensively used in Eastern Europe and Russia as a method to prevent and treat viral respiratory diseases such as cold and flu. However, mechanisms of such action of interferon are not well understood; it is thought that doses must be larger by several orders of magnitude to have any effect on the virus. Consequently, most Western scientists are skeptical of any claims of good efficacy.

3．Adverse effects

The most frequent adverse effects are flu-like symptoms: increased body temperature, feeling ill, fatigue, headache, muscle pain, **convulsion**, dizziness, hair thinning, and depression. Erythema, pain and hardness on the spot of injection are also frequently observed. Interferon therapy causes **immunosuppression**, in particular through **neutropenia** and can result in some infections manifesting in unusual ways.

All known adverse effects are usually reversible and disappear a few days after the therapy has been finished.

chemotherapy[ˌkeməu'θerəpi] n. 化学疗法

hepatitis[ˌhepə'taitis]n. 肝炎

histology[his'tɔlədʒi]n. 组织学

symptom['simptəm]n. 症状，征兆

sclerosis[skliə'rəusis]n. [医]硬化症，硬化，硬结

convulsion[kən'vʌlʃən]n. 惊厥，痉挛
immunosuppression[ˌimjunəusə'preʃən] n. 抑制（生物体的）免疫反应
neutropenia[ˌnjuːtrəu'piːniə]n. 嗜中性白细胞减少症

Expressions and Technical Terms
produced by 产生于
belong to 属于
in response to 响应，适应

Notes

[1] special background 1957 年，英国病毒生物学家 Alick Isaacs 和瑞士研究人员 Jean Lindenmann，在利用鸡胚绒毛尿囊膜研究流感干扰现象时了解到，病毒感染的细胞能产生一种因子，后者作用于其他细胞，干扰病毒的复制，故将其命名为干扰素。

1966～1971 年，Friedman 发现了干扰素的抗病毒机制，引起了人们对干扰素抗病毒作用的

关注，而后，干扰素的免疫调控及抗病毒作用、抗增殖作用以及抗肿瘤作用逐渐被人们认识。1976年 Greenberg 等首先报道用人白细胞干扰素治疗 4 例慢性活动性乙肝，治疗后有 2 例 HBeAg 消失。但是由于人白细胞干扰素原材料来源有限，价格昂贵，因此未能大量应用于临床。

1980～1982 年，科学家用基因工程方法在大肠杆菌及酵母菌细胞内获得了干扰素，从每 1L 细胞培养物中可以得到 20～40ml 干扰素。从 1987 年开始，用基因工程方法生产的干扰素进入了工业化生产，并且大量投放市场。

[2] Interferons are produced by a wide variety of cells <u>in response to</u> the presence of double-stranded <u>RNA</u>, a key indicator of viral infection. 大多数细胞里的干扰素是以自身存在的双链 RNA 为模板产生的，也是细胞受病毒感染的关键指示剂。produced by 是"产生于…"，interferons 是两个短句的主语。

[3] There are three major classes of interferons that have been described for humans according to the type of receptor through which they signal. 依据受体的不同，人天然干扰素主要分为三种类型。"humans" 表示人体内天然存在的干扰素，简称人干扰素。

[4] Administered intranasally in very low doses, interferon is extensively used in Eastern Europe and Russia as a method to prevent and treat viral respiratory diseases such as <u>cold</u> and <u>flu</u>. 在东欧和俄罗斯，喷入鼻腔非常低剂量的干扰素是一种被广泛应用的治疗由病毒引起的呼吸系统疾病的方法，比如感冒和流感。主语是 interferon，administered intranasally in very low doses 是定语。

Exercises

1. Put the following into Chinese

More than half of hepatitis C patients treated with interferon respond with viral elimination (sustained virological response), better blood tests and better liver histology (detected on biopsy). There is some evidence that giving interferon immediately following infection can prevent chronic hepatitis C. However, people infected by HCV often do not display symptoms of HCV infection until months or years later making early treatment difficult.

2. Put English sentences into Chinese

(1) However, mechanisms of such action of interferon are not well understood; it is thought that doses must be larger by several orders of magnitude to have any effect on the virus.

(2) Interferon therapy causes immunosuppression, in particular through neutropenia and can result in some infections manifesting in unusual ways.

3. Put the following into English

干扰素　糖蛋白　细胞因子　巨噬细胞　抑制（生物体的）免疫反应　肝炎

4. Writing

Write summary of this text (no more than 120 words).

19.2　Principles of drug design

Drug design is the approach of finding drugs by design, based on their <u>biological targets</u>. Typically a drug target is a key <u>molecule</u> involved in a particular **metabolic** or signalling <u>pathway</u> that is specific to a disease condition or **pathology**,

Remarks Column

metabolic[ˌmetəˈbɔlik]*adj.* 代谢作用的，新陈代谢的

pathology[pəˈθɔlədʒi]*n.*病理学

or to the **infectivity** or survival of a <u>microbial</u> pathogen.

Some approaches attempt to stop the functioning of the pathway in the diseased state by causing a key molecule to stop functioning. Drugs may be designed that bind to the active region and inhibit this key molecule. However these drugs would also have to be designed in such a way as not to affect any other important molecules that may be similar in appearance to the key molecules. Sequence homologies are often used to identify such risks.

Other approaches may be to enhance the normal pathway by promoting specific molecules in the normal pathways that may have been affected in the diseased state.

The structure of the drug molecule that can specifically interact with the **biomolecules** can be modeled using computational tools. These tools can allow a drug molecule to be constructed within the biomolecule using knowledge of its structure and the nature of its active site. Construction of the drug molecule can be made inside out or outside in depending on whether the core or the R-groups are chosen first. However many of these approaches are plagued by the practical problems of chemical synthesis.

Newer approaches have also suggested the use of drug molecules that are large and **proteinaceous** in nature rather than as small molecules. There have also been suggestions to make these using mRNA. Gene silencing may also have therapeutical applications.

1. Common designer drugs

Most of the best known research chemicals are structural analogues of **tryptamines** or phenethylamines, but there are also many other completely unrelated chemicals which can be considered as part of the group. It is very difficult to determine **psychoactivity** or other **pharmaceutical** properties of these compounds based strictly upon structural examination. Many of the substances have common effects whilst structurally different and vice versa (see also SAR paradox). As a result of no real official naming for some of these compounds, as well as regional naming, this can all lead to (and is anecdotally known to have led to) potentially hazardous mix ups for users. One such example is bk-MDMA known primarily as "methylone" which is also legally a trademark name of **methylpre- dnisolone**.

2. Computer-assisted drug design

infectivity[,infek'tiviti]n.传染性，易传染

biomolecule[,baiəu'mɔlikju:l] n.[生]生物分子

proteinaceous[,prəutiːˈneiʃəs]adj. 蛋白质的，似蛋白质的

tryptamine['triptə,mi:n]n.色胺，β-吲哚基乙胺

psychoactivity[,psaikəuækˈtivəti]n.作用于精神，影响(或改变)心理状态
pharmaceutical[,fɑːməˈsjuːtikəl]n.药物 adj.制药(学)上的

methylprednisolone[,meθilpredˈnisələun]n.甲强龙,甲基强的松龙,6-甲强的松龙,6-甲氢化泼尼松

Computer-assisted drug design uses computational chemistry to discover, enhance, or study drugs and related biologically active molecules. Methods used can include simple molecular modeling, using molecular mechanics, molecular dynamics, semi-empirical quantum chemistry methods, ab initio quantum chemistry methods and density functional theory. The purpose is to reduce the number of targets for a good drug that have to be subjected to expensive and time-consuming synthesis and trialling.

Expressions and Technical Terms
involved in　参与…
microbial pathogen　微生物病原体
Sequence homologies　序列同源性
interact with　相结合…
the nature of　实质、本质
chemical synthesis　化学合成
Gene silencing　基因沉默
structural analogues　结构类比法
molecular mechanics　分子力学
molecular dynamics　分子动力学
semi-empirical quantum chemistry　半经验量子化学
quantum chemistry　量子化学
Computer-assisted　计算机辅助

Notes

[1] special background 药物设计是随着药物化学学科的诞生相应出现的。早在 20 世纪 20 年代以前，就开始进行天然有效成分的结构改造。直到 1932 年，欧兰梅耶发表了将有机化学的电子等排原理和环状结构等价概念用于药物设计，首次出现具有理论性的药物分子结构的修饰工作。随后，药物作用的受体理论、生化机制、药物在体内转运等药物设计的理论不断出现。在 20 世纪 60 年代初出现了构效关系的定量研究，1964 年汉希和藤田稔夫提出定量构效关系的汉希分析。药物设计开始由定性进入定量研究阶段，为定量药物设计奠定了理论和实践基础。药物设计逐渐形成一门独立的分支学科。70 年代以后药物设计开始综合运用药物化学、分子生物学、量子化学、统计数学基础理论和当代科学技术以及电子计算机等手段，开辟了药物设计新局面。

随着分子生物学的进展，对酶与受体的理解更趋深入，对有些酶的性质、酶反应历程、药物与酶复合物的精细结构得到阐明，模拟与受体相结合的药物活性构象的计算机分子图像技术在新药研究中已取得可喜的成果。运用这些新技术，从生化和受体两方面进行药物设计是新药设计的趋向。

[2] Typically a drug target is a key molecule involved in a particular metabolic or signalling pathway that is specific to a disease condition or pathology, or to the infectivity or survival of a microbial pathogen. 具有代表性的药物靶点是一个参与特殊的新陈代谢或是信号通路的关键分子，这种分子对某种病情或病理，或对传染性和抵御微生物致病菌有特效。involved in… "有关的"，在这里依据句意的需要译为 "参与"。

[3] However these drugs would also have to be designed in such a way as not to affect any other important molecules that may be similar in appearance to the key molecules. 但是这些经设计的药物应该不能影响其他一些在结构上和这些关键分子相似的重要分子。"have to be designed in such a way" 是用来修饰主语 "drugs"，affect 谓语，the key molecules 宾语。

[4] Most of the best known research chemicals are structural analogues of tryptamines or phenethylamines, but there are also many other completely unrelated chemicals which can be considered as part of the group. 最著名的化学结构类似物的研究大部分都是关于色胺和苯乙胺的，但是这些类似物中仍然有与色胺和苯乙胺性质完全不相干的化学物质。"there" 指的是

tryptamines or phenethylamines 的结构类似物。

Exercises

1. Put the following into Chinese

Other approaches may be to enhance the normal pathway by promoting specific molecules in the normal pathways that may have been affected in the diseased state.

2．Put English sentences into Chinese

(1) Many of the substances have common effects whilst structurally different and vice versa (see also SAR paradox).

(2) The purpose is to reduce the number of targets for a good drug that have to be subjected to expensive and time-consuming synthesis and trialling.

3. Put the following into English

微生物病原体　新陈代谢的　传染性　生物分子　蛋白质的　制药(学)上的　化学合成

4. Writing

Write summary of this text (no more than 100 words).

参考译文

19.1　干扰素

干扰素（IFNs）一类由大多数脊椎动物的机体免疫细胞产生的具有抗病毒、抗寄生虫、抗肿瘤及免疫调节作用的蛋白质。干扰素属于一种大糖蛋白类细胞因子。大多数细胞里的干扰素是以自身存在的双链 RNA 为模板产生的，也是细胞受病毒感染的关键指示剂。干扰素帮助免疫系统抑制细菌在宿主细胞里的复制，提高自然杀伤细胞和巨噬细胞活性，增加淋巴细胞的抗原，诱导宿主细胞产生对细菌感染的抵抗力。

1．干扰素的种类

依据受体的不同，人天然干扰素主要分为三种类型。

干扰素 I：所有 I 型干扰素（IFNs）都是由特殊的细胞表面受体联合构成的，正如 IFN-α 受体（IFNAR）是由 IFNAR1 和 IFNAR2 链组成的。

干扰素 II：受 IFNGR 拘束。在人干扰素中为 IFN-γ。

干扰素III：是由 IL10R2（也称作 CRF2-4）和 IFNLR1（也称 CRF2-12）组成的复杂受体。

2．药用价值

正如它们的天然功能，干扰素具有抗病毒、防腐、抗肿瘤等诸如药物的作用。

干扰素已经用于众多癌症患者的治疗（结合化学疗法和放射疗法）。

大多数接受干扰素治疗的 C 型肝炎患者能产生消灭病毒的反应（持续的合理的反应），和较好的血液和肝组织测试结果（用活组织检查）。结果非常明显，注射干扰素后可以阻止 C 型慢性肝炎的传染。然而，人们被感染上 HCV 后通常在数月或数年内都不出现感染症状的，从而增加了早期治疗的难度。

干扰素（干扰素 β-1a 和干扰素 β-1b）通常也被用作治疗和控制多发性硬化、自体免疫紊乱等疾病。

在东欧和俄罗斯，喷入鼻腔非常低剂量的干扰素是一种被广泛应用的治疗由病毒引起的呼吸系统疾病的方法，比如感冒和流感。然而，干扰素的这种作用机理还不是很清楚；有人认为干扰素剂量成倍加大，才能对病毒产生作用。因此，许多西方科学家都质疑其良好的功效。

3. 副作用

最常见的副作用是产生类似流感的症状：使身体温度升高、感觉不适、疲劳、头痛、肌肉酸痛、痉挛、头晕眼花、头发稀少和意识消沉。红斑、痛苦和皮肤硬化也频繁被观察到。干扰素治疗引起抑制（生物体）的免疫反应，特别表现在能引起中性粒细胞减少和导致一些明显的特殊途径的传染。

所有已知的副作用通常都是可逆的或者是在治疗结束的一段时间内就会消失的。

19.2 药物设计原则

药物设计是一种发现新药的方法，这种设计是基于生物学的靶点。具有代表性的药物靶点是一个参与特殊的新陈代谢或是信号通路的关键分子，这种分子对某种病情或病理，或对传染性和抵御微生物致病菌有特效。

许多方法都尝试在疾病状态下只停止一个关键分子的功能从而就能停止某种代谢途径的功能。设计的药物应能约束活性区域和抑制这种关键分子。但是这些经设计的药物应该不能影响其他一些在结构上和这些关键分子相似的重要分子。序列同源性常常被用来鉴定这种风险。

其他方法是可能在患病状态时，通过提高正常代谢途径中的特殊分子来增强正常代谢途径。

利用计算工具可以模拟出与生物分子相对应的药物分子的结构。这些工具能利用药物分子本身的结构和活性部位的本质，让药物分子重构成生物大分子。构建药物分子是由里到外还是由外到里，取决于首先是选择核还是 R-基团开始。但是这些方法都被化学合成的一些实际问题所困扰、约束。

最新的方法也建议使用大的、蛋白质的药物分子，而不是小分子。也有建议用mRNA来制备药物分子的。基因沉默也可能是治疗中的应用。

1. 常见的药物设计

最著名的化学结构类似物的研究大部分都是关于色胺和苯乙胺的，但是这些类似物中仍然有与色胺和苯乙胺性质完全不相干的化学物质。严格基于结构的检查非常难判断到底是这些化合物的药物性质在起作用，还是人的心理在起作用。许多物质有共同作用而结构不同，反之亦然（请参见 SAR 悖论）。由于一些这类化合物没有正式命名，以及区域命名，对用户来说有混乱使用的潜在危险。一个例子就是bk-MDMA起初被称作"木精"，后来法律上的商标是甲强龙。

2. 计算机辅助药物设计

计算机辅助药物设计利用计算化学来发现、增强或研究具有生物活性的药物和相关的分子。这些方法包括简单分子建模、分子力学、分子动力学、半经验的量子化学方法、量子化学方法和密度泛函理论。这样做的目的是减少药物的筛选对象，从而为化学合成和实验节约大量的时间和金钱。

Reading material

Fake Vaccines From China PoseDanger in War on Avian Flu

BEIJING——Late last fall, a village official visited Wang Jicheng, a poultry farmer in the northern Chinese province of Liaoning, to warn him that thousands of chickens in the area were suddenly dying, probably from **bird flu**.

Mr. Wang wasn't too worried, a month before, he had paid $225 for 28 bottles of condensed vaccine to protect his chickens and had spent two and a half days injecting each of his 10,000 birds.

But the day after the official's visit, Mr. Wang saw three-wheeled bicycles ferrying bags of bird **carcasses** past his farm. Then his own poultry began to die. Within a few weeks, all of his chickens had died or been **slaughtered** to prevent the spread of the disease.

It **turns out** that Mr. Wang's vaccine was a low-quality drug, produced in an unlicensed factory.

Late last year, the Ministry of Agriculture announced that it had fined 13 companies, including several government-supported research institutes, for peddling vaccines without licenses and confiscated some profits. It is monitoring dozens of other companies.

About five weeks after the **epidemic** hit in Liaoning, the government halted production at the Inner Mongolia Biopharmacy Co. which had manufactured Mr. Wang's vaccine without a license, according to the **Chinese Ministry of Agriculture**, and announced the arrest of six company executives.

In the past couple of months, the government has begun to act, **moving against** manufacturers like **Inner Mongolia** Biopharmacy, issuing warnings to farmers about the risks of using unauthorized vaccines and announcing new controls.

"It's good that China has finally recognized fake vaccines". says Yoshihiro Ozawa, an animal-disease expert and adviser to the World Organization for Animal Health, based in Paris. The question is, can it move quickly and broadly enough?

Avian vaccination also protects an industry that is critical in a country like China, where hundreds of millions of farmers depend on birds for their livelihood and as a relatively inexpensive source of protein. The Chinese government has committed itself to vaccinating every one of its billions of domestic birds——agreeing to pay for the vaccines while allowing the farmers to vaccinate their own birds.

Beijing says it is ramping up vaccine supply from approved manufacturers. Zhuo Baoshan, general manager of Jinan-based Qilu Animal Health Products Factory, one of the authorized vaccine makers, says his company is now producing the vaccine at full capacity and shipping product every other day. "We need to report our daily output to the ministry, which has sent people here to test every batch of vaccines". he says.

But it isn't clear if these efforts go far enough. Meanwhile, unlicensed vendors approach local officials who may not be savvy enough to know the difference between approved and unapproved products, or how a vaccine works. In the case of Inner Mongolia Biopharmacy, price may have been a factor. The company's bird-flu vaccine was priced lower than the vaccines that had been approved by the government; at the time, the approved vaccines were still being sold, rather than distributed to farmers at no cost.

An official of Inner Mongolia Biopharmacy has admitted that its vaccines were unauthorized and that it has recalled the product. But the official said tests have shown that the vaccines weren't the cause of the outbreaks in Liaoning. The executives are still under arrest, and the company's 1,300 workers are idle while the company seeks approval to produce other products.

Mr. Wang says that, if his chickens had lived, he could have sold each of them at the local market for $2.35 apiece. "We were very upset with the vaccine company". He says. "It has wasted us so much money and time".

New Words

bird flu 禽流感
carcasses ['kɑːkəs] *n.*（屠宰后）畜体
slaughter ['slɔːtə]*n.& v.* 屠宰，残杀，屠杀
epidemic[ˌepi'demik] *adj.* 流行的，传染的，流行性
avian ['eiviən] *adj.* 鸟类的

Expressions and Technical Terms

turns out 驱逐，生产，起床，翻出，关掉
Chinese Ministry of Agriculture 中国农业部
moving against 行动起来反对
Inner Mongolia 内蒙古

Unit **5** Information retrieval

Chapter 20 Introduction

Information retrieval (IR) is the science of searching for documents, for information within documents and for **metadata** about documents, as well as that of searching relational databases and the World Wide Web. There is **overlap** in the usage of the terms data retrieval, document retrieval, information retrieval, and text retrieval, but each also has its own body of literature, theory, praxis and technologies. IR is interdisciplinary, based on computer science, mathematics, library science, information science, information architecture, cognitive psychology, **linguistics**, statistics and physics.

As recently as the1990s, studies showed that most people preferred getting information from other people rather than from information retrieval systems. Of course, in that time period, most people also used human travel agents to **book** their travel. However, during the last decade, **relentless** optimization of information retrieval effectiveness has driven web search engines to new quality levels where most people are satisfied most of the time, and web search has become a standard and often preferred source of information finding. For example, the 2004 Pew Internet Survey (Fallows 2004) found that "92% of Internet users say the Internet is a good place to go for getting everyday information". To the surprise of many, the field of information retrieval has moved from being a primarily academic discipline to being the basis **underlying** most people's preferred means of information access. This book presents the scientific **underpinning**s of this field, at a level accessible to graduate students as well as advanced undergraduates.

Information retrieval systems are used to reduce what has been called "information overload". Many universities and public

Remarks Column

metadata 诠释资料

overlap ['əuvə'læp]v. (与…)交叠，重叠

linguistics [liŋ'gwistiks] n. 语言学

book[buk] v. 登记，预订 n.书，书籍

relentless [ri'lentlis] adj.不屈不挠的，不懈的；严酷的，残忍的，不留情面的

underpinning [ʌndə,pInIŋ]n. 基础，支柱，支撑

libraries use IR systems to provide access to books, journals and other documents. Web search engines are the most visible IR applications. Information retrieval did not begin with the Web. **In response to** various challenges of providing information access, the field of information retrieval evolved to give principled approaches to searching various forms of content. The field began with scientific publications and library records, but soon spread to other forms of content, particularly those of information professionals, such as journalists, lawyers, and doctors. Much of the scientific research on information retrieval has occurred in these contexts, and much of the continued practice of information retrieval deals with providing access to unstructured information in various corporate and governmental domains, and this work forms much of the foundation of our book.

Nevertheless, in recent years, a principal driver of innovation has been the World Wide Web, **unleashing** publication at the scale of **tens of millions of** content creators. This explosion of published information would be **moot** if the information could not be found, **annotated** and analyzed so that each user can quickly find information that is both relevant and comprehensive for their needs. By the late 1990s, many people felt that continuing to index the whole Web would rapidly become impossible, due to the Web's exponential growth in size. But major scientific innovations, **superb** engineering, the rapidly declining price of computer hardware, and the rise of a commercial underpinning for web search have all **conspired** to **power** today's major search engines, which are able to provide high-quality results with in subsecond response times for hundreds of millions of searches a day over billions of web pages.

unleash [ˈʌnˈliːʃ] *vt.* 释放；放纵；发动；解开…的皮带（链锁）

moot [muːt] *adj.* 未决议的，无实际意义的 *n.* 大会，审议会

superb [sjuːˈpəːb] *adj.* 庄重的，堂堂的，华丽的，极好的

conspire [kənˈspaiə] *v.* 协力促成，参加或合作，协力；共谋，阴谋

Expressions and Technical Terms

information retrieval
信息检索

in response to 响应，适应

tens of millions of 成千上万

Notes

[1] Special background　信息检索（information retrieval）是指将信息按一定的方式组织和贮存起来，并根据信息用户的需要找出有关信息的过程。所以，它的全称又叫信息存贮与检索（information storage and retrieval），这是广义的信息检索。狭义的信息检索则仅指该过程的后半部分，即根据课题的需要，主要借助于检索工具，从信息集合中找出所需信息的过程，相当于人们所说的信息查寻（information search）。信息检索的过程往往需要一个评价反馈途径，多次比较匹配，以获得最终的检索结果。

从检索工具的功能出发，检索类型可分为三种：事实检索、目录检索、文摘索引检索。事实检索是对包括事实（fact）、数值（numeric data）与全文（full-text）的检索，提供原始信息，给出直接、确定性的答案；目录检索一般用于查找图书、报刊的线索，指引原始文献；文摘索引检索提供相关文献的线索，包括文献来源出处（source），也常带有文献的内容摘要，但不是文献

原文。

[2] Information retrieval (IR) is the science of searching for documents, for information within documents and for metadata about documents, as well as that of searching relational databases and the World Wide Web. 信息检索是搜寻文献、搜寻文献内的信息和搜寻文献的原始资料的学科，也是搜寻相关数据库和万维网的学科。as well as 表示"也",作为连接词用。 这里"that"指代的是"science"。

[3] As recently as the1990s, studies showed that most people preferred getting information from other people rather than from information retrieval systems. 在最近 20 世纪 90 年代，研究表明大多数人宁愿从别人那儿得到信息，都不愿从信息检索获得。此句"rather than"表示"not"，rather than 后面省略了 getting.

[4] Information retrieval systems are used to reduce what has been called "information overload". Many universities and public libraries use IR systems to provide access to books, journals and other documents. Web search engines are the most visible IR applications. 人们使用信息检索系统来缩减被称为"信息泛滥"的大量文献资料。有很多大学和公共图书馆使用信息检索系统为公众提供图书、期刊和其他一些文献资料的检索服务。最明显的应用于文献检索的就是环球网的搜索引擎。"what"引导宾语从句。

[5] In response to various challenges of providing information access, the field of information retrieval evolved to give principled approaches to searching various forms of content. The field began with scientific publications and library records, but soon spread to other forms of content, particularly those of information professionals, such as journalists, lawyers, and doctors. 为适应信息访问的挑战，信息检索领域逐渐发展成搜索各种形式内容的原则性方法。该领域起初以科学出版社和图书馆档案开始的，但不久迅速发展成其他的形式，尤其是那些信息专业人员，例如记者、律师和医生。"those"指代"forms"。

[6] But major scientific innovations, superb engineering, the rapidly declining price of computer hardware, and the rise of a commercial underpinning for web search have all conspired to power today's major search engines, which are able to provide high-quality results with in subsecond response times for hundreds of millions of searches a day over billions of web pages. 但是科学的进步，熟练的操作技术，计算机硬件价格的下降以及网页搜索的商业基础的增长，推动了如今主要的搜索引擎，能在不到一秒的响应时间内满足每天成千上万个查询者搜索几十亿个网页的高质量的要求。"which"指代 search engines"。

Exercises

1. Put the following into Chinese

Information retrieval (IR) is the science of searching for documents, for information within documents and for metadata about documents, as well as that of searching relational databases and the World Wide Web. There is overlap in the usage of the terms data retrieval, document retrieval, information retrieval, and text retrieval, but each also has its own body of literature, theory, praxis and technologies. IR is interdisciplinary, based on computer science, mathematics, library science, information science, information architecture, cognitive psychology, linguistics, statistics and physics.

2. Put the following into English

信息检索　认知心理学　信息构建　搜索引擎　信息访问　非结构化信息

万维网　　指数增长　　网页搜索　　计算机硬件

3. Cloze

Information retrieval systems are used to reduce __(1)__ has been called "information overload". Many universities and public libraries use IR systems to provide access __(2)__ books, journals and other documents. Web search engines are the most visible IR applications. Information retrieval did not begin __(3)__ the Web. __(4)__ various challenges of providing information access, the field of information retrieval __(5)__ to give principled approaches to __(6)__ various forms of content. The field began with scientific publications and library records, but soon spread to other forms of content, particularly __(7)__ of information professionals, such as journalists, lawyers, and doctors. __(8)__ of the scientific research on information retrieval has occurred in these contexts, and much of the continued practice of information retrieval __(9)__ with providing access to unstructured information in various corporate and governmental domains, and this work forms much of the __(10)__ of our book.

（1）　A. what　　　　B. that　　　　　C. those　　　　D. it　　　　　　（　　）
（2）　A. with　　　　B. to　　　　　　C. of　　　　　　D. for　　　　　（　　）
（3）　A. from　　　　B. in　　　　　　C. with　　　　　D. on　　　　　（　　）
（4）　A. In regard to　B. In view of　　C. In relation to　D. In response to（　　）
（5）　A. developed　　B. evolved　　　C. approached　　D. spread　　　（　　）
（6）　A. search　　　B. find　　　　　C. searching　　　D. finding　　　（　　）
（7）　A. that　　　　B. many　　　　　C. much　　　　　D. those　　　　（　　）
（8）　A. Much　　　　B. Those　　　　C. Many　　　　　D. That　　　　（　　）
（9）　A. dealed　　　B. begins　　　　C. deals　　　　　D. began　　　（　　）
（10）　A. information　B. explanation　　C. formation　　　D. foundation　（　　）

4. What is the use of information retrieval according to this text?

参考译文

　　信息检索是搜寻文献、搜寻文献内的信息和搜寻文献的原始资料的学科，也是搜寻相关数据库和万维网的学科。在使用资料检索、文献检索、信息检索和全文检索等词语时，它们在意义上会有一些重复，但它们在文化、理论、实践和技术方面又有各自鲜明的特点。信息检索是以计算机科学、数学、图书馆学、信息科学、信息构建、认知心理学、语言学、统计学和物理学等诸多学科为基础的交叉学科。

　　在20世纪90年代，研究表明大多数人宁愿从别人那儿得到信息，都不愿从信息检索获得。当然，那时期大多数人们使用旅行代理商（旅行社）去预定旅行。然而，在以后的十年里，信息检索的高效优化发展使网页搜索引擎达到新的水平，网页搜索已成为深受人们喜爱的信息查询（方式）。例如，在2004年Pew因特网调查中发现92%因特网用户认为因特网是每天获得信息的好地方。让人惊讶的是，信息检索已经主要从学术学科（研究）向大多数人们获取信息的方向转变。这本书阐述了这个领域的基础，适合于本科生和研究生的水平要求。

　　人们使用信息检索系统来缩减被称为"信息泛滥"的大量文献资料。有很多大学和公共图书馆使用信息检索系统为公众提供图书、期刊和其他一些文献资料的检索服务。最明显的应用于文献检索的就是环球网的搜索引擎。信息检索不是先从网页开始的。为适应信息访问的挑战，信息检索领域逐渐发展成搜索各种形式内容的原则性方法。该领域起初以科学出版和图书馆档案开始的，但不久迅速发展成其他的形式，尤其是那些信息专业人员，例如记者、律师和医生。在这些背景下，信息检索的科学研究诞生了，在与政府合作领域内从事于非结构化信息的大量信息检索工作，这个工作形成了这本书的基础。

然而，近年来，创新的主要动力是万维网，疯狂出版成千上万个创作者的作品。如果信息不能被找到，信息的出版就没有意义。注释和分析以便于每个用户都能快速找到相关的和全面的信息从而满足其需要。20世纪90年代末，许多人觉得由于网页量呈指数增长，继续搜索整个网页不可能实现。但是科学的进步，熟练的操作技术，计算机硬件价格的下降以及网页搜索的商业基础的增长，推动了如今主要的搜索引擎，能在不到一秒的响应时间内满足每天成千上万个查询者搜索几十亿个网页的高质量的要求。

Chapter 21　The research process in the cornell university library

The following seven steps outline a simple and effective strategy for finding information for a research paper and documenting the sources you find. Depending on your topic and your **familiarity** with the library, you may need to rearrange or recycle these steps. Adapt this **outline** to your needs. We **are ready to** help you at every step in your research.

1. Identify and develop your topic

State your topic as a question. For example, if you are interested in finding out about use of alcoholic beverages by college students, you might pose the question, "What effect does use of **alcoholic beverage**s have on the health of college students?" Identify the main concepts or keywords in your question. In this case they are alcoholic beverages, health, and college students.

2. Find background information

Look up your keywords in the **index**es to subject **encyclopedia**s. Read articles in these encyclopedias to set the context for your research. Note any relevant items in the **bibliographies** at the end of the encyclopedia articles. Additional background information may be found in your lecture notes, textbooks, and reserve readings.

3. Use **catalog**s to find books and media

Use guided keyword searching to find materials by topic or subject. Print or write down the **citation** (author, title, etc.) and the location information (call number and library). Note the circulation status. When you pull the book from the shelf, scan the bibliography for additional sources. Watch for book-length bibliographies and annual reviews on your subject; they list citations to hundreds of books and articles in one subject area. Check the standard subject subheading "——BIBLIOGRAPHIES", or titles beginning with Annual Review of…in the Cornell Library Catalog.

4. Use indexes to find **periodical article**s

Use periodical indexes and abstracts to find citations to articles. The indexes and abstracts may be in print or

Remarks Column

familiarity [fə,mili'æriti]*n.*熟悉，通晓，亲密

outline ['əutlain]*n.*大纲，轮廓，略图，外形，要点，概要 *vt.*描画轮廓，略述

index ['indeks]*n.*索引

encyclopedia[en,saikləu'pi:diə]*n.*百科全书

bibliography [,bibli'ɔgrəfi]*n.*参考文献，参考书目

catalog ['kætəlɔg]*n.*目录，目录册 *v.*编目录

citation [sai'teiʃən]*n.*引文，引用

computer-based formats or both. Choose the indexes and format best suited to your particular topic; ask at the reference desk if you need help **figuring out** which index and format will be best. You can find periodical articles by the article author, title, or keyword by using the periodical indexes in the Library Gateway. If the full text is not linked in the index you are using, write down the citation from the index and search for the title of the periodical in the Cornell Library Catalog. The catalog lists the print, microform, and electronic versions of periodicals at Cornell.

5. Find internet resources

Use search engines. Search engines do not really search the World Wide Web directly. Each one searches a database of web pages that it has harvested and **cach**ed. When you use a search engine, you are always searching a somewhat stale copy of the real web page. When you click on links provided in a search engine's search results, you retrieve the current version of the page. Check to see if your class has a bibliography or research guide created by librarians.

cache [kæʃ] *vt.*储存，贮存；隐藏，窖藏 *n.*高速缓冲存储器；隐藏处所，贮藏物

6. Evaluate what you find

You can begin evaluating a physical information source (a book or an article for instance) even before you have the physical item in hand. **Appraise** a source by first examining the bibliographic citation. The bibliographic citation is the written description of a book, journal article, essay, or some other published material that appears in a catalog or index. Bibliographic citations characteristically have three main components: author, title, and publication information. These components can help you determine the usefulness of this source for your paper.

appraise [ə'preiz] *v.*评价

7. Cite what you find using a standard format

Give credit where credit is due; cite your sources. Citing or documenting the sources used in your research serves two purposes. It gives proper credit to the authors of the materials used, and it allows those who are reading your work to **duplicate** your research and locate the sources that you have listed as references.

duplicate ['dju:plikeit] *vt.*复制，重复

Expressions and Technical Terms
Cornell University 康奈尔大学
be ready to…乐于做…
periodical article 期刊论文
figure out 想知道，领会到；合计为，计算出

Notes

[1] special background　图书检索的方法有手工检索和计算机检索。手工检索主要有目录、索引、文摘、百科全书、年鉴等类型。计算机检索是利用计算机中图书数据库来了解图书馆的藏书情况和图书流通情况。

[2] Use guided keyword searching to find materials by topic or subject. Print or write down the citation (author, title, etc.) and the location information (call number and library). Note the circulation

status. When you pull the book from the shelf, scan the bibliography for additional sources. Watch for book-length bibliographies and annual reviews on your subject; they list citations to hundreds of books and articles in one subject area. Check the standard subject subheading "──BIBLIOGRAPHIES", or titles beginning with Annual Review of…in the Cornell Library Catalog. 通过主题使用引导关键词查询资料。打印或记下引文（作者，题目等）和位置信息（索书号和图书馆），记下流通情况。当你从书架上拿出这本书时，浏览一下参考书录，寻找关于主题的书籍长度的参考文献以及评论年鉴，因为它们列出了就一个主题领域的许多书籍和文章的引文。查看副标题为参考目录或康乃尔大学图书馆藏目录中的评论年鉴的题目。这里"annual"为"年鉴"的意思，指按年度系统汇集一定范围内的重大事件、新进展、新知识和新资料，供读者查阅的工具书。按年度连续出版，所收内容一般以当年为限。

[3] Search engines do not really search the World Wide Web directly. Each one searches a database of web pages that it has harvested and cached.搜索引擎并不是直接查询万维网。每个搜索引擎能够搜索储存信息网页的数据库。句中"that"引导的是修饰主语的定语从句，"it"指代"each one"。

Exercises

1. Put the following into Chinese

See how to critically analyze information sources and distinguishing scholarly from non-scholarly periodicals: a Checklist of Criteria for suggestions on evaluating the authority and quality of the books and articles you located.

If you have found too many or too few sources, you may need to narrow or broaden your topic. Check with a reference librarian or your instructor.

When you're ready to write, here is an annotated list of books to help you organize, format, and write your paper.

2. Put the following into English

百科全书　引导关键词　流通情况　参考文献　评论年鉴　期刊论文　索引引文
馆藏目录　搜索指南　实体信息　标准格式

3. Cloze

Use periodical indexes and abstracts to find citations 　(1)　 articles. The indexes and abstracts may be in print or computer-based formats or both. Choose the indexes and format best suited to your particular topic; ask at the reference desk if you need help figuring 　(2)　 which index and format will be best. You can find periodical articles by the article author, title, or keyword by using the periodical indexes in the Library Gateway. If the full text is not linked in the 　(3)　 you are using, write down the citation 　(4)　 the index and search for the title of the 　(5)　 in the Cornell Library Catalog. The catalog lists the print, microform, and electronic versions of periodicals at Cornell.

（1）　A. to　　　　B. with　　　　C. of　　　　　D. in　　　　　　（　）
（2）　A. into　　　B. of　　　　　C. with　　　　D. out　　　　　（　）
（3）　A. index　　 B. catalog　　 C. file　　　　D. bibliography　（　）
（4）　A. to　　　　B. of　　　　　C. from　　　　D. in　　　　　　（　）
（5）　A. monthly　 B. yearly　　　C. periodical　 D. daily　　　　（　）

4. Writing

Write summary of this text (no more than 150 words).

参考翻译

康乃尔大学图书馆查询方法

关于研究论文和查找资源（所需要）的信息查询，下面列出了简单有效的七个步骤。根据你的主题以及对图书馆的熟悉程度，安排或循环这些步骤，从而适合自己的需要。我们乐于帮助你们研究中（所需要信息查询）的每一个步骤。

1. 确定主题

以问题形式确定主题，例如，如果你对大学生饮酒感兴趣，你也许提出这个问题，"酒精对大学生身体健康产生什么影响？" 以问题形式确定主要的概念或关键词。在这里它们是酒精饮料、健康和大学生。

2. 查找背景信息

在相应学科的百科全书索引中查找关键词。阅读其中的文章，确定研究方向。在百科全书文章末尾的参考书目中标明相关的条目，也可在你的课堂笔记、教科书和阅读书目中找到更多背景知识。

3. 运用目录查询书籍和媒体

通过主题使用引导关键词查询资料。打印或记下引文（作者，题目等）和位置信息（索书号和图书馆），记下流通情况。当你从书架上拿出这本书时，浏览一下参考书录，寻找关于主题的书籍长度的参考文献以及评论年鉴，因为它们列出了就一个主题领域的许多书籍和文章的引文。查看副标题为参考目录或康乃尔大学图书馆藏目录中的评论年鉴的题目。

4. 运用索引查找期刊论文

使用期刊索引和文摘找到文章的引文。这些索引和文摘可以是打印文件或计算机文件格式或两者都可以。选择适合主题的期刊索引，如果你想知道哪个索引和格式是最好的，请询问咨询台。通过文章作者、题目或关键词使用图书馆网的期刊索引可以查找期刊文章。如果你使用的索引没有链接全文，记下索引引文，在康乃尔大学图书馆藏目录下搜索期刊题目。康乃尔大学图书馆藏目录下期刊文献有打印、微型和电子版格式。

5. 查找网络资源

使用搜索引擎。搜索引擎并不是直接查询万维网。每个搜索引擎能够搜索储存信息网页的数据库。当你使用搜索引擎时，你总是搜索到一些实时网页的陈旧拷贝。当你点击搜索引擎提供的搜索结果链接时，你搜索到的是该网页的当前版本。如果你的班级有图书馆管理员编写的参考目录和搜索指南，请先阅读。

6. 评价所查找的内容

你先开始评价实体信息资源（例如一本书或一篇文章），然后才能进行手头上的实体研究项目。先要查看参考目录引文，然后评价资源。该参考目录引文指的是一本书、杂志文章、评论或其他的出版材料以目录索引形式呈现。参考目录引文有三个主要的组成特征：作者，题目和出版信息。这些组成部分有助于你评价（写文章所用）该资源的用途。

7. 引用文献使用标准格式

给出引用文献资料应该给的荣誉。引用文献资料有两个目的：一方面它给作者提供了荣誉；另一方面，允许那些阅读文献资料的人可以复制你的研究和查找你列出的资料作为参考。

Learning to Retrieve Medical Literature through Interactive Problem Solving

Searching the literature has a direct, beneficial influence on patient care. The amount of medical scientific information has increased to a great extent, while the development of networking technologies has broadened access to online databases. Successful searches depend upon understanding technical librarianship concepts and the skills for mastering searching interfaces. From a problem-oriented approach, concepts like **MEDLINE** coverage, **PubMed** resources, Boolean logic, search strategies, and Web sources for full-text articles are introduced along seven online situations: locating a specific publication, answering a complex clinical question, finding information on a general subject, finding publications by a particular author, finding publications in a particular language, finding a specific publication type, and locating the full-text document. Oncologists should face the challenge of performing their own searches. Specific knowledge is mandatory to avoid frustrating, time-consuming work. The objective of this work is to present concepts, strategies, and skills required for medical literature retrieval, easing the incorporation of new and welcomed practices.

INTRODUCTION

Scientific journals are the primary publication media for professional communication. Once imprisoned in libraries, medical publications can now be accessed worldwide through the internet. More recently, Web-based resources provide regular professional updates, evidence-based patient care information, and medical problem solving. Therefore, oncologists should be able to perform their own searches.

Specific training is needed because internet access and the World Wide Web revolution have introduced a multitude of technologies and resources into the medical field. The necessary skills for performing a successful search and locating full-text publications may include a technical librarian background on one hand and practical computer experience for managing sophisticated Web interfaces on the other.

HOW TO START

Choosing an evidence resource database must be the initial step. A database is a collection of data organized to allow easy retrieval; MEDLINE, **EMBASE**, the Cochrane Library, and Best Evidence are valuable sources of information. Because of its appropriateness, MEDLINE, the world's most commonly used biomedical database, was selected for this work. MEDLINE is produced by the U.S. National Library of Medicine (NLM) and contains citations for a vast number of journal articles. Its relevance is described fully on the NLM Web site.

HOW TO SEARCH

Ebbert and colleagues wrote a comprehensive review on PubMed features and resources. The main advantages of searching MEDLINE through PubMed are its user-friendly interface, sophisticated search resources, and built-in links to full-text documents. Performing a PubMed search in the same way that one performs an ordinary Web search has a lot of appeal, since typing a word in a search box and clicking on "Go" using the Google or Yahoo! search engines has become a popular procedure. Techniques originally developed for internet search engines are adapted here for PubMed searching.

FINDING FULL-TEXT ARTICLES

Having the list of references, the final step is to obtain the full-text articles. Online access to full-text electronic articles emerged in the mid-1990s and has become more and more available over the Web. Basically, there are two main models of full-text availability. In the distributed full-text model, each journal has its own site, and users create an account for each journal they address. In the aggregated full-text model, journals are licensed from publishers and placed in collections with other journals. Journal collections can then be searched through a single interface.

FINAL COMMENTS

This work delivers both theoretical and practical knowledge for searching and retrieving quality full-text articles online. We believe that a successful search depends, on one hand, upon understanding technical concepts and the reasoning behind the search itself and, on the other hand, upon the skills needed to actively implement the search through a specific interface.

New words

MEDLINE ['med,lain] *n.* 联机医学文献分析和检查系统

PubMed ['pʌbmed] 美国国家医学图书馆(NLM)下属的国家生物技术信息
中心(NCBI)开发的、基于 WWW 的查询系统。

EMBASE（Excerpt Medica Database）是由荷兰 Elsevier Science 出版公司建立的 EM 的书目型数据库，以光盘数据库、国际联机数据库及网络数据库的形式为用户提供。 EMBASE 收录从 1974 年以来至今 EM 中报道的文献信息，收录 70 多个国家出版的约 4550 种期刊的医药文献，每年约 50 多万条文献记录，累积约 994 万条，80%的文献带有文摘。内容涉及药学、临床医学、基础医学、预防医学、法医学和生物医学工程等。

参 考 文 献

[1] Ladisch Michael R. Bioseparations Engineering: Principles, Practice, and Economics. Wiley. 2001.

[2] Harrison Roger G, Paul W. Todd, Scott R. Rudge, Demetri Petrides. Bioseparations science and engineering. Oxford University Press, 2003.

[3] Christopher D. Manning，Prabhakar Raghavan，Hinrich Schütze. Introduction to Information Retrieval. Cambridge University Press, 2008.

[4] 张永勤，刘福胜. 生物与制药工程专业英语. 北京：化学工业出版社，2007.

[5] Martin Chaplin, Christopher Bucke. Enzyme Technology. Cambridge University Press, 1990.

[6] 吴达俊. 制药工程专业英语. 北京：化学工业出版社，2000.

[7] 邬行彦. 生物工程生物技术专业英语. 北京：化学工业出版社，2004.